The Creation and Destruction of Social Capital

'A word is a word'
(old Danish saying)

**Dedicated to our parents,
Ingeborg Vibeke and Svend Asbjørn**

The Creation and Destruction of Social Capital

Entrepreneurship, Co-operative Movements and Institutions

Gunnar Lind Haase Svendsen

PhD student,
University of Southern Denmark, Odense, Denmark

Gert Tinggaard Svendsen

Associate Professor of Economics,
Aarhus School of Business, Aarhus, Denmark

Edward Elgar
Cheltenham, UK • Northampton, MA, USA

Published by
Edward Elgar Publishing Limited
Glensanda House
Montpellier Parade
Cheltenham
Glos GL50 1UA
UK

Edward Elgar Publishing, Inc.
136 West Street
Suite 202
Northampton
Massachusetts 01060
USA

A catalogue record for this book
is available from the British Library

Library of Congress Cataloguing in Publication Data

Svendsen, Gunnar Lind Haase, 1965-
  The creation and destruction of social capital : entrepreneurship, co-operative movements and institutions / Gunnar Lind Haase Svendsen, Gert Tinggaard Svendsen.
  p. cm.
  Includes bibliographical references and index.
  1. Cooperation—Denmark. 2. Cooperation—Poland. 3. Social capital (Sociology) 4. Entrepreneurship. 5. Cooperation. I. Svendsen, Gert Tinggaard, 1963- II. Title.

HD3519.A4S88 2004
302.3'5'09489—dc22
2004040441

ISBN 1 84376 616 7 (cased)

Printed and bound in Great Britain by MPG Books Ltd, Bodmin, Cornwall

Contents

Figures

Tables

Preface

Our first motivation to write this book was the everyday observation that social capital and trust matters – an issue that seemed to be missing in the literature on economic growth and welfare in economics. For example, traditional economic theory ignored the value of local communities and the unintended detrimental effects on public and private decision-making processes following the elimination of these local networks. This gap between theory and reality formed the point of departure of this book. Our discussions on this question motivated us to look for the answer that could not be found in the literature.

To answer the main question of how social capital is created and destroyed, we had to develop an interdisciplinary approach combining political science, economics, anthropology, sociology and history. Our academic backgrounds in these different disciplines provided us with the necessary foundation to undertake this task.

We hope that this book will contribute to the academic and popular discussions on social capital and how to improve the quality of public policy making. The book has a strong policy orientation towards the necessary institutional changes that should be made if the missing link is to be taken into account. Therefore, besides being addressed to the academic world, the book is also aimed at public policy makers and private decision makers in the market.

This social capital research has been funded by two projects.

The first one, 'People in the agrarian landscape', was set up under the cross-disciplinary initiative 'The agrarian landscape in Denmark 1998–2001', financed by the Danish Research Councils. We thank the participants in this project, especially Per Grau Møller, Henrik Christoffersen and Karen Elberg.

The second project, 'Social capital, corruption and economic growth', is being financed by the Danish Social Science Research Foundation in two stages (2000–2001 and 2002–2004), and one of the authors, Gert Tinggaard Svendsen, is the director. Important new elements from this research are added to the political economy model in this book. We are continuing to collect data on social capital and corruption in about 20 countries, and most of those results and the resulting new policy recommendations will be presented in a forthcoming book by Paldam and Svendsen (cited in the

Bibliography). This research group consists of both a Danish core group and an international group of collaborators. Our deepest thanks to all the participants in the social capital project (SoCap) for their enthusiasm and inspiration, especially Martin Paldam, Peter Nannestad and Christian Bjørnskov.

This book is one consequence of these two projects, and we therefore owe much to the Danish Research Councils for supporting us. Also, we are indebted to the Research Board, Faculty of Business Administration at the Aarhus School of Business, which has also given financial support to both projects.

We are most grateful to Edward Elgar Publishing for its prompt offer to commit itself to publish this book and for its receptiveness to changes to the original book proposal. In particular, we owe a great debt to Professor Elinor Ostrom for her enthusiasm and helpful comments and her kind offer to write the foreword.

Many ideas in the book are due to dynamic colleagues. Warmest thanks go to Carsten Daugbjerg, Henrik Christoffersen, Jarka Chloupkova, Urs Steiner Brandt, Esben Bergmann Schjødt, Yoshifumi Ueda and Lene Hjøllund. Furthermore, we would like to thank colleagues at the University of Southern Denmark and the Department of Economics, Aarhus School of Business for valuable comments on earlier draft chapters. We deeply appreciate all those not mentioned here who also helped us in this work. Needless to say, any remaining errors or shortcomings are due to the authors. Special thanks for skilful preparation of the camera ready work go to Ann-Marie Gabel. Last, but not least, we thank our wonderful wives, Jannie and Kristina, for all their love and support.

We would also like to thank the cited journals for permission to use parts of the following five articles. (1) 'Building and destroying social capital: The case of co-operative movements in Denmark and Poland', *Agriculture and Human Values*, 20 (3), 2003: 241–252 (by J. Chloupkova, G.L.H. Svendsen and G.T. Svendsen) [Chapter 3]; (2) 'Measuring social capital: the Danish co-operative dairy movement', *Sociologia Ruralis*, 40 (1), 2000: 72–86 (by G.L.H. Svendsen and G.T. Svendsen) [Chapter 4]; (3) 'Alleviating poverty: entrepreneurship and social capital in rural Denmark 1800–1900', *Belgeo*, 1 (3), 2001: 231–46 (by G.L.H. Svendsen and G.T. Svendsen) [Chapter 4]; (4) 'The right to development. Construction of a non-agriculturalist discourse of rurality in rural Denmark', *Journal of Rural Studies*, 20 (4), 2003: 79–94 (by G.L.H. Svendsen) [Chapter 6]; and (5) 'The wealth of nations: Bourdieuconomics and social capital', *Theory and Society*, 32 (5/6), 2003: 607–631 (by G.L.H. Svendsen and G.T. Svendsen) [Chapter 2]. In particular, we are indebted to Jarka Chloupkova for permitting us to reproduce parts of her work from our joint article as cited in the reference list [Chapter 3].

The book is dedicated to our parents, Ingeborg Vibeke and Svend Asbjørn whose love and trust made our dreams come true.

Foreword

Elinor Ostrom

Reading the new book written by Gunnar Lind Haase Svendsen and Gert Tinggaard Svendsen on *The Creation and Destruction of Social Capital: Entrepreneurship, Co-operative Movements and Institutions,* has been fun as well as being a substantial mental challenge. The Svendsens are urging all social scientists to think more as social scientists than just as anthropologists, economists, historians, political scientists, or sociologists. Their effort to broaden the way social scientists think about social organization is an important step, especially for those of us interested in public policies. All too often, scholars with a strong disciplinary view of the world are willing to make sweeping policy prescriptions that require, as a foundation, knowledge derived from more than one discipline. Many of the policy failures of the last half-century can be attributed in large part to the limited vision of those who have proposed that changing one part of the social-economic structure will fix multiple ailments.

Instead of seeing social capital as a new fad or something that the economists at the World Bank have discovered, the Svendsens review the major contributions of sociologists, political scientists, economists and anthropologists to the study of social capital even when the scholar did not specifically use the word.

The design of this study is ingenious. It is indeed important to study the creation of anything as important in modern life as capital. Equally important is an understanding of the factors that are associated with the destruction of capital. The design of comparing voluntary, agricultural cooperatives in Denmark over time as contrasted to Poland is ingenious. This enables them to trace the 'stock' of social capital in the form of farmers' cooperatives established in a bottom-up process in the nineteenth century and the process of building and sustaining them during the early twentieth century. They are thus able to really get in and look at the detail of local entrepreneurship in the formation and continuance of capital stock, particularly in the twentieth century before the Second World War. And, tragically, they show that the centralized regime established in Poland after the Second World War – which prided itself on the support of the worker and the creation of worker cooperatives as a national policy – destroyed the very capital it proclaimed it supported. Cooperatives, in effect, lost their voluntary foundation and effectively became state enterprises. The empirical differences shown in the participation rates and levels of trust of citizens in Poland and in Denmark are astounding. Further, the Svendsens provide a fascinating picture of the consequences of centralization of the dairy industry in Denmark after 1960, the transformation of bridging social capital into bonding social capital, and the consequences for continued social capital development in the rural areas of Denmark. Their study of the tension and lack of trust between long-term rural residents of Ravnborg and the newcomers moving there from Copenhagen is also a further insight to how social capital can further disintegrate.

Many lessons can be learned from this study. There are specific lessons to be learned about the history of cooperatives and rural life in Poland and in Denmark and the changes that have occurred over time. Far more important is a deep understanding of the relationship between central government and its institutions and the capacity of citizens to learn entrepreneurial and to undertake important economic and social activities relying primarily on their own skills. Even more important is the lesson we learn about the fragility of even very successful experiments.

This is the type of book that should be assigned to graduate students across the social sciences as an illustration of the kind of work that they should aspire to do. I know I have learned a great deal from reading this manuscript and appreciate the effort that the Svendsens have put in to crafting this study.

1. Introduction: The 'Missing Link'

1.1. RESEARCH QUESTION

The question addressed in this book is *'how is social capital created and destroyed?'*. We argue that the presence of entrepreneurs facilitates the creation of a new important production factor, social capital, which again is crucial for understanding collective action and voluntary co-operative movements.

Co-operative movements have been strongest in Scandinavia, and particularly in Denmark. The exemplary Danish co-operative movement is the strongest voluntary co-operative movement in the world, matched only by Poland in the nineteenth century and Iceland in the twentieth century after the Second World War. Here, our comparison between two different political systems sheds further light on this issue, namely by focusing on how social capital is built in decentralized market economies (the case of Denmark) and destroyed in centralized planned economies (the case of Poland).

Furthermore, the well-documented development in the unique case of the voluntary Danish co-operative movement makes it possible to trace a number of crucial factors that determine the creation and destruction of social capital. Our focus on entrepreneurship and rural communities raises general questions for the future of democracies in the Western world as more and more rural areas have undergone the kind of transformation that has occurred in Denmark in recent years. The implications of this cross-disciplinary investigation ranging from political economy, to sociology, history and anthropology, are of general interest to social scientists.

1.2. CONTRIBUTION

Our purpose is simple: we want to show that until now there has been a gap or 'missing link' in economic debates. Thus, partly because of poor communication between social scientists and economists, *we simply overlooked a production factor!* In line with more traditional production factors such as physical, financial and human capital, this missing factor can be called 'social' capital. Consequently, applying rich empirical material from

1

Denmark and Poland as evidence, we hypothesize that the missing link of *social* capital must be added as an important production factor when considering economic growth and the net outcome of any economic solution such as economies of scale and centralization of production.

Moreover, in our view the implication of such a discovery is a re-evaluation of traditional economics. Therefore, in order to develop a more realistic economics we propose a new socio-economics that we shall call 'Bourdieuconomics', in memory of the great French sociologist. Allowing for cross-disciplinary analyses of both material and non-material forms of capital, we propose that such a Bourdieuconomics should concentrate on the study of a long-ignored capital: social capital.

Various social capital studies have already been undertaken (for overviews, see for example Boix and Posner 1998; Portes 1998; Woolcock 1998; Sobel 2002). We have chosen political scientist Robert D. Putnam's (2000) recent book, *Bowling Alone*, as our main inspiration. In many ways our contribution profits from Putnam's study. Most significantly, we have made his notions of 'bridging' and 'bonding' social capital – i.e., inclusive and exclusive types of social capital – the key concepts of our book. Thus, when we speak of building positive or beneficial social capital we mean 'bridging' social capital, that is, open networks that are 'outward looking and encompass people across diverse social cleavages' (ibid.: 22).

When we speak of destruction of social capital we refer to bridging social capital giving way to 'bonding' social capital, that is, monopolistic-like and 'inward looking' networks that 'tend to reinforce exclusive identities and homogeneous groups' (ibid.). We shall show that such processes ultimately lead to what economists call 'negative externalities' or what sociologist Enzo Mingione (1991) has called 'fragmented societies'. We shall also show that bridging social capital enforces personal contact and acts as a 'lubricator' for human co-operation, whereas bonding social capital enforces distance between people and, consequently, acts as a 'super-glue', increasing *dis*trust and, thus, transaction costs.

For example, bonding social capital and distrust arise between different ethnic groups. In this context, Putnam (2000: 340) remarks that a case very often referred to in the United States is that of the Ku Klux Klan. Another extreme example is that of Italy, where bonding social capital is thriving among mafia groups in the South, resulting in nepotism and corruption, whereas strong civil traditions and bridging social capital prevail in the North (Putnam 1993a). In short, just like a cancer, excessive bonding social capital tends to 'eat up' healthy stocks of bridging social capital. In this sense, excessive bonding social capital is counterproductive, unless it is offset by a continuous revitalization – and reorganization – of existing stocks of productive bridging social capital.

Of course, different religious beliefs, for example, may differ so much that it is hardly possible to establish bridging social capital. Such seemingly insurmountable religious/cultural barriers can clearly be identified in India, for example, with its violent and relentless conflicts. Also, following September 11, a vast majority of Americans (and Western Europeans in general) would not be willing to trust members of the Al Qaeda network or political leaderships hosting terrorist groups. Thus, an important observation is that bridging social capital is much easier to build when we are dealing with agents with similar cultural and religious backgrounds and it becomes increasingly difficult as the number of common norms decline. We shall consider the type of conflicts that fall within the surmountable part of this scale, where the total benefits exceed the total costs of creating bridging social capital.

This not to say that society holds either bridging or bonding social capital, exclusively. Bonding social capital exists, for example, among close friends or relatives. However, the economic problem arises if the optimal balance between the stocks of bridging and bonding social capital in a society is disturbed by 'too much' bonding social capital at the expense of bridging social capital. Other examples are clashes between ethnic fractions, between different producer or consumer groups or between urban newcomers and local rural inhabitants in the countryside. The implications of this bridging and bonding social capital approach are wide indeed.

Whereas Putnam's quest in *Bowling Alone* was – primarily by use of statistics – to operationalize, quantify and thereby measure a shrinking stock of bridging social capital in the United States since the mid 1960s, our method is somewhat different. Rather than relying fully on statistical material, we shall demonstrate how (bridging) social capital is built and destroyed by people *in situ* – both historically and in contemporary society. In other words, we want to show how bridging social capital is built, and how it is transformed into bonding social capital. In order to do this, we shall make use of James Coleman's and Pierre Bourdieu's sociological social capital findings combined with empirical data from historical sources and anthropological fieldwork. In this way it is our hope, in a book about social capital, to establish social capital as *the* concept capable of 'bridging' rather than 'bonding' disciplines within the human sciences.

At the micro level, we are interested in entrepreneurship that facilitates voluntary collective action and the creation of inclusive types of social capital. A crucial factor is that these entrepreneurs are motivated not only by economic but also by social incentives. This mix of both economic and non-economic incentives forms the basis for the accumulation of social capital. We hope that this new view on entrepreneurship and the creation of social capital will contribute to the current academic and political discussions on group action and human behaviour.

Our contribution is to suggest that the presence of a social 'glue' in the form of bridging social capital – defined as regular face-to-face, co-operative relations across social boundaries – may explain the paradox of collective good provision (see Coleman 1988a; Putnam 1993a, 2000). The question of how social capital is created/destroyed has not yet been answered in the literature. We suggest that bridging social capital may be built locally as an outcome of organizational innovations ('the rules of the game') and then entrepreneurship could be fostered, which again may lubricate collective action. This theory seems to be confirmed by empirical evidence from rural Poland and Denmark, 1800–1900, obtained through our recent social capital surveys based on a comprehensive questionnaire, as well as by the growth of new forms of bridging social capital in recent years.

In the specific case of Denmark, we also make a new contribution by analysing the roles of leading entrepreneurs and decision makers within the co-operative movement. Here, we clearly demonstrate that the positive externality of bridging social capital is not taken into account when private economic decisions in the market are made, such as further centralization of production. Because the economic value of social capital linked to local production has been ignored so far in private market decisions, politicians must, from a societal perspective, intervene and support local production to a higher degree so that, for example, too much market centralization does not occur. The dominance of economic efficiency and 'hard' data in the public debate is also reflected by the fact that those opposing the closure of local co-operative associations could not vocalize their opposition due to the so-called 'theory effect' – they did not know the theory of social capital whereas the central leadership were well versed in the theory of traditional economics. This idea is also highlighted and linked to cases of bridging and bonding social capital in our most recent fieldwork studies.

1.3.   GROUP ACTION

Collective action simply means group action. It is relevant in our context whenever two or more individuals are involved, and it serves the interests of the individual better than individual action. Any collective action will benefit all members of the group. So, in its most *abstract* sense, collective action is to be found whenever two or more individuals join forces to accomplish a goal. With this wider definition, all collective goods are covered. The achievement of any common goal (in relation to a specific group) in a local area means that a collective good has been provided for all members in that group. In

Chapters 3, 4 and 7, we return to actual examples of collective good provision by local entrepreneurs in rural Denmark and Poland, and in Denmark, respectively.

We know from Mancur Olson's seminal work, *The Logic of Collective Action* (1965) that it does not pay an individual to provide collective goods voluntarily, if the individual economic gain from doing this is negative (see also Mueller 1989; Svendsen 1998). Thus, it does not pay an individual in larger groups to act as entrepreneur and facilitate local collective action, because individual costs from doing so are higher than the individual benefits from acting. Nevertheless, everyday observations and the empirical evidence presented in this book tell us that larger groups do organize and that entrepreneurs in the form of group leaders do exist. How can this paradox be explained? Why do we find entrepreneurship within larger groups? This paradox shows that incentives other than economic ones are important to the economic development of local areas and there is a strong need in the literature to fill this gap (see Green and Shapiro 1994).

1.4. HOLISTIC APPROACH

Cross-disciplinary human science research has approached this problem by focusing on the social aspects of economic transactions (Granovetter 1985; Coleman 1994). However, in our opinion, the overall theoretical framework of such investigations could be further strengthened by introducing the concept of social capital. In contrast to conceptual cousins such as the micro-oriented terms of 'network' and 'entrepreneurship' (to which social capital should be regarded as a supplement and not as a replacement!), the notion of social capital can be applied – and has been applied – at micro, meso and macro levels. This includes historical studies (Rotberg 2001). Thus, the possibility for consistent transnational comparisons is enhanced. Moreover, as Coleman (1994: 175) has argued, social capital is a fruitful term to use, because it closely links the economists' word 'capital' to the social scientists' key notion of 'social' – a point to which we shall return. Thus, by including in this very direct way both the economic and cultural spheres, social capital promotes a holistic understanding of collective goods provision processes.

1.5. METHOD

Is it possible to transfer experiences of how to build social capital from one country to another? Is it, for example, possible to apply knowledge gained from the Danish and Polish experiences with co-operative movements to an

American or European setting? What is the justification for using such a comparative method?

In principle, it seems necessary to analyse all similarities and differences because countries vary. For example, the United States and Scandinavia differ in many respects due to different institutional and cultural backgrounds. How then is it possible to transfer experience between these two different regions and to Western Europe? Is it possible to justify the selection and comparison of only a few variables in a most complex reality?

When answering this question, the discussion in the following will first present the traditional view of the comparative method, as represented by Lijphart (1975), which holds that all similarities and differences should be investigated. Next, the discussion will counter this approach by presenting Yin's (1989) innovative way of viewing the comparative case study as an experiment (see Svendsen 1998).

Lijphart (1975) represents the traditional approach. First, all similarities must be identified so that they can be assumed constant. Second, all differences must be found, and their occurrence must be explained. As such, the Scandinavian countries are ideal for comparison because they are similar in most ways, making it easier to reduce the number of possible explanations for the differences. This is not so easy, however, when comparing such different countries as Poland, Denmark and the United States.

Lijphart begins the analysis by choosing a causal relationship such that the variation in the dependent variable is maximized and the variation in the independent variable is minimized, so that the variation in the remaining independent variables can be used to explain the differences. This choice avoids the situation in which the dependent variable shows no variation, because then nothing can be explained. In this way, according to Lijphart, comparable cases are those in which the variables that are most similar are chosen as independent variables, whereas the variables that are most different are chosen as dependent variables.

The resulting variation in the dependent variable, then, forms the basis for an explanation. As such, the researcher can focus on the connections between variables with significant variation and try to explain why this variation takes place. However, this way of dealing with the comparative method is extremely cumbersome and difficult to handle. An infinite number of potentially related variables, and a universe of possible outcomes, make any result questionable.

Traditional case study is defined as 'an empirical inquiry that: investigates a contemporary phenomenon within its real-life context; when the boundaries between phenomenon and context are not clearly evident; and in which multiple sources of evidence are used' (Yin 1989: 23). These points are examined in more detail and contrasted with elements of three other dominant research strategies: historical analysis, statistical analysis, and case study as experiment. It will be argued that the 'case study' combined with the 'experiment' approach is the most appropriate tool for this book.

In contrast to a case study, historical analyses deal with events that have taken place in the past. Statistical analyses (or surveys) concern quantifiable data where the number of observations is large. An experiment differs from a case study by its laboratory setting. The experiment controls the context and separates a phenomenon from reality by varying only a few variables.

But the case study also concerns non-quantifiable (or qualitative) data, such as interviews or written statements, and thus makes it possible to investigate motivations and perceptions behind an action, such as the incentives for forming an environmental organization. Case studies are found both in political science, for studying international relations, for example, and in economics, for investigating the structure of an industry. In both cases, quantifiable data are insufficient to explain strategic motives.

In general, case studies have been the preferred strategy for explanatory research, that is, when 'how' or 'why' questions are being posed, when the investigator has little control over events and when the focus is on a contemporary phenomenon within a real-life context (ibid.: 13). To 'explain' a phenomenon is to stipulate a set of causal links about it, which case studies do through sets of logical statements. When Lijphart uses this method in a comparative context, however, the logic becomes flooded by the complexity of the analysis.

Here, Yin offers an alternative to the traditional approach to comparative analysis, arguing that a universe is not needed to explain local phenomena. Yin's point is that the single case is analogous to a single experiment in that the number of observations is one. A theory specifies a clear set of propositions and the circumstances within which the propositions are believed to be true. To confirm, challenge, or extend a theory, the case can be used to assess whether its propositions are correct, or whether some alternative set of explanations should be considered. When several cases are empirically tested against the theory, a multiple-case study simply means that an experiment is conducted several times over. In this way, the case can provide a significant contribution to knowledge and theory-building and can help to refocus future investigations in an entire field (ibid.: 47–53). Such new knowledge ensures the continuation of scientific progress.

Overall, the actual test of the theory is deductively carried out by pattern-matching with the experimental approach (ibid.: 109). This logic is used to compare an empirically based pattern to the theoretically predicted one. If the patterns coincide, the result does not reject the theory, and it becomes stronger the more confirming cases that are investigated. If a case does not confirm the theory, a rival theory may be reinforced or new theoretical propositions and explanations may be developed.

Hence, in this book we have chosen the cases of Denmark and Poland, arguing that these cases can be considered multiple experiments testing the same theoretical approach. This means that, in principle, it would be possible to transfer these experiences to an American setting, for example, and vice versa.

1.6.   OUTLINE

The comparative method used in this book is not as clear-cut as described in the previous section. It is in fact a combination of both deductive and inductive elements. The starting point is a theoretical model for social capital, but the choice of theory and the observations that follow have been influenced by induction. As such, the approach has been shaped by a dynamic interplay between theory and reality. However, as in a pure theory-testing model, the theory contained in Chapter 2 will guide the collection of data in Poland and Denmark (Chapter 3) whereas Chapters 4, 5, 6 and 7 generally use the method of induction. The deductive and inductive main elements identified eventually suggest a theoretical model concerning the creation and destruction of social capital (Chapter 8).

Thus, in order to answer the research question of how bridging social capital is built and destroyed, Chapter 2 starts by defining the theoretical background of social capital and entrepreneurship. Chapter 3 raises the general question whether a political system, that is, the formal institutional set-up in a country, matters to the level of social capital and civic society in practice. Here, the early and parallel emergence of co-operative movements in Denmark and Poland is analysed before comparative measures for social capital are developed from our new survey results. This comparison is interesting because we thereby compare the level of bridging social capital in those two countries to demonstrate the effect on co-operative movements and social capital level in two different political systems, namely that of democracy and capitalism (Denmark) and that of former communism and planned economy (Poland).

Given the political system of democracy and capitalism, Chapter 4 asks whether bridging social capital really is a production factor and why entrepreneurs voluntarily provide it in practice. We answer this question in two steps: first by focusing on the presence of entrepreneurship in Denmark as an explanatory variable for the occurrence of co-operative movements and subsequently the creation of bridging social capital and second, the recent growth of new forms of bridging social capital in Denmark, such as the wave of sports halls building and the inclusive networks linked to it, is highlighted.

Chapter 5 discusses how market centralization processes and transformations of beneficial bridging social capital, built by energetic entrepreneurs before the Second World War, turn into excessive harmful bonding social capital after the war. Thus, market centralization processes in a capitalist society eventually may fragmentize and thus destroy bridging social capital if the positive externality of local production and social capital is not taken into account. Chapter 6 analyses how cultural clashes between local people and newcomers in the Danish villages turned local stocks of social capital into prevailingly bonding types of social capital. Chapter 7 brings social capital to everyday life by presenting the results from our most recent fieldwork study. In this, the conflict between urban newcomers and locals in rural areas is analysed. This case is interesting both in relation to the theory of bridging and bonding social capital but also because outlying municipalities in Denmark and other Western European countries have had to cope with an influx of an increasingly large number of newcomers from big cities. Finally, Chapter 8 concludes the book, suggesting an overall model for explaining the creation and destruction of social capital.

2. Social Capital and Entrepreneurship

2.1. CAPITAL AND ENTREPRENEURSHIP

2.1.1. Introduction

In recent years, numerous capital concepts have been introduced in the social science literature. This can be documented by a data search of articles published within the latest few years. Thus, besides the familiar economic terms (financial, real, public, venture, human, social capital, and so on), scholars operate with at least 16 newly invented, alternative forms of capital: religious, intellectual, natural, digital, psychological, linguistic, emotional, symbolic, cultural, moral, political, endogenous, network, family, knowledge and organizational capital (see, for example, Current Contents Database 2003).

In the following, we shall focus on one of the latest additions to the family, namely social capital. What is social capital, and how can it be viewed as a new production factor? We try to answer this question in an interdisciplinary way by combining the disciplines of sociology, history and economics in three steps. First, the general economic starting point is taken from new institutional economics, with its focus on asymmetrical information and transaction costs. Second, we incorporate Bourdieu's capital theory by demonstrating how informal socio-economic, human exchange may compensate for the absence of full information. Third, we introduce the social capital concept in the sociological setting as a further specification of Bourdieu's approach. We do this by defining social capital as the presence of *entrepreneurship* and *trust* in a society. A summary completes the section.

Thus, we argue that what Putnam (2000) calls the inclusive form of *bridging* social capital, embodied as trust produced by regular face-to-face contact between citizens across group boundaries, may solve the fundamental problem in new institutional economics, namely by compensating for the presence of asymmetrical information and consequently reducing the level of transaction costs in society. This means that social capital in perspective can be viewed as a new capital form.

In fact, the whole purpose of this book is to apply historical and anthropological case studies in order to demonstrate that social capital both *is* and *always has been* an important production factor. More specifically, we want to emphasize that until recently – unfortunately, and partly due to poor co-operation between economists and social scientists – the social capital factor has been the 'missing link' in political and economic debates, with serious human and economic consequences. In other words, it was not until the beginning of the new millennium that we discovered that for far too long we had not taken the important production factor of *social* capital into consideration! It is precisely this 'missing link', which may be used as one explanation for the wealth of nations in specific contexts, that is, in historic as well as in contemporary societies (Svendsen and Svendsen 2003).

How can anything social be productive in an economic sense? Because a bridging social capital, although invisible and non-material in that it only exists in human relations, functions as a lubricator, linking people together in relations of both specific and generalized trust, that is, as a positive externality 'lubricating' human exchange across group boundaries. As such, strongly inclusive types of bridging social capital facilitate *all* transactions and, ultimately, lead to economic growth in a society. But does human co-operation *always* benefit society? No, not always. Social capital also has a downside (compare Portes and Landolt 1996). We refer to cases where co-operative networks are monopolized by relatively isolated groups, leading to exclusive types of social capital or – in Putnam's (2000) terminology – 'bonding social capital'. As will be clearly evidenced in the following, in such cases social capital can often be seen as a negative externality and a barrier for economic growth at the macro level. Bonding social capital tends to entail generalized *dis*trust and lack of co-operation between groups. As such, and in contrast to lubricating bridging social capital, bonding social capital can be seen as 'too much' glue – or *superglue* (ibid.) – which 'stiffens' society and, ultimately, makes it a 'fragmented society' to borrow an expression from sociologist Enzo Mingione (1991). In the Danish and Polish case studies presented in this book, we identify the destruction of social capital as the transformation of beneficial bridging social capital characterized by open co-operation to harmful bonding social capital characterized by lack of communication and co-operation among citizens, and, potentially, distrust, prejudice and symbolic violence between groups.

2.1.2.   Economics and Culture

2.1.2.1.   Wealth of nations

Why are some countries richer than others? Adam Smith (1776) and other social scientists have tried to answer this question highlighting the role of material capital, such as physical capital, and reified capital, such as human capital. But are the more or less tangible forms of capital *always* the key to economic growth? What about invisible culture and unformal institutions – tacit knowledge, which is closely linked to basic formal institutions, securing political and civic rights? As economist Amartya Sen (1999) has convincingly argued, it is exactly such liberty rights, embedded in 'invisible' capitals such as social capitals, that should be seen as the *true* factors for economic growth and human happiness.

Theoretically and, in contrast to Sen, with pure epistemological purposes, Bourdieu broke the Smithsonian line of thought by answering the two questions, what is capital and what forms of capital exist, in 'The forms of capital' (1986). The result was an original reformulation of Marx's concept of capital, where the term 'capital' is expanded to include both material as well as non-material phenomena. Thus, our contribution is to highlight the role of non-material capital when explaining differences in the wealth of nations.

An expanded concept of capital is most relevant to interdisciplinary social science research, which operates with a myriad of more or less exotic forms of capital. We try to operationalize Bourdieu's expanded concept of capital as a general framework, or epistemology, for an interdisciplinary research within a widened field of socio-economics, namely 'Bourdieuconomics' (Svendsen and Svendsen, 2003). Thus, in the following, we overall argue that the cultural capital dimension of institutions should be added to explain differences in the wealth of nations.

2.1.2.2.   Capital

The word 'capital' itself is derived from the Latin, *capitalis*, which again is derived from *caput* meaning 'head' or 'the sum of heads'. Within economics, capital has generally been defined as a resource that enables a person or organization to maximize profits. More specifically, stocks of capital goods, such as physical and financial capital, are used as input in the production process in different ways. For example, physical capital means produced production factors such as buildings, machines, tools, roads and railways, whereas financial capital refers to liquid assets such as stocks and bonds, enabling investments in physical capital.

Such basic definitions suggest a dividing line in research between economics and the other social sciences. Economists have tended to focus on capitalist market forces while sociologists, anthropologists and others have focused on the so-called 'non-economic' issues in terms of social phenomena (Smart 1993: 388).

2.1.2.3.   Socio-economic analyses

This division of labour has partly broken down by the end of the twentieth century due to interdisciplinary approaches headed by academics such as Pierre Bourdieu, Marc Granovetter, James Coleman, Douglass S. North and

Barry Weingast. Among these pioneers, Bourdieu has been the most radical in trying to remove the, in his opinion, artificial borders between economics and sociology. Bourdieu, whom we shall discuss more fully below, outlined an ambitious capital theory where the social field is also methodologically integrated into the field of economics as a form of capital on equal terms with other traditional economic capitals. Furthermore, we find other sociological and anthropological theories trying to deal with the principles of organizing markets in a broader perspective (Wrong 1961; Appadurai 1986; Granovetter 1990). For example, Mauss has analysed the exchange of gifts (Mauss [1925] 1969), Simmel has developed ideas on reciprocity (Simmel [1908] 1955), economic historian Karl Polanyi (1944, 1968) has by use of anthropological terminology investigated the 'embeddedness' of economic practices in cultural systems. And, most recently, in collaboration with Bourdieu, Frédéric Lebaron (2000) has questioned what he sees as the economic belief (*la croyance économique*), while Jean-Claude Passeron (for example 2001) has commented on the missing links between sociology and economy within science (but not in reality). However, the most path-breaking approach seems to have come from Durkheim (1908: 5), who, considering economic ideas and practices as collective representations in the form of the popular opinions dominating a society, strongly questioned what he termed the 'theory of economic materialism' – a theory held by economists who could only conceive of external, objective realities, and which made the economic life the 'underlying structure' (*substructure*) of social life. Also, this critique is reflected in Mauss's idea of 'the total social fact' (*le fait social total*). In contrast, economists, especially those belonging to the field of new institutional economics, have attempted to incorporate cultural aspects as *production factors* in the market and its production processes.

2.1.2.4. New institutional economics
In contrast to the standard assumption of full information in neoclassical economic theory, new institutional economics is basically the study of economic interaction in a world where agents do not have full information. Because agents lack information, they bear extra transaction costs when exchanging goods and services in the market. This argument is relevant to political decision making both in the political arena and in the market.

New institutional economics is one of three main lines within the academic field of political economy. The other two are the public choice school and collective good analysis (Svendsen 2003). Note that the *methodology* used in political economy is that of economics, which for example, allows the behaviour of interest groups in the political arena to be formally treated in the same way as the analysis of behaviour in the marketplace. This formal, mathematical exposition helps to develop a coherent, parsimonious, and deductive theory (Ordeshook 1993: 72; Green and Shapiro 1994: 10). Deduction means that the empirical consequences following theoretical statements are tested against reality (Hellevik 1980: 68). The researcher moves from theory to empirical evidence and thereby tests his/her theory. In contrast, induction and the discovery of theories in a bottom-up process has been the traditional starting point for research in sociology, history and political science. Theoretical statements are then based upon single empirical observations. Typically, this inductive phase is followed by a deductive theory test (ibid.). However, political economy theorists are sceptical that universal theories of politics can be developed through the inductive methods that have characterized political science through most of its history (Green and Shapiro 1994: 24).

Concerning the political arena, there are transaction costs linked to the process of influencing political decision makers. Based on North and Weingast (1989), Svendsen (2003) argues that the size of these costs depend upon the institutional set-up in society. A classical historical example could be that of the successful economic development in early England after the 'Glorious Revolution' in 1689. Here, one may argue that the successful economic policies adopted after 1689 are due to the very introduction of a parliamentary system at the expense of the previous totalitarian system under the king. By spreading power across a number of different institutions in England, the transaction costs in connection to lobbying activities were raised significantly. Lobbyists could no longer be content with influencing the king or a few of his officials only. All of a sudden they had to influence the majority of the members of parliament. In short, it was no longer enough to lobby in one place – now, it was necessary to lobby in many, and therefore more difficult to achieve the desired results.

Reducing lobbyism improved economic policies in England and turned the state into a far more trustworthy partner than previously because the king could no longer break contracts in an arbitrary way, for example, by sudden confiscation of private property or financial capital without compensation. Therefore, private English citizens started lending money to the state convinced that they would be repaid as agreed. Within two decades, England had in this way accumulated sufficient capital for investing in industrial and naval supremacy, resulting in tremendous economic growth (ibid.).

With regard to the market, trading agents must use resources to write and enforce a contract. Also, agents may need to use resources to protect themselves against non-voluntary transactions such as theft. These transaction costs will always be positive when agents do not have full information about one another. Thus, 'rules of the game', that is, institutions, are necessary (North 1990). These institutions, through rules, provide incentives for the group members to take certain actions to achieve the desired outcome, and the development of institutional arrangements require an investment of time by the members of the community. Coordination and information activities are initial aspects of building institutions (Ostrom 1992).

Modern economic market systems cannot rely on informal institutions alone. Many gains from trade would never be realized in the absence of formal institutions. For example, the establishment of long-term loans, insurance of the transaction and so on, would never happen in pre-capitalist societies, where transactions are typically performed in face-to-face relationships between trading partners giving with one hand and taking with the other (see North 1990: 54).

Here, the presence of strong formal institutions is essential. New institutional economics theorists base this hypothesis on empirical evidence from economic history. Here, they show how distant trade is facilitated by complex institutional set-ups rather than local behavioural norms. For example, Milgrom et al. (1990) describe the establishment of the so-called 'law merchants' in England, which gave trading parties vital information on trading conditions in other countries or regions. If traders did not respect the conditions in their contracts, they were simply 'blacklisted' and excluded from further trade. This efficient and formal enforcement of trade rules enabled economically beneficial trade with distant regions (Schjødt and Svendsen 2002).

Overall, the necessary institutional set-up can be based both on formal institutions with written-down rules and also on informal institutions with unwritten rules. The latter is especially relevant in relation to social capital, which we shall return to in Chapter 4, where voluntary self-enforcement of behavioural norms takes place at the local level. When this happens, society may save both monitoring, enforcement, and transaction costs, and consequently achieve more economic growth.

Thus, we may hypothesize that adequate formal institutions enforced by the state and informal institutions enforced by local agents on a voluntary basis, are crucial in determining the success or failure of a society in terms of its political institutions, its market economy and its potential economic growth. As we shall see in Chapters 3 and 4, a similar development concerning the development of efficient informal institutions occurred in co-operative movements established during the nineteenth century where well-functioning formal institutions were established already.

2.1.3.   Bourdieu

To continue the new institutional economics theme, and basing our comments on the work of Pierre Bourdieu, we shall now argue that economic and cultural dimensions of human exchange cannot be separated. Rather, they should be integrated into the same analytical model that we outline as a new socio-economics, 'Bourdieuconomics'.

In this way it becomes possible to trace a dynamic interplay between material and non-material capitals in a society. Thus, non-material capital as social capital lubricates the interaction between individuals, thus facilitating generalized trust and reduced transaction costs. Therefore, non-material and invisible cultural values cannot be perceived as being of less economic importance than traditional economic values such as buildings, tools, machines, infrastructure, raw materials, financial capital and so on. Here, as we mentioned earlier, Coleman (1994: 175) has suggested it would be natural to combine the word 'social' from social scientists with the word 'capital' from economists, thereby fusing together different approaches. In other words, the link between economics and culture may be operationalized as social capital, broadly viewed as an informal exchange embedded in cultural systems which, none the less, presumably holds important economic implications. In the following, we suggest how Bourdieu, through his extended 'capital' definition, clears the road for this kind of interdisciplinary social capital research.

2.1.3.1.   Towards a neo-capital theory

What is capital? What forms of capital exist? In 1979, Bourdieu sought to answer these two questions in two articles, 'Le capital social' and 'Les trois états du capital culturel' (Bourdieu 1979a, 1979b). In 1983, these ideas were further elaborated in 'Ökonomisches Kapital, kulturelles Kapital, sociales Kapital', which appeared in the anthology *Soziale Ungleichheiten* (Bourdieu 1983a). In 1986, the German article was 'concealed' in the relatively obscure publication from Greenwood Press, *Handbook of Theory and Research for the Sociology of Education* (Bourdieu 1986), which may explain why Bourdieu's great capital project within the human sciences has gone largely unnoticed by the broad academic audience. (For a discussion of Bourdieu's definitions of capital and forms of capital, see also Müller 1986; Gartman 1991; Bourdieu and Wacquant 1992; Anheier et al. 1995; Lebaron 2003.)

Bourdieu sought to address the two questions – what is capital, and what forms does it take? – in the abovementioned article 'The forms of capital' (Bourdieu 1986). Building on classical social economic thinkers, such as Émile Durkheim, Max Weber, Marcel Mauss and Karl Polanyi, the result was an original reformulation of Marx's concept of capital, where the term 'capital' is expanded to include both material as well as non-material phenomena.

In the following we will try to further the operationalizion of 'capital' by applying and developing Bourdieu's (1986) seminal ideas of a 'general theory of the economy of practices'. This leads us towards a new socioeconomics, that is, 'Bourdieuconomics' (Svendsen and Svendsen 2003), which aims to identify and explain the existing 'plethora of capitals' (Woolcock 1998: 155) within a unified, neo-capital theory framework.

2.1.3.2. The extended concept of 'capital'

Within classical economics, capital has been broadly defined as a resource available for a person or an organization and used for maximizing profits. More specifically, economists have operated with stocks of capital goods in the form of real capital and financial capital, where real capital – as we already have mentioned – consists of produced production factors such as buildings, machines and infrastructure, while financial capital consists of money and similar liquid assets that can be invested in real capital. Similarly, Marx applied the terms 'constant' or 'fixed' capital in contrast to 'circulating capital' (for example, Marx [1867] 1968c).

Surprisingly, economists do not seem to agree on a core concept such as 'capital', which – apparently – often is taken for granted (like other key concepts as 'market', 'transaction cost', 'investment', 'externalities' and 'value'). Thus, in the social capital literature, the term 'capital' is often quickly overviewed, *if defined at all*, as illustrated by an important anthology on social capital from the World Bank (2000) dominated by contributors within economics.

Here, we find it fruitful to return to Bourdieu (1986: 241), who in line with Marx defines capital broadly as 'accumulated, human labour' in either a 'materialized' or 'incorporated' form (that is, within a person), which can potentially produce various forms of profits (for a more detailed discussion, see Svendsen and Svendsen 2003). But whereas the Marxian capital framework is macroeconomic, historic and materialistic, that is, obsessed with visible forms of capital like most classical economic studies are, the Bourdieusian framework allows for a sociological scope, implying the focus on concrete human relations. Furthermore, it operates with various material and non-material capitals or forms of power (ibid.: 243) within specific fields (economic, political, juridical, artistic, religious, scientific). Like the number of fields, the number of capital forms seems to be unlimited, ranging from technological, juridical, cultural, educational, organizational, commercial, symbolic and social capital (see for example Bourdieu 1979a, 1979b, 1986, 1997, 2000).

Accumulated human labour through history, or 'capital', is both valuable and durable. Moreover, capital is 'labour-time', and it can only be built at the expense of human energy and time. As formulated by a poet: capital is 'dried sweat' (cited from Almås 1999: 162). Here, Bourdieu's inspiration from the work of Marx is clear. However, in contrast to Bourdieu, Marx sought to argue for a historical hypothesis: a specific way of organizing working relations, capitalism, had entailed a significant difference between applied and consumed human labour (Marx [1867] 1968c: 635). Here, past labour (*die vergangne Arbeit*), forming a basis of capitalistic economic growth, should be seen as unpaid working time, that is, working time stolen from generations of working slaves through 'thousands of centuries':

> Das Kapital besteht nicht darin, daß aufgehäufte Arbeit der lebendigen Arbeit als Mittel zu neuer Produktion dient. Es besteht darin, daß die lebendige Arbeit der aufgehäuften Arbeit als Mittel dient, ihren Tauschwert zu erhalten und zu vermehren. (The capital does not imply that accumulated labour of the living labour serves as a tool for new production. It implies that the living labour serves the accumulated labour in order to profit from and increase its exchange value.) (Marx [1849] 1968a: 409, our translation)

In a more sociological, synchronic perspective, Bourdieu states that it is a key characteristic of capital that it is inscribed in the world or, in his own formulation, 'a force inscribed in the objectivity of things' (1986: 241). Therefore, capital implies the existence of media, through which it can be transferred in time and space. These media consist of human-made things (materialized form) and human beings (incorporated form).

Consequently, we find physical capital in an objectified material form, whereas we find human capital consisting, for example, of education and working experience in an incorporated form, that is, as an invisible part of a person. However, only one form of capital, social capital, exists as relations, that is, as invisible products *outside* human beings. Therefore, social capital can be transferred through time only in an indirect form, namely as an integral part of a thing or a person.

2.1.3.3.   Critique of economism: The *real* economy of practice

Bourdieu's expanded concept of capital differs from the traditional economic definition of the word as a factor of production, that is, a resource which facilitates production and which is simultaneously not consumed in the production process. This is in line with the critiques of undersocialization within economics, most vigourously formulated by economic anthropologist Karl Polanyi (1944) in *The Great Transformation* – an impressive economic historical account analyzing the roots of a culturally and economically disordered world after the two world wars.

The Great Transformation is the transformation of three historical modes of exchange – reciprocity, redistribution, market exchange – being reduced to one in the Western World, namely that of liberalistic-capitalistic market exchange. The legtimate recognition of only one of three forms of resouce allocation (or modes of circulation of goods) is due to ethnocentric economistic economics dating back to the founding father of the discipline of economy, Adam Smith. Thus, following Polanyi, the economic thinking of

Smith and his successors are based on an abstract idea of a universal 'market' and 'natural' economic instincts in each individual person transcending all cultures, places and time periods – a thesis, which, however, has been falsified by all ethnographic and historical sources:

> Adam Smith suggested that the division of labor in society was dependent upon the existence of markets, or, as he put it, upon man's „propensity to barter, truck and exchange one thing for another." This phrase was later to yield the concept of the Economic Man. (Polanyi [1944] 1957: 43)

This Smithsonian legacy has lead to what Polanyi sees as the formalist definition of economy, or 'the economic problem': history *matters*, as 'to narrow the genus economic specifically to market phenomena is to eliminate the greatest part of man's history from the scene' (op.cit.: 6).

It is precisely the social scientific reciprocity tradition, formed by social scientists such as Durkheim, Weber, Mauss and Polanyi that has lead to a critique of undersocialization within classical economy theory. Here, non-reflexive Rational Actor research of various types are accused of reducing human actions to simple profit maximization without cultural implications – similar to the reduction of living, spoken language (*parole*) to an underlying grammar (*langue*) in Ferdinand de Saussure's language theories before World War One that later were to form the basis of the formalistic school within linguistics and Lévi-Strauss' structuralism within anthropology. During the last part of the nineteenth century, similar critiques have been formulated by the economist Yoram Ben-Porath (1980), who in line with Polanyi and more recent ethnographic fieldworks has spoken of the 'F-connection' (family, friends and firms) stressing the importance of identity, reciprocity and trust not only in families, but also in market exchanges. Similarly, sociologist Marc Granovetter (1985) has also applied the ideas of Polanyi, by emphasizing the embeddedness of economic transactions in changing cultural contexts.

It is Bourdieu, however, who since Polanyi has formulated the most elaborated social scientific critique of *homo oeconomicus*. This has been done in an attempt to reach a more realistic definition of economic reasoning (*une définition réaliste de la raison économique*) (2000: 235). As we noted, similar research has been carried out by other French sociologists, not least Frédéric Lebaron (2000), who has questioned the collective economic beliefs (*la croyance économique*) invented and reproduced by neo-classical economic thought.

Through the 1960s, Bourdieu was extremely interested in economics and econometrics. In several projects he even worked as an economist himself, co-operating with professionally trained, French econometricians (Lebaron 2003). However, he gradually realized the shortcomings of quantitative metods and consequently the need of qualitative sociological methodologies in order to explain an, if standing alone, highly unrealistic economics, far from real human lives.

Therefore, from the late 1970s, Bourdieu (1979a, 1979b, 1980, 1986) began to play with the idea of a broad interdisciplinary-based human science, termed 'A general science of the economy of practices'. The purpose of such a new discipline is to reformulate the economists' word capital 'in all its forms and not only in the one form which is recognized by economic theory' (1986: 242; see also 1980: 261ff.). The acquisition of the forms of capitals, that is, material *as well as* non-material, gives access to power and ultimately to material wealth.

This allows Bourdieu to direct a focus towards the economy in *all* practices, that is, towards the economic calculation, which lies behind not only obvious economic practices but also the more hidden and symbolic ones. This clearly entails a break with culturalism, which has tended to oversocialize practice, ignoring 'the brutal fact of universal reducibility to economics' (Bourdieu 1986: 253). The project is described thus:

> A general science of the economy of practices, capable of reappropriating the totality of the practices which, although objectively economic, are not and cannot be socially recognised as economic . . . must endeavour to grasp capital and profit in all their forms and to establish the laws whereby the different types of capital (or power, which amounts to the same thing) change into one another. (ibid.: 243)

Lebaron (2003) has recently published an interesting review of Bourdieu's early work on a general theory of practices. By this, he intends to explain the origins of Bourdieu's polemic 'double position' between economy and sociology (and economic and sociological discourse) – a position that has often been misunderstood and criticized by scholars. However, Lebaron argues, such criticisms have not done Bourdieu justice in that it is exactly by choosing this position that he opens the possibility of an 'integrated vision of social and economic factors of practices' (ibid.: 555).

In our view, a 'Bourdieuconomics' offers two original observations (compare Calhoun 1993: 69; Svendsen and Svendsen 2003: 615ff.). First, there are many different forms of capital, from material (physical, economic) to non-material (cultural, symbolic, social). Second, with varying degrees of difficulty, it is possible to convert one form of capital into another.

Apart from the above mentioned break with culturalism, this entails a second conceptual break with the economism of Marx and the classical economists. Thus, Bourdieu argues, around the new millennium such a dehumanizing economics seems to have obtained an almost hegemonial power on a global scale (Bourdieu 2000, 2003). This reflects what Polanyi early detected as Western ethnocentrism inhered in the idea of global free markets as the endgoal or *telos* for The development – the academic soundability of which can only be established by artificially isolating an economical economy from a cultural one. (See also Bourdieu 1990a: 113; Lash 1993). Bourdieu's alternative is to depart from such a substantialism and materialism by localizing the economic forces behind *all* human actions, without necessarily seeing these as derived from naked self-interest, as the economists would have it (Bourdieu 1977: 178; Snook 1990: 169; May 1996: 125).

For Bourdieu, this does not prevent that all forms of capital can always be converted into economic capital (see also Svendsen and Svendsen 2003: 616–17). At the same time, he fully acknowledges the paradox that while an economic calculation lies behind every action, every action cannot be reduced to economic calculation (Bourdieu 1979a: 2, 1986: 253, 1989: 224).

This is due to the fact that, for individual actors, it is a value in itself to participate and invest time, energy and money in 'the economic game', which thereby – precisely as a culturally embedded game with written and unwritten rules – obtains a legitimacy in itself (Bourdieu 1990: 89). In sum, in the Bourdieusian terminology, traditional economic words such as 'interest' and 'value' retain their ambiguity, such that Bourdieu cannot be accused of being a pure rational choicer but, rather, a reasonable (*raisonnable*) choicer:

> Economism knows no other interest than that which capitalism has produced, through a sort of concrete application of abstraction, by establishing a universe of relations between man and man based, as Marx says, on 'callous cash payment'. Thus, it can find no place in its analyses, still less in its calculations, for the strictly symbolic interest which is occasionally recognised (when too obviously entering into conflict with 'interest' in the narrow sense, as in certain forms of nationalism or regionalism) only to be reduced to the irrationality of feeling or passion. (Bourdieu 1977: 177)

With regard to the concrete analysis of the economy of practices in all its forms, Bourdieu proposes that we operate with four forms of capital: economic, cultural, symbolic and social. (For more details, see also Svendsen and Svendsen 2003).

Beyond economic capital, into which the other capitals can be capitalized, cultural capital should be understood here as cultural products, which are embedded in the human mind and body, as well as in objects (Bourdieu 1986: 243ff.). In contrast, symbolic capital is a more hidden form of capital which is defined as 'economic or political capital that is disavowed, mis-recognized and thereby recognized, hence legitimate, a "credit" which, under certain conditions, and always in the long run, guarantees "economic" profits' (Bourdieu 1980: 262). In his definition of *social capital*, Bourdieu succeeds in unifying the classical group theories (Marx, Durkheim, Weber) with the reciprocity theories (Mauss, Simmel). Focusing on network relations within a group from which the individual group member can profit, social capital becomes:

> the aggregate of the actual or potential resources which are linked to possession of a durable network of more or less institutionalised relationships of mutual acquaintance and recognition – or in other words, to membership in a group – which provides each of its members with the backing of the collectively-owned capital, a 'credential' which entitles them to credit, in the various senses of the word . . . The network of relationships is the product of investment strategies . . . aimed at establishing or reproducing social relationships that are directly usable in the short or long term. (Bourdieu 1986: 248–9)

In the following, we offer a presentation of social capital within the framework of Bourdieu's capital theory. However, first it is necessary to analyse social capital in its genesis, so to speak. This implies a specific focus on entrepreneurship.

2.1.3.4. Entrepreneurship

Overall, it does not follow that perfect consensus, both about the desire for the collective good and the most efficient means of getting it, will always bring about the achievement of a group goal. As we mentioned earlier, Mancur Olson's seminal contribution from 1965 is that rational, individual behaviour *does not* lead to rational group behaviour. Even if the total benefits by far exceed total costs for achieving a common goal, it does not logically follow that collective action takes place (Svendsen 2003). The Olsonian theory of collective action has been called '*the* central subject of political science' (Ostrom 1998: 1).

This logic broke with traditional group theory, which was based on the degree of consensus. An individual will voluntarily act in support of common group interests and values as a logical consequence of the widely accepted premise of rational self-interest. Exceptions to this rule occur when the leadership ignores the group interests and, due to asymmetrical information (leaders know more than the rest of the group members), is serving other ends (Olson 1965: 5).

In other words, prior to Olson (1965), groups were simply viewed as voluntary organizations furthering their common interests. But this is not so, says Olson. Rational individual behaviour does not lead to rational group behaviour! Olson formulates it as follows: 'rational, self-interested individuals will not act to achieve their common or group interests' (ibid.: 2). This means that even though the aggregate gains that a local group attains from a collective good greatly exceed the total costs of that action (and thereby enhances prosperity), it does not follow that the action will occur: individual rationality *does not* lead to collective rationality.

David Hume was the first to treat this collective choice problem in group action. In his *A Treatise of Human Nature* (1739) he writes that when men have protected themselves against each other's weaknesses and passions – by the *execution* and *decision* of justice, they 'begin to taste at ease the sweets of society and mutual assistance'. Hume illustrates this situation by looking at how two farmers co-operate, assuming that they 'know each other's mind' and that failing means 'abandoning the project':

> Your corn is ripe to-day; mine will be so tomorrow. It is profitable for us both, that I should labour with you to-day, and that you should aid me to-morrow. I have no kindness for you, and know you have as little for me. I will not, therefore, take any pains upon your account; and should I labour with you upon my own account, in expectation of a return, I know I should be disappointed, and that I should in vain depend upon your gratitude. Here then I leave you to labour alone: You treat me in the same manner. The seasons change; and both of us lose our harvests for want of mutual confidence and security. (Hume [1739] 1984)

In contrast, Hume observed that it is indeed impossible that *a thousand* persons should agree on any such action, 'it being difficult for them to concert so complicated a design, and still more difficult for them to execute it; while each seeks a pretext to free himself of the trouble and expense, and would lay the whole burden on others' (ibid.: 590).

This brings us back to Mancur Olson's main point that individual rationality does not necessarily lead to collective rationality. Why is this so? Let us take a closer look at the distribution of costs and benefits in a group. Say, for example, that the total cost of eliminating mad cow disease is $100,000 whereas the total benefit is $1 million. In other words, the group of farmers will in this hypothetical example earn $900,000 as a group. Assume finally that these benefits are shared equally among all the farmers.

It follows that if the group size amounts to two farmers only, each of them will experience a benefit valued at $500,000. Since each individual member's net benefit from providing the good alone at the cost of $100,000 is positive in this case ($400,000), the good will be provided even in the absence of organization and cost-sharing.

However, if there are 1,000 farmers in the group, each farmer will receive an individual gain of $1,000. Although the group as a whole would stand to get benefits worth ten times the amount of money invested in eliminating mad cow disease, the net benefit to any individual member who chooses to provide the good on his or her own is clearly negative. Thus, in the absence of organization and cost-sharing, the collective good will not be provided.

In summary, the link between individual rationality and group rationality depends on the individual net benefit from contributing to the collective good. Table 2.1 reviews this logic. In other words, Olson (1965) suggests that in the small group of two farmers, both will act as entrepreneurs and will voluntarily provide the collective good on their own, because they both get a positive economic net gain from doing so. In contrast, in the larger group of 1,000 farmers no one will act as entrepreneur on their own and start organizing the group, reaping the aggregated economic benefits for the group (or local society) as a whole, because the economic net gain is clearly negative.

Table 2.1 Collective good provision of eliminating mad cow disease

	2 farmers	1000 farmers
Total gain	$1 million	$1 million
Individual gain	$500,000	$1,000
Total cost	$100,000	$100,000
Individual net gain	$400,000	Negative ($1,000 – $100,000)

Source: The authors.

Coase (1960) put forward a similar transaction cost idea that – in the absence of transaction costs and incomplete information – it is sufficient to define and enforce property rights. Then a socially efficient outcome will occur independently of how the rights are distributed. For example, in the relationship between a farmer and a rancher, the one who is liable will build the fence, or between a polluter and a victim, the one who is liable will pay the abatement costs.

So, when only two persons are involved and the liability is defined, transaction costs are low. If numbers are raised to, say, the thousand farmers in Hume's example, transaction costs will be high and an optimal outcome may not occur. It is then difficult to reach an agreement with all parties involved. This is exactly what the so-called 'Coase theorem' states.

Although mobilization of these larger groups is difficult and takes time, it does happen. Olson explains the presence of entrepreneurs and group mobilization in larger groups by the phenomenon of chance. Only when the *right leadership* and the *right circumstances* are present, will a group be formed (Olson 1982).

Elinor Ostrom has defined such a 'public entrepreneur' as someone familiar with the situation who 'has to envision the possibilities of joint action and bring together the necessary factors of production into one unit' (Ostrom 1965: 3, cited in Kuhnert, 2001: 17). Olson repeatedly mentions the necessity for 'professional organizers' and says that there is no 'automatic' collective action (Olson 1965 and 1982, cited in Kuhnert 2001: 14).

As noted by Simon (1993), human choice is also driven by a number of motives not limited to economic gain that are based on anticipated consequences (pleasure and pain) for the chooser. Altruism, such as the one undertaken by voluntary entrepreneurs in the empirical sections of this book, could therefore be defined as behaviour that is influenced by expectations of pleasure and pain for other persons. Such a definition would come close to everyday common-sense understanding of altruism and entrepreneurial behaviour: 'It includes economic gain among the selfish motives but does not restrict selfishness to it alone' (ibid.: 158). By focusing on the interests of others as well rather than single-minded self-interest, one avoids the theoretical deadlock of selfish utility maximization:

> Neoclassical economics assumes that people maximize utility but postulates nothing about what utility is. With only this assumption, it is impossible to distinguish altruism from selfishness. One might call altruistic any choice that decreased the utility of the chooser while increasing the utility of others; but such a definition is useless. With the appropriate utility function, a person whose utility derived from giving to other people could selfishly give away millions of dollars. (Ibid.)

The social and non-selfish dimension of human behaviour is, as argued by Svendsen (2003), also reflected in the classical prisoner's dilemma games. Here, economists have long wondered why people tend to co-operate more than they should according to economic theory. It has not been possible to explain why excess co-operation takes place in prisoner's dilemma games. For example, experimental evidence on such games reveals a surprising amount of trusting behaviour. In several sets of experiments, one-half of the first-move players in anonymous sequential prisoner's dilemma games chose to trust their partners, while three-quarters of second-movers declined to violate this trust, co-operating rather than defecting to the Nash equilibrium. Thus, experimental and everyday observations indicate that people tend to co-operate and follow a set of social norms, though it would be economically rational for the individual to defect (ibid.). This leads us to alternative explanations such as the one of social capital and trust.

Following Carter and Ghorbani (2003), we define trust as the willingness of a party to be vulnerable to the actions of another party based on the expectation that the other party will perform a particular action important to the trustor, irrespective of the ability to monitor or control that party. A similar definition is suggested by Mayer, et al. (1995) who define trust as the mutual confidence that no party to an exchange will exploit another's vulnerabilities, that is, that no party will cheat or free ride even if there is an economic net gain from doing so. Finally, Luhmann argues that trust is a social relationship subject to its own set of rules and that it occurs within a framework of social interaction and personality (Luhmann 1979; see Carter and Ghorbani 2003).

As will be remembered, this idea is reflected in the 'F-connection' (family, friends and firms), as well as in Granovetter's (1985, 1995) notion of the 'embeddedness' of economic transactions in differing cultural contexts. For example, in an American context, Granovetter has shown that getting a job normally requires that the actor uses his or her social network in the form of friends, acquaintances and the like. In this way, Granovetter explains, getting a job depends more on using the resource of 'weak ties' rather than that of 'strong ties', that is, kinship-based relations (1973, 1974). Also, Ostrom (1998) has developed common-pool resource management further by including social capital in so-called 'second generation' rational choice models.

Economist Bengt Johannisson's research on the networking of community entrepreneurs links closely to Granovetter's findings (see, for example, 1973, 1974, 1985, 1990). Here, the 'network metaphor' is used to bridge 'social and economic dimensions of human conduct', while 'entrepreneurship' is regarded as 'an act of creation' and 'small business as a way of life, that is, as phenomena beyond rational economic behaviour' (Johannisson and Mønsted 1997: 109). Johannisson and Nilsson (1989) have documented that, in contrast to traditional entrepreneurs who 'reorganise resources', entrepreneurs networking in local communities (that is, 'contextual' entrepreneurs) 'reorganise values' (see also Daugbjerg and Svendsen 2001, concerning network formation within the agricultural sector).

Generally, much research in the Scandinavian countries applies a socio-economic approach, aiming to link the economic with the non-economic – not least in connection with investigations in networking and entrepreneurship (Johannisson and Mønsted 1997). Moreover, at the beginning of the 1980s, a group of Danish ethnologists (Christiansen 1982; Højrup 1983, 1989; Møllgaard 1984) developed the concept of 'life-form' or, alternately, 'life-mode', referring to the 'totality' of a practice and a worldview belonging to a distinct group (peasants, industrial workers, functionaries etc.). Thus, ethnologist Thomas Højrup (1983: 17), for example, has suggested constructing 'the concepts of several distinct life-modes, which are the bases for [group] practices and ideologies and which place their own distinct demands on social institutions and social organization as a whole'.

2.1.4.   Summary

In this section, we identified the theoretical roots of social capital by developing an interdisciplinary theoretical framework that combined economics and sociology in three steps. First, we introduced the general economic starting point from new institutional economics, focusing on asymmetrical information and transaction costs. Next, we incorporated the capital theories of Bourdieu and Coleman and demonstrated how cultural values generally may compensate for asymmetrical information. Finally, we argued that the concept of social capital can be perceived as a more specific version of Bourdieu's capital approach when measuring social capital as the level of trust in a group or society.

Overall, we suggested that social capital, embodied as trust, may solve the two fundamental problems in new institutional economics, namely by compensating for asymmetrical information and by reducing the size of transaction costs following social and economic interaction. Thus, social capital may be viewed as a new production factor that may help explain the wealth of nations. In perspective, the concept of social capital may help to explain the paradox of entrepreneurship. This question has challenged the social sciences since Olson (1965) showed that it does not pay an individual to provide collective goods voluntarily, if the individual economic gain from doing this is negative. However, the fact that larger groups actually do organize in local areas cannot be explained in strict economic terms. Thus, in an attempt to fill this gap in the literature, we now offer another solution, namely the presence of social incentives called 'social capital'. This idea will be elaborated in the next section, where the crucial notion of social sanction will be added as an explanatory variable for group action on top of the transaction cost idea outlined above.

2.2.   SOCIAL CAPITAL

2.2.1.   Introduction

In this section, we shall elaborate on the theory behind the creation and economic effect of social capital. Overall, the social capital approach can be regarded as an attempt to combine sociology and economics. Coleman was the first to define social capital as people's ability to co-operate in achieving a common goal (Coleman 1988a: 95). This voluntary co-operation is self-enforcing and establishes an informal institution without any written rules in contrast to forced co-operation enforced by a third party following the written-down rules of a formal institution.

Bjørnskov (2004) gives an overview where he identifies three main advantages from the presence of social capital. First, actors may gain access to resources held by other people such as complementary human capital specific to one's job. Second, social capital allows access to a latent resource, for example when being able to count on neighbours and family to mind one's children or do other odd jobs, which in turn enables individuals to, for example, act more flexibly towards fluctuations in work hours and work pressure. Third, in the presence of trust people can save on transaction costs, as many formal and informal deals can be handled without extensive contracts or monitoring.

Social capital is arguably built up in small groups where 'face-to-face' interaction generates common social norms (or 'social glue') and creates predictable behavioural patterns. In this way, culture and behavioural rules are built through repetition, tradition and example (Svendsen and Svendsen 2000, 2001). This is a credible informal contract because social ostracism helps to enforce it. If someone does not follow these informal rules, that person will simply be ostracized by the group and, as such, confront extra costs from not co-operating.

The interdisciplinary concept of social capital is probably the scientific concept that has attracted most attention and most followers ever within a short period of time. It provides a common language for all social sciences (Paldam 2000). For an authoritative and comprehensive review of the interdisciplinary development and theoretical foundations of social capital within economics, political science, sociology, development theory and philosophy, see Ostrom and Ahn (2003).

The outline of this section is as follows. First it is explained theoretically how social capital is created by the potential use of a social sanction mechanism and how such accumulation of social capital can be described as a positive externality resulting in an economic net gain for society. This all leads us to the crucial distinction between bridging and bonding social capital. The following subsections link social capital to classical reciprocity theories and introduce our new concept of Bourdieuconomics, that is, the linking of social capital and the wealth of nations. We conclude with a summary of the section.

2.2.2.   Social Capital and Trust

The most important impact that the type and extent of shared norms will have on the strategies available to individuals has to do with the level of opportunistic behaviour that appropriators can expect from other appropriators (Ostrom 1990: 36). Ostrom here uses Williamson's (1975) definition of opportunism, namely 'self-interest with guile', and continues:

> In a setting in which few individuals share norms about the impropriety of breaking promises, refusing to do one's share, shirking, or taking other opportunistic actions, each appropriator must expect all other appropriators to act opportunistically whenever they have the chance. In such a setting it is difficult to

develop stable, long-term commitments. Expensive monitoring and sanctioning mechanisms may be needed. (Ostrom 1990: 36)

However, we shall argue that building of trust in smaller groups facilitates the removal of opportunism due to the possibility of social sanctioning, thus leading to a higher level of aggregate economic growth. This idea is derived from the work of Ostrom and Swedberg. Ostrom (1990: 35) writes:

Norms of behavior reflect valuations that individuals place on actions or strategies in and of themselves, not as they are connected to immediate consequences. When an individual has strongly internalized a norm related to keeping promises, for example, the individual suffers shame and guilt when a personal promise is broken. If the norm is shared with others, the individual is also subject to considerable *social censure* for taking an action considered to be wrong by others. (Our italics)

Other social scientists have subsequently taken up Ostrom's idea and the sanctioning of undesirable individual behaviour. A representative example is that of Swedberg, who has defined a social structure as a recurrent and patterned interaction between agents that are maintained through sanctions (Swedberg 1994).

The implication in our social capital approach is that if group members trust one another and can sanction defectors, this group may achieve more economic growth compared to another group without such internal trust because more transactions may take place at lower cost and the predictability of behaviour increases; it is no longer necessary to monitor and enforce most transactions formally. Trust lubricates society, as Putnam puts it (Putnam 1993b). One may therefore suggest that social capital is a new production factor by saving transaction costs in society, thus allowing more voluntary transactions to take place.

Figure 2.1 suggests why an informal agreement is accomplished where the only sanction is that of social ostracism. In Figure 2.1, the marginal benefit curve from opportunism and free riding, *MB*, is, for simplicity, shown as a straight horizontal line. Here, we simply assume that an agent receives the same return in terms of money and saved time per unit of opportunism. Furthermore, the marginal cost curve, *MC*, is shown as an increasing straight line, indicating that the cost to the opportunistic individual increases because the voluntary provision of collective good is hampered more and more, thus reducing the individual share of the gains following collective good provision. *Without* the presence of social capital, an individual will undertake opportunistic and non-cooperative behaviour corresponding to Q^* thereby achieving the net gain of area *A*. *With* the presence of social capital and the possibility of inflicting social costs on any opportunists that defect in co-operating, these social costs must be added to the *MC* curve so that we now get the new MC_{sc} curve. As drawn, the MC_{sc} curve does not cross the *MB* curve, implying that no opportunistic behaviour will take place in this case given the presence of social capital. Here, we assume, again for the sake of simplicity, that community members can punish one another socially at negligible cost.

Thus, social sanctioning and the building of trust lubricate society while reducing opportunistic behaviour and free riding. More transactions can take place at a lower cost and trust will increase predictability and production in society because it is no longer necessary to have a formal third party for monitoring and enforcing all transactions. In this way, a group with members that trust one another may be capable of accomplishing more economic growth than a similar group without trust. Also, for example, it may be argued that a firm reduces transaction costs by having numerous informal transactions taking place, which are not formally sanctioned (see Coase 1937).

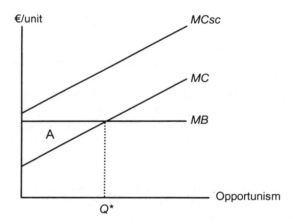

Source: The authors.

Figure 2.1 Social capital and opportunism

This crucial feature of social capital, here operationalized as trust, had already been observed by David Hume in 1739: 'When a man says he promises any thing, he in effect expresses a resolution of performing it; and along with that, by making use of this form of words, subjects himself to the penalty of never being trusted again in case of failure' (Hume [1739] 1984).

Another early writer, Adam Smith, the founder of economics, observed in *The Wealth of Nations* (1776):

> Commerce and manufactures can seldom flourish long in any state which does not enjoy a regular administration of justice; in which the people do not feel themselves secure in the possession of their property; in which the faith of contracts is not supported by law; and in which the authority of the state is not supposed to be regularly employed in enforcing the payment of debts from all those who are able to pay. Commerce and manufactures, in short, can seldom flourish in any state, in which there is not a certain degree of confidence in the justice of government. (Smith [1776] 1991)

Overall, social capital, defined as people's ability to co-operate, may enhance economic growth in society. For example, it may be argued that voluntary organization among farmers lowers transaction costs by having numerous informal transactions taking place, which are not formally sanctioned. It is not necessary to monitor and enforce all the transactions.

This positive externality following the presence of social capital is presumably created in small-group activities with regular face-to-face interaction. An externality occurs when an agent (for example, a firm or a household) does not bear all the consequences of its action and imposes an external benefit (or cost) on some other agent *outside the market system* (Tietenberg 2002: 67).

For example, as we argue in Chapter 5, small-scale dairy production may stimulate local networking and social capital building, thus providing the basis for more overall economic growth in society. Here, we assume that increased small-scale production imposes an external benefit on society so that too little production of this kind will take place in a market economy without political intervention. In Figure 2.2, we illustrate the positive externality of social capital in, for example, small-scale dairy production.

In the figure, the horizontal axis measures the small-scale dairy production in million tons per year. To state the argument as simply as possible, assume that the supply curve, that is, the marginal cost curve for this production, *MC*, is drawn horizontally, meaning that it constantly costs the same to produce one extra unit of dairy production. The private demand curve is the marginal private benefit curve, *MPB*, which measures the marginal private benefits of dairy consumers. In this case, in an unregulated market situation small-scale dairies will choose to invest q^1 in production. Here, at the intersection of demand and supply, the total net gain from private production is maximized. However, this type of production also generates external benefits to society on top of the *MPB* when social capital is created. This external advantage due to an increase in the level of social capital is shown as the marginal external benefit curve, *MEB*. In Figure 2.2, we have assumed that the marginal external benefits from the first units of small-scale dairy production are the largest because eventually, social networks have already been formed and no further networks will be established following an increase in production. Therefore, the *MEB* curve is downward sloping.

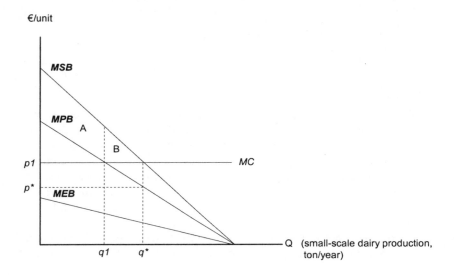

Figure 2.2   The positive externality of social capital in small-scale dairy production

The marginal social benefit curve, *MSB*, is the 'true' and corrected demand curve seen from the perspective of society. It is the sum of the *MPB* curve (expressing the marginal *private* benefits and the *MEB* curve). The new equilibrium (p^1, q^*) shows that p^1 is higher than p^* in the unregulated situation and that more output now is produced because q^* is bigger than q^1. Overall, in the unregulated situation, the positive externality is not taken into account and therefore too little production by the production mode happens in this case. Because p^1 is higher than p^*, state intervention that ensures the higher output q^* rather than q^1 is justified. For example, tax exemptions for voluntary associations or lower company taxes on small-scale producers compared to large-scale producers would ensure that society reaps the welfare gain of areas A and B.

Another example of positive externalities is house repair in Holland and Denmark, where it is possible to get extra loans for renovating private homes thus benefiting the neighbours and the passers-by. Innovation is another example of a positive externality because when other firms can take over or copy new products, the reward linked to innovation is less. Again, p^1 will be too high ($p^1 > p*$) and too little research and development will take place. The least favourable outcome in a market left alone results because the small-scale dairy producers do not receive all the benefits of their investments themselves. In Figure 2.2, we have now shown theoretically how the realization of a positive externality, in this case the extra economic gain from the presence of social capital in society, will amount to the total of areas A + B.

We shall use the co-operative movements, of which small-scale dairy production is one example, as an indicator of social capital, because they are voluntary and as such reflect the level of trust and co-operation in primarily rural societies. We shall hypothesize that a group with members who trust one another can accomplish more economic growth than a similar group without trust.

As discussed above, social capital is a new production factor, which must be added to the conventional concepts of human and physical capital. Consequently, the concepts of social capital and trust are of extreme interest to social scientists. For example, a recent World Bank project on social capital analyses these concepts and tries to measure it in different ways (see World Bank, 1999). Therefore, this section raises the following three questions: what is social capital, what principle can explain social capital, and how can it be built? In answering these questions, we look first at the close linkage between social capital and trust, and then at the linkage between social capital and reciprocity.

2.2.2.1. Social capital as derived from socialization

Social capital is rooted in at least five classical economic–sociological approaches where the first three focus on group practice and the last two on mutually binding relations or reciprocity.

The first classical theory about group practice is expressed by Marx and Engels in *The Communist Manifesto* ([1848] 1948). Here, they explain the class conflict based on class solidarity in terms of the proletariat becoming increasingly conscious of its own strength and common interests (ibid.: 17–18). Within the working class, such bounded solidarity is derived from a (higher) conscience of a common destiny to free itself from economic exploitation. By this, group relations are imposed on the group of workers from the outside, provoking an economic defence alliance with social implications (see also Portes and Sensenbrenner 1993: 1324).

Second and third, the sociological theories of Durkheim and Weber from the beginning of the twentieth century are focused on the moral character of economic transactions within the group. As such, Durkheim ([1893] 1984: 162) writes in his analysis of 'noncontractual elements of contract': 'The contract is not sufficient by itself, but is only possible because of the regulation of contracts, which is of social origin'. Weber ([1922] 1947) distinguishes between 'formal' and 'substantial' rationality when considering economic transactions. Transactions consistent with a formal rationality are based on universal norms and inclusive networks and are therefore not directed by narrow group interests. Transactions consistent with a substantial rationality are, in contrast, directed by group norms and narrow group interests. The purpose in the latter is typically that of establishing or maintaining monopoly status in the market. Weber's overall point is that individual group members are capable of suppressing their own egoistic wants here and now, in anticipation of future and lasting advantages, that is, future net gains, from undertaking social action (ibid.):

> Relationships which are valued as a potential source of present or future disposal over utilities are . . . objects of economic provision. The opportunities of advantages which are made available by custom, by the constellation of interests, or by conventional or legal order for the purposes of an economic unit, will be called economic advantages. (Ibid.: 165)

The last two classical theories by Mauss and Simmel focus on reciprocity. In *The Gift* ([1925] 1969), Mauss describes how reciprocity in many primitive societies takes the form of a perpetual exchange of goods. Simmel ([1908] 1955) gets even closer to the concept of social capital in his investigations of group belonging. A constant flow of exchanges materialized as services, information, approvals and so on mutually binds the actors to repay according to specific norms for reciprocity. Such theories of reciprocity relations form a natural transition to the capital theory of Bourdieu, operating with different types of capital and thereby also linking the economic and social universes.

Bourdieu has primarily made his analysis at the meso level, thus linking his concept of capital to that of Marx, Durkheim, Weber, Mauss and Simmel, with a specific focus on social capital as a potential instrument for individuals and groups in order to achieve various profits (Portes 1999, 2002). Though still sociological in perspective, this focus is slighty modified in the works of the American sociologist James Coleman (1988a), who sees social capital as reciprocal obligations and expectations between people, that is, reciprocity, as well as on the norms and sanctions which ensure these relations. Coleman has sought to demonstrate this at both macro and micro levels.

Following Coleman, at the macro level the ability to co-operate derives from shared values and ultimately out of mutual trust in a society. It is because these shared values and trust facilitate co-operation that social capital can be counted upon as a factor of production on an equal footing with other types of capital. In this sense, Coleman argues that social capital is a collective good, that is, a product which benefits persons other than the individual producer him-/herself, including those whom the producer does not know (Coleman 1988a: 116ff., 1988b: 388ff.).

Coleman has especially focused on socialization processes in his micro-sociological investigations. Comparing Catholic and non-Catholic schools in the United States, suggested that pupils in the Catholic schools have a lower dropout rate than those in non-Catholic schools (Coleman and Hoffer 1987; Coleman 1988a). Arguably, the pupils in Catholic schools possess a larger stock of social capital in the form of networks of family, friends and neighbours. Also, their family, friends and neighbours also know one another, just as they regularly meet and in this way ensure common norms and social control. This concept is summarized with the term 'closure' (Coleman 1988b: 386; 1988a: 119; 1990: 317ff.).

2.2.2.2.   Strong and weak ties

Networks are important, no matter whether these are constituted by the 'strong ties' of kinship or the 'weak ties' of friends, acquaintances and the like. As will be remembered, Granovetter (1973) was the first to make the distinction between strong and weak ties: the former occurring within immediate family networks, and the latter with more distant relatives and friends. Granovetter further argued that weak ties are just as important as strong ties, because strong ties may be closed off and inward looking. In other words, sets of strong ties tend to form exclusive networks or 'cliques', in which participants have direct relationships with one another. In contrast, weak ties are more commonly used to build bridges between cliques made up of strong ties. Thus, weak ties are more effective than strong ones at extending the social capital or contacts of a person or group. Paradoxically, Granovetter therefore showed that weak ties were more effective than strong ties for obtaining information on employment (ibid., based on Lemieux 2001).

With regard to information, Lazega and Lebeaux (1995) have conducted an interesting study in a major law firm. They determined whether the lawyers had relationships of consultation, collaboration or friendship with each other. Any two given lawyers had possibly two or even three of these types of relationship. A weak tie consisted of only one type of relationship, and a strong tie of two or three types. It was even possible for two lawyers not to have any of the three types of relationships (Lemieux 2001).

Each partner (or source) was asked the following question: 'If you were in charge of the firm, which person (or lever) would you approach to speak about a partner (or target) whose personal problems were threatening office productivity and therefore the common good?'. Each partner then had to answer the question in relation to each of the other lawyers in the office (ibid.). The result of the survey was that the respondents would use levers who only had weak ties with them but strong ties with the target, thus confirming the role of weak ties for connecting/bridging actors who have no direct relationship and facilitating the use of contacts' social capital rather than their own in cases where they have no ties with the targets (ibid.).

With regard to employment, a person can use his or her weak ties to make contact with a target, for example an employer whom he or she scarcely knows. Thus, the applicant can approach a third party who has some influence with the employer. However, since these weak ties are less varied and intense than strong ties, there is usually less mutual trust among the actors. Good social capital seems to be based on the right blend of strong and weak ties (ibid.). Distinguishing between such ties leads us to the distinction between 'bridging' and 'bonding' social capital, discussed below.

Overall, the point here is that in a complex society, it is extremely important to possess both strong and weak ties, enabling contact with people of different background and experience, that is, a group of people who demand less engagement than family and close friends. Where this is not the case, a group can risk becoming isolated, as in certain black urban neighbourhoods, where industry and white middle-class families 'have left the remaining population bereft of social capital, a situation leading to its extremely high levels of unemployment and welfare dependency' (Portes 1998: 14).

This leads us to what Portes calls 'negative social capital', and what Putnam (2000) calls 'bonding social capital'. The monitoring, which takes place in certain local communities, and which results in a binding and forced solidarity, has a positive function of social control. However, it may also have a negative effect on the individual in so far as it limits freedom of action. In this connection, Jeremy Boissevain reports on a village community on Malta, where neighbours know everything about everyone, and where the demand for participation in joint activities ultimately leads to a demand for conformity. The curtailed freedom of action, which follows from this, can help explain 'why the young and the more independent-minded have always left' (Boissevain, in Portes 1998: 16).

The networks can also assume a direct exclusionist and negative character. Beyond monopolization, this may also lead to a group more or less consciously isolating itself from its surroundings. An example is the Puerto Rican drug dealers in New York, who do everything to keep one another within the drug milieu, to the extent that it would be treason to mix with the whites in an attempt at social upward mobility (Portes 1998: 17).

2.2.2.3. Bowling alone

Putnam's first book about social capital, namely *Making Democracy Work* from 1993, is a comparative study of social capital in Northern and Southern Italy. Social capital is measured as traditions of civic engagement (in the form of voter participation, newspaper reading and the number of civic associations). He concludes that the two regions have evolved in diametrically opposed directions for historical reasons. Northern Italy has relatively more associational life than Sourthern Italy and has therefore accumulated more wealth (Putnam 1993a: 37).

Since his survey in Italy, Putnam has focused on his own country, the United States. Here, the presumed erosion of social capital due to decreasing associational activity from 1969 until today, has caught his interest (Putnam 1996, 2000). Putnam finds that the main factor for this erosion is television, which jeopardizes the big stock of social capital created during 'the long civic generation', that is, the civil right movements from the 1960s in the United States. The time that could have been spent on social activities is now spent on watching TV. Thus, Putnam concludes, the rise of television has meant that leisure time has become privatized:

> Television is . . . the only leisure activity that seems to inhibit participation outside the home. TV watching comes at the expense of nearly every social activity outside the home, especially social gatherings and informal conversations . . . [T]elevision privatizes our leisure time. (Putnam 1996: 47–8)

The idea about erosion of the American stock of social capital is the main theme in Putnam's latest book *Bowling Alone* from 2000. Indeed, one may perceive the book as an impressive collection of statistical evidence, which is verified by numerous cases. This 'degradation of our public life' is reflected in a significant decline in political participation, church attendance, union work, the frequency of informal social relations, voluntary engagement in cultural life and so on (Putnam 2000: 403). Putnam has furthermore incorporated the criticisms raised in the journal *American Prospect*, which led to his two articles 'Bowling alone' (1995) and 'The strange disappearance of civic America' (1996). Putnam has, as a reviewer writes, given an 'antitank gun of an argument, relentlessly researched and heavily armored against academic counterassault' (Nyhan 2000).[1]

Also, in his chapter on 'The dark side of social capital' in *Bowling Alone*, Putnam questions the one-sided focus on positive social capital (see especially Portes and Landolt 1996 and Portes 2000 for a critique). Here, he recognizes that social capital is often created in opposition to something or somebody else (Putnam 2000: 361). In other words, negative social capital of excluding nature may arise in the form of excessive 'bonding social capital', as found, for example, within certain religious networks: '[P]roselytizing religions are better at creating bonding social capital than bridging social capital, and tolerance of unbelievers is not a virtue notably associated with fundamentalism' (ibid.: 410).

The opposite of 'bonding social capital' is therefore 'bridging social capital'. What does Putnam mean by this expression? Simply, that through a new political structure based on decentralization of political power and flexibility in the labour market, one must create fertile *conditions* for the creation of social capital. The bridging consists in moving beyond 'our social and political and professional identities to connect with people unlike ourselves' (ibid.: 411). In other words, Putnam asks Americans in all societal sectors to create fertile soil for giving people the opportunity to meet one another in person. Only by so doing, does Putnam believe that the American stock of social capital can be restored (ibid.: 412). We shall return to these physical contacts in the empirical chapters.

2.2.3.   Social Capital and Reciprocity

We have now explained the close link between social capital, trust and economic growth in recent social capital literature within sociology and political science. However, tracing the theoretical roots of social capital raises another important and preliminary question: can we find anything in the social science literature that would explain *why* people learn to trust one another and co-operate in the first place? Such a question leads us to the concept of *reciprocity*.

2.2.3.1.   Classical reciprocity theories

Reciprocity is observed empirically by the perpetual exchanges of goods between the individuals and groups in every single community of a society, as was first shown by Mauss in his earlier mentioned famous work, *The Gift*, first published in 1925. Here, reciprocity in the form of exchanges of goods were shown in the Potlatch case among the Northwest coast Indians and in the case of the *Kula* among the Trobriand islanders (Mauss [1925] 1969). Mauss points out that it is precisely the reciprocity observed in the innumerable exchanges of goods in a society that – at an overall level – knits this society together in every aspect, producing common norms, common identity, trust and solidarity on the one hand, and strong economic ties on the other (ibid.: 70). As will be remembered, this line of thought was taken up by Polanyi (1944) in *The Great Transformation*. Applying ethnographic material, including works cited in Mauss, he here tries to document the existence of reciprocity as an important historical system of allocation of goods. In this way he seriously challenges the Smithsonian doctrine of the sole existence of market exchange within economies as a consequence of an universal and genetically transmitted 'propensity to barter' of (Economic) Man.

The first words in *The Great Transformation* leave no doubts about Polanyi's project:

> Our thesis is that the idea of a self-adjusting market implied a stark utopia. Such an institution could not exist for any length of time without annihilating the human and natural substance of society; it would have physically destroyed man and transformed his surroundings into a wilderness. Inevitably, society took measures to protect itself. (Op.cit.: 3)

The two other systems ('protecting' society) that have co-existed together with markets in various mixes throughout history Polanyi identifies as *redistribution*, that is, reallocation of goods via a center, and *reciprocity*, that is exchange between symmetrical and often kinship based groups belonging to a specific locality, for example a village.

More recently, reciprocity in the social capital sense of 'the ability of people to work together for common purposes in groups and organizations' has been defined more specifically as 'social capital' (Coleman 1988a). Social capital is a narrower definition of reciprocity, which focuses on trust. Trust is the expectation that arises within a community of regular, co-operative behaviour, based on commonly shared norms. Acceptable behaviour is disciplined by reinforcing encounters in a closed group. In this way, an informal agreement is accomplished where the only sanction is that of social ostracism. The social norms can be based on religious or justice values but they also cover secular norms like professional standards and codes of behaviour. These norms are created and transmitted through cultural mechanisms. The word 'culture' itself suggests that the ethical rules by which people live are nurtured through repetition, tradition and example. Therefore, human beings will never behave as purely selfish utility maximizers as postulated by economists. (For a critique of neoclassical economy, see Granovetter 1985; for economic rationality, see Svendsen 1998; and for profit maximization and altruism among US environmental groups, see Svendsen 1999. See also Becker 1968, 1996; Olson 1982, 1993, 1996, 2000; Green and Shapiro 1994; Fukuyama 1995a, 1995b; and Kurrild-Klitgaard and Svendsen 2003.)

Therefore, a crucial issue would be to prevent the groups from growing bigger if these social pressures are to be maintained effectively. Thus, large open and more complex settings would require a more impersonal or indirect form of trust. More complex networks of mutual trust must be woven together. Often, members must trust in the trust of others. Social networks may allow trust to become transitive and spread: I trust you, because I trust her and she assures me that she trusts you.

By extending Mauss's argument further, we reach the conclusion that it is the demarcated, small-scale nature of the local communities that seems to stimulate the face-to-face exchanges, which – according to Mauss – strengthen the socio-economic ties of the entire society. Reciprocal relations are being accumulated in bundles of local, social networks. In this way local, social networks create bottom-up social control: the order and social cohesion of the entire society is guaranteed in the sense that everybody is committed to everybody else. As Mauss puts it: 'Although the prestations and counter-prestations take place under a voluntary guise they are in essence strictly obligatory, and their sanction is private or open warfare' (Mauss [1925] 1969: 3). In this way, Mauss actually provided a consistent explanation of Tönnies's *Gemeinschaft* and Durkheim's 'mechanical solidarity' – but not of the *Gesellschaft* and 'organic solidarity'.

2.2.3.2. Closure and entrepreneurship

Unlike Mauss, who studied non-European pre-capitalist communities, later studies within sociology and anthropology have questioned the apparent equilibrium of a society's production of social capital. Such studies are in line with Durkheim's sociological approach to equilibrium problems in *Suicide* ([1888] 1951), using case studies from Western Europe. Similarly, within anthropology, conflict theory was introduced by the Marxist-influenced Max Gluckman, using case studies from South Africa (Gluckman 1958).

Thus, both classical and more recent studies show that societies in principle should be regarded as fragile, often disharmonious, or even as collapsing entities. Social ties do not exist *per se* – they can be lost and must, therefore, continually be renewed. A society's social capital must be built up and protected. Whereas it takes a long time to build up a 'stock' of trust in society, it may be destroyed in a very short time. Again, we remember Putnam's regret of a rapid 'disappearance of civic America' after the culmination of the civil rights movement of the 1960s, implying a dramatic loss of social capital.

In a similar way, Coleman (1994: 175) uses the term 'social capital' in an attempt to fill a 'lacuna in social and economic theory'. (On Coleman's concept of social capital, see Sandefur and Laumann 1998. For a review of the origins of the concept of social capital, see, for example Flora 1998; Portes 1998; Woolcock 1998.)

As mentioned, Coleman (1994) argues that the two words 'social' and 'capital' denote a useful linkage in that the economists' term 'capital' implies a resource that facilitates production, 'but is not consumed or otherwise used up in production', while the social scientists' notion of 'social' refers to 'aspects of social organisation, ordinarily informal relationships, established for non-economic purposes, yet with economic consequences' (see also

Svendsen and Svendsen 2000: 73; Paldam and Svendsen 2000; Paldam 2000). Furthermore, and as we have mentioned before, applied to empirical data Coleman (1988b: 388ff., 1988a: 116ff.) sees social capital as a public good, that is, a product that also benefits persons other than the producer, including persons who are unknown to the producer. For example, it can be statistically documented that the production of human capital in schools is highly facilitated, when pupils possess social capital in the form of strong networks consisting of family, friends and neighbours, who know one another and meet regularly, thus ensuring shared norms and social control, that is, what Coleman termed 'closure' (1988b: 386ff.). At the same time it follows that, if a key person in the local production of social capital (for example, a parent of one of the schoolchildren) moves from a community, persons other than this one will feel the loss by the 'severance' of closure-based relations (ibid.: 389). This should confirm the importance of social capital as a collective good.

Such disappearance of key persons from a community highlights the importance of individual social entrepreneurs. In local areas people have rich opportunities to get to know one another and meet regularly and so prepare the ground for social incentives facilitating group action and the realization of collective goods. However, as has already been stressed, the provision of collective goods necessarily implies that the rural community in question is based on non-excludability or, in other words, that the inhabitants generally tend to pursue 'integrating' and not 'excluding' survival strategies and thus are promoting the spread of social networks rather than restricting them so as to include only a circle of privileged group members (Meert 2000: 328).

Recalling the case of eliminating mad cow disease cited earlier, this suggestion only holds for larger groups where social action with most people is possible, such as a local group consisting of 1,000 individuals (like the 1,000 farmers, see Table 2.1). Very large groups having millions of members (for example, all citizens in a country) are not fertile ground for the use of social incentives and thus, of accumulating social capital. Therefore, only the focus on larger groups is relevant when discussing entrepreneurship and social capital in the context of local areas and poverty alleviation. This focus was also justified in an earlier paper where we demonstrated how local dairy production in Denmark probably encouraged entrepreneurship and the initiation of larger local group organization around this production (Svendsen and Svendsen 2000). Note that very large groups without regular social interaction among most individuals are not relevant in this setting.

2.2.3.3. Self-selection and reputation

Crucially in this respect is the feature of self-selection of leaders among a number of entrepreneurs in, for example, the locally based and voluntary co-operative movements. This self-selection of local leaders takes place in a non-hierarchical setting in contrast to the situation in former communist Russia, for example, where top leaders would appoint local officials within a highly hierarchical organization.

We suggest that the self-selection process is based on reputation. Sociologists see personal reputation as the general estimation made by the public about the individual in question. This estimation is based on the way in which a given role or identity is managed by the individual and presented to a group or society. Through presentation of the self, society constructs a reputation by looking at the objective behaviour of the individual (Carter and Ghorbani 2003).

Commercial reputation is very similar to personal reputation in that it focuses on the estimation made by the public about the business in question. However, companies utilize public relation components to influence how society perceives them. Hence, companies have more power than the individual in establishing and marketing their own reputation. This helps to explain the unequal distribution of social power between companies and individuals (ibid.).

Erving Goffman makes a useful analogy of reputation and identity management with the dramatic world of the theatre (Goffman 1959, cited in Carter and Ghorbani 2003). Individuals are here depicted as actors on a stage negotiating their roles in society. On stage, individuals are playing a part, whereas backstage they exist as themselves. Front and backstage attain a certain fluidity and reputation is created through the management of both (ibid.).

The audience has certain expectations or roles for the actors. Reputation is constructed on the basis of the audience's belief that the actors have fully fulfilled their role. If actors cannot act, they have failed in their role as an actor and will develop a negative reputation with the audience. In the same way, individuals and businesses have a certain role within society. If society objectively judges that they have met this role, they are rewarded with a positive reputation (ibid.).

Positive reputation leads to confidence and trust in the individual along with a higher level of social status and power. Such individuals become sought after within society. Negative reputation leads to a loss of esteem, along with social status and power. Naturally, it is in an individual's best interest to maximize his/her positive reputation through identity management. Within human societies, reputation is so important that rules are established to protect it. Defamation laws prevent one individual from destroying another's reputation through false accusations to third parties (ibid.).

2.2.4. Theory Effects and the Missing Link of Social Capital

The case studies in this book not only illuminate the *consequences* of a production factor being overlooked (for example, centralization of production, conflicts between rural groups, state politics hostile to rural communities), but they also show us *how* it was overlooked. Thus, the missing link of social capital can be traced as a serious *conceptual gap* in such economic and political debates which, following Bourdieu (1977: 170), are part of a 'struggle for the power to impose the legitimate mode of thought and expression'.

Therefore, having discussed the socio-economic significance and real effects of informal exchange we shall conclude this chapter by making a few theoretical reflections that can help to highlight the significance of the existence and non-existence of academic words and their impact on reality – a mechanism our case studies clearly reveal.

For example, as we shall see in Chapter 5, during the 1960s a large group of Danish smallholders and enthusiastic members of local co-operative dairies desperately needed a legitimate argument to defend their way of living. They knew that the word they used themselves – 'life form' (*livsform*) – was too diffuse to be taken seriously in the public debate. Consequently, they were struck by what Bourdieu (ibid.) has called the 'aphasia of those who are denied access to the instruments of the struggle for the definition of reality'.

This partly explains the incredibly rapid and overwhelming defeat they suffered in the mid-1960s at the hands of a small group of national agricultural leaders and experts, whose 'mantras' – abstract economic terms presented in a dogmatic and almost reified form, such as *the* structural changes, *the* development, *the* rationalization, *the* centralization, *the* vertical integration – were reported frequently in the public media. The same tendency can be seen even today.

In our view, what local entrepreneurial networkers such as these smallholders and milk producers needed in a struggle on words was a term that in a more accurate and convincing way could express the significance of their *socio-economic* practice at the macroeconomic level: *social* capital. Socio-economic entrepreneurs *do* benefit society, strictly economically. That is to say that their social capital *does* transform into economic capital in the long run – in the 1960s as well as now. However, the problem is that informal networking has never been acknowledged in the public debate as a production factor. Economic discourse is rich on physical, economic and human capital, but *not* on social capital.

This is precisely why we want to link current social capital debates to another important finding of Bourdieu, summed up in titles such as 'The thinkable and the unthinkable' (1971), 'The production of belief' (1980) and 'The economy of linguistic exchanges' (1977), a title which appears on a book published in French (1982) with the important addition: *Ce que parler veut dire* (What speaking means). In doing this, we hypothesize that, if local entrepreneurs make an argument more explicit by using the word 'social capital', they will probably be more successful in obtaining a 'theory' or 'theorization effect' (Bourdieu 1977: 178, 1990a: 134), that is, by their symbolic practice contribute to shaping reality – just like Marx's 'the class struggle' did.

2.3.   SUMMARY

In the previous section we argued theoretically how social capital, as a positive externality, is created and what the economic effects will be. We first explained how extra social sanction costs could be imposed on non-cooperative members in a group and thus ensure trust between members and successful group action. Furthermore, the accumulation of social capital could be described as a positive externality resulting in an economic net gain for society. However, there is also the reverse of the coin, namely bonding social capital detrimental to economic growth. This all led us to the crucial distinction between bridging and bonding social capital and the discussion of classical reciprocity theories.

We considered social capital as a new production factor, which must be added to the conventional concepts of human and physical capital. Social capital is productive because it increases the level of trust in a society and allows more transactions to take place without third-party enforcement. In fact, as argued in the setting of new institutional economics, social capital compensates for the presence of asymmetrical information in real life. Theory therefore leads to the general recommendation that any loss in social capital must be deducted from the economic gain following market forces. For example, as will become evident in the empirical parts of the book, the voluntary organization of small-sized groups in the Danish co-operative dairy movement was eliminated due to economies of scale. It may be that an alternative means of production, taking social capital into account, could have increased economic growth even further.

Examining why some countries are rich and others poor has been a core issue in research for centuries. We suggested that traditional production factors cannot fully explain the observed differences in the wealth of nations and that the non-material and informal dimension of institutions had to be added. Also, we suggested how self-selection of local leaders can take place in a non-hierarchical setting such as self-selection among a number of potential entrepreneurs in, for example, the locally based and voluntary co-operative movements. Such a self-selection process of entrepreneurs was arguably based on reputation.

Therefore, we introduced a socio-economic approach in the study of the relationship between economic growth and institutional set-ups. This new socio-economics – Bourdieuconomics – operates with material and non-material forms of capital *at the same level*. As such, social capital could be described as an institutionalized but non-material informal human exchange (unwritten rule).

In this way, we suggest that social capital should be added to the traditional production factors of land, technological knowledge, physical capital, human capital and formal institutions (written rules). When lubricating civic society, the presence of social capital facilitates voluntary provision of collective goods. Reducing transaction costs and enhancing the access to resources in networks, stimulate economic growth and consequently the creation of differences in the wealth of nations. In perspective, future research should therefore be directed towards this new field of Bourdieconomics and, within such a framework, highlight the 'missing link' of social capital, which can be seen as a new important and, until now, almost unexplored and overlooked production factor.

NOTE

1. The debate in *American Prospect* following issue no. 26 from May–June 1996, can be found at www.prospect.org/authors/putnam-r.html

3. Co-operative Movements and Social Capital in Denmark and Poland

3.1. CO-OPERATIVE MOVEMENTS IN DENMARK AND POLAND

3.1.1. Introduction

As argued in the previous chapter, literature on social capital shows how totalitarian regimes (for example communism) destroy social capital and affect civil society when passive reliance on the state is strongly enforced. In this chapter, we ask whether a political system, that is, the formal institutional set-up in a country, is important to the level of social capital and civic life in practice.

For example, the heavy state intervention in centrally planned economies meant that the state made almost all decisions and coerced people into doing certain things. There was little room for entrepreneurship, experiments and voluntary organization into social groups. Along a similar line, Vincent Ostrom (1985) argues that human beings are subject to the serious biological constraint that only one speaker can be heard and understood at a time. Therefore, as groups increase in size, the voice of leadership in directing the proceeding increases and the proportionate voice of each individual member decreases. For example, he observes that the extreme Leninist solution of expropriating all property of productive significance, thus treating the entire economy as a single firm (that is, as one large group), was inadequate in terms of self-organization. It was not clear how this would increase the voice of workers, reduce the voice of management, and result in the withering away of the state as Lenin anticipated (Ostrom 1985: 8).

Earlier work such as Bonanno (1993) did not take social capital into account but rather focused on elements such as homogeneity of the agricultural sector, the role of the market and changing social stratifications of rural regions. Thus, the purpose of this chapter is to suggest the link between social capital and rural development, rather than undertaking strict chronological comparison in co-operative movements. This is achieved via two approaches.

First, we identify possible roots of social capital building with reference to Denmark and Poland. Social capital cannot be measured directly, therefore various proxies have been suggested for its conceptualization (see Paldam 2000). Based on the fact that, during the nineteenth century, Denmark and Poland were both agricultural countries with strong traditions of private farming and co-operative movements encompassing a major part of the rural population, this book utilizes the proxy of voluntary agricultural co-operatives. Thus, we trace how stocks of social capital in the form of peasant co-operatives initially were formed bottom up in nineteenth century Europe, as a buffer against uncontrolled capitalism; and how, specifically, social capital was built and maintained by agricultural co-operative movements in Denmark and Poland during the nineteenth and early twentieth centuries.

Second, we illustrate how the present level of social capital in Denmark and Poland differs significantly. At present, the level of social capital is significantly higher in Denmark than in Poland. It is argued that this difference can be explained by the fact that communism was introduced in Poland, severely influencing the level of trust and civic life, whereas controlled capitalism and democracy continued unhindered in Denmark. As Putnam (1993a) argues, social capital takes a long time to accumulate (see also Fukuyama 1995a and b). Therefore, despite the relatively fast economic transformation, the level of social capital in Poland has presumably not changed significantly since 1989. When assessing the economic and social situation in the Central and Eastern European countries (CEEC), Mlcoch (2000) confirms Putnam's findings. These findings are documented in a questionnaire survey in Denmark and Poland from 2000 and 2001. Finally, we suggest that the reason for this difference in social capital is due to the fact that the original accumulation of social capital in Poland was destroyed by the communist regime.

3.1.2.   Early Agricultural Co-operatives in Europe

Historical evidence shows that inclusive network co-operation based on trust and regular face-to-face interaction – that is, positive social capital – has been one of the crucial means by which small farmers have managed to survive. Hence, in many European countries, prior to the development of a regular co-operative movement, agriculture was controlled by middlemen, who discouraged and often impoverished the farmer, while at the same time exploiting the consumer. Lacking any immediate alternative, farmers had to market their produce through these middlemen. However, if farmers were able to perform all the necessary tasks themselves without third part involvement at all, such as making butter and cheese and slaughtering animals, their situation would improve (Haagard 1911).

As capitalism developed, and larger companies were both selling goods to farmers and buying their produce, farmers with a relatively small bargaining position had to protect themselves from being exploited. So a widespread counter-reaction to capitalistic exploitation entailed that farmers pooled their buying power in order to attract lower prices from suppliers. By grouping together, farmers also pooled their selling power, so that on the market one farmer could not be played off against another. This process is clearly evidenced in Danish sources (for example, Sonne 1867; Haagard 1911; Christensen 1983), including Danish agricultural journals. Likewise, Thugutt (1937), Inglot (1966) and Maliszewski (1995) support the claim that the birth of the Polish co-operative sector was as a reaction to the transformation of social structures in early capitalism.

Capital concentration and accumulation, industrial specialization and changes in agriculture were among macro level factors that led to widespread proletarianization in Europe during the nineteenth and early twentieth centuries, in the countryside as well as in urban areas. The relatively poor private smallholders and farmers had no organization to protect them from the upper class or from the exploitation and competition of the capitalists. This stimulated the development of agricultural co-operatives.

For example, the co-operative wholesale movement in Denmark from 1866 – inspired by the first co-operative wholesale society in Rochdale, England, 1844 – was established as a declared anti-capitalistic reaction against 'class privileges and monopolies' (Sonne 1867: 13). Likewise, in the years before and during the First World War, the influential Danish agricultural co-operative movement (*Andelsbevægelsen*) declared war on American inspired industrial cartels. These monopoly companies continually increased prices, particularly at the expense of the economically less liquid, Danish rural population. This they did by imposing a 'hidden and illegal tax' on Danish peasants, as one of the pioneer co-operative leaders declared (compare Severin Jørgensen in *Ab* 1904).

Also in the CEEC, various co-operative movements were formed as a buffer against harsh capitalism. Thus, the first wholesale and credit co-operative in continental Europe, the Farmers' Society (*Spolok Gasdovský*), was established in Slovakia in February 1845, only 90 days after the one in Rochdale (Kaser and Radice 1985: 283). In the Czech countryside, a co-operative movement flourished, especially after 1919 (ibid.: 282). Other examples of early Eastern European agricultural co-operatives are *Agraria*, established in 1922 in Voivodina, *Gospodarska Sloga* in Croatia (1935), and the Bulgarian Agrarian Co-operative Bank, founded in the late 1920s (ibid.: 180).

3.1.3.   Co-Operative Movements in Denmark and Poland

A co-operative is defined by the International Co-operative Alliance as a group of people who join together in a common undertaking, in accord with the following six principles (ICA 1999):

1. Membership is open and voluntary.
2. There is democratic control, usually on the basis of one person, one vote.
3. Interest on share capital is limited.
4. There is equitable distribution of any surplus, usually in proportion to transactions with or work done in the society.
5. Co-operatives devote some part of their surpluses to education.
6. Co-operatives co-operate among themselves.

Thus the co-operative process is basically an interaction between: (a) co-operatively committed members, (b) co-operative values inherited from the past and expressed in principles, (c) practical co-operative structures, also inherited from the past, and (d) the institutional environment where co-operatives operate.

In the following, we shall show how social capital building, the outcome of inclusive and democratic forms of network co-operation, took place within agricultural co-operative movements in Denmark and Poland before the Second Word War.

3.1.3.1.   The Danish co-operative movement

Although agricultural co-operative movements traditionally have been strong in most Scandinavian countries, the Danish co-operative movement (*Andelsbevægelsen*) appears to have been particularly vigorous and influential.

In particular, this movement grew strong when co-operative dairies were established from 1882. These were soon followed by co-operative enterprises within other agricultural sectors, such as co-operative fodder purchase associations from 1883, co-operative slaughterhouses from 1887, a regular co-operative bank with branches in provincial towns from 1914 and so on, until wholly voluntarily established co-operatives finally became *the* way of organizing all common practical matters among the Danish rural population. Furthermore, right from the beginning, *Andelsbevægelsen* was closely linked to a peasant political movement centred around the farmers' party (*Venstre*), and to rural cultural movements, such as the free church, free school and folk high school movements (Svendsen and Svendsen 2001).

It is clearly documented that all these peasant movements were formed bottom up by energetic entrepreneurs in the local rural communities. Such 'public-spirited' people who met regularly, and who knew and trusted one another, often participated in numerous local and regional co-operative associations, and often as highly trusted leading board members. These consisted of agricultural as well as cultural associations, forming stable and long-lasting networks with a significant overlap of members. Hence, valuable social capital was created bottom-up, enhancing economic growth and the general educational standards of the rural population in an extraordinary process of self-organization (see also Svendsen and Svendsen 2000, 2001).

In particular, the Danish co-operative dairies are good examples of self-organized peasant co-operation, institutionalized in the form of commonly agreed upon, written rules of the game, that is, the articles of such an association. Such democratic processes led to trust and, ultimately, to a lowering of transaction costs to the benefit of all milk-producing farmers (Svendsen and Svendsen 2001).

Prior to 1882 peasants made their own butter and sold it themselves in the nearby town and/or they had to rely on the food traders, who canvassed the country. This process was costly, and the returns received were uncertain, and so small farmers, of which there were many thousands, were at a disadvantage with respect to their bargaining position (Christensen 1983).

From 1882, an increasing number of Danish peasants bound themselves to deliver all their milk to their own co-operative dairy, except the amount required for domestic use. They held themselves individually responsible for any debts that might be incurred, and if the dairy made any profit, it was to be divided among the members in proportion to the amount of milk each of them had delivered, thus securing an important capitalistic incentive for the farmers. In this way, members were obliged to trust one another, sharing the risk of economic disaster – a trust that, once established, became an important and multifunctional 'glue' in the local community, facilitating all kinds of self-organized activities.

The co-operative dairies were an immediate success. It became possible to standardize output and thus demand higher prices. Technical improvements upgraded both the quality and the quantity of the butter. Soon, the co-operative dairy butter surpassed the celebrated 'Estate Butter' for which Denmark had been famous (Haagard 1911). Consequently, the number of co-operative dairies increased rapidly from one in 1882 to about 700 in 1890, including one-third of all Danish milk producers.

The movement made farmers aware of the scientific possibilities of dairy production and of cattle breeding, thus increasing educational levels – a process that was enhanced by the establishment of self-organized peasant folk high schools and agricultural schools. Milk was delivered in good condition, and the social control mechanism of the members of a co-operative (who often participated in the same associational networks) guaranteed that none of them would cheat. When all the farmers in the district were members, a single horse-drawn carriage collected the milk from every farm, which reduced the transportation cost. Among the economies, skimmed milk was saved for feeding hogs, which consequently stimulated the bacon industry and thus brought about the opening of co-operative slaughterhouses. Small farmers, in particular, who had previously held a negligible bargaining position at the market, now had greater opportunities to market their produce. This, in effect, contributed to the development of smallholdings (Christensen 1983).

A typical method of establishing a dairy co-operative was for a group of trustworthy and highly respected farmers in a locality to get together and borrow the necessary capital from a savings bank. All the work in the dairy co-operative was performed with unlimited liability. The original funds for construction purposes were repaid in instalments, while the working capital was supplied by a premium paid by each member. When the original loan was repaid, a new one was taken out from the bank at the same rate of interest. The financial resources obtained were handed over to the original members who all undertook to repay the new loan. Savings banks thus have had a direct interest in the development of the dairy co-operatives (ibid.).

The co-operative dairies were governed in a democratic way. In most dairies, each member had one vote, irrespective of the number of cows owned. The members themselves elected the board of their association, including a dairy manager, who was expected to be an expert within his field. Local co-operatives were all affiliated to a central national confederation, which aimed at developing the dairy production industry through exhibitions, conferences and dissemination of material.

The constitutional articles of a local dairy co-operative obliged members to send all their milk to the co-operative dairy, with the exception of milk needed for household use. Such a contract between the farmers and the dairy was agreed for a fixed period, usually 10 or 15 years. Heavy fines were imposed on anyone who broke this rule. Furthermore, the articles contained strict but, as ever, commonly agreed-upon rules relating to proper feeding of the cows, sanitary milking and so on, thus hindering free riding and the formation of exclusive, negative social capital (Svendsen and Svendsen 2001).

Danish farmers soon found it necessary to carry co-operation a step further, in a dynamic proliferating process that was initially inspired by the success of the dairy co-operatives. For example, it now became a matter of urgency to control the distribution of their produce in England, which was the chief market for many Danish agricultural products. Danish farmers managed this in a characteristically independent way by forming a distributive and selling agency.

As co-operation was not confined only to the selling of farm products and buying of merchandise and farm supplies, improvement – or supportive – societies emerged, such as co-operative fertilizer plants and canning factories. Another example was the maintenance of cattle and swine improvement and breeding societies and seed-testing organizations (Haggard 1911). The breeding of cattle, horses, swine and sheep was promoted by co-operative societies, whose main purpose was to improve the breeding of farm animals by keeping accounting systems of the quantity of milk produced per cow and its butter fat content, as well as the relative cost of maintenance. The first central society was established in 1895. In 1913, there were 592 such societies, all of which received some subsidy from the state. Almost every need of the farmer was supplied through one or more organizations of this kind. In addition, there were societies for accident insurance against for example, storms and fire, and for the insurance of livestock (Svendsen 2001).

Thus, in rural Denmark, during the second half of the nineteenth century, network co-operation spread to include nationwide co-operation. Consequently, about 1890, the Danish state – however obstructive it had been towards these peasant initiatives – reluctantly had to acknowledge the national economic importance of the co-operatives (Svendsen and Svendsen 2000). At this time, a valuable stock of social capital had been established among Danish peasants, sustained by groups of energetic local and regional peasant entrepreneurs and institutionalized in the constitutional articles of the co-operative association, as well as in more informal traditions of generalized trust, civic participation and democracy.

3.1.3.2.   Polish co-operative movements

Co-operative movements have also played an important role in other parts of Europe, including the CEEC.

In Poland, there has been a long and strong tradition of private farms and mostly smallholdings, particularly before the Second World War (Nelson 1983: 175). Thus, the pre-war mode of organization among Polish peasants was in many ways similar to the one prevailing among Danish peasants in the same period. Moreover, the co-operative approach to counteracting harsh nineteenth-century capitalism can also be found in Poland. Here, the Hrubiewzów Agricultural Association, founded in 1816, became a predecessor of voluntary peasant co-operatives. The first real co-operative was a wholesale and credit co-operative association, founded in Poznan in 1861 by two of the pioneers of Polish agricultural co-operatives, A. Szamarzewski and P. Wawrzyniak (Inglot 1966). These were enthusiastic, idealistic entrepreneurs and social capital builders, that is, the same type of trusted, dedicated people we also find in great numbers within the Danish co-operative movement.

Later on, various co-operative enterprises were formed in other parts of Poland as well. In Galicia, the first co-operative was established in 1890, while in the Russian part of Poland, consumer co-operatives played a major role, especially among the workers of Plock (Lódz) and Warsaw after the 1905 revolution (ibid.). As a result, the Union of Consumer Co-operatives (*Zwiazek Spóldzielni Spozywców* or *Spolem*) was established in Warsaw in 1908 by two other public-spirited men, namely the leaders of the nationwide Polish Co-operative Association. However, from 1945, *Spolem* was gradually superceded by the Polish Socialist Party (Landau and Tomaszewski 1985: 205–6). As we shall show in the next section, this implied a dramatic shift from voluntary to state-enforced co-operation.

Due to the specific politico-historical context of Poland, the development of co-operatives until the First World War followed different patterns in the Prussian, Russian and Austrian parts of Poland. In the western region under Prussian occupation, a widespread network of co-operative banks and agricultural marketing and supply co-operatives developed, primarily as a counter-reaction to the policy of Germanization on the part of the German state, providing economic subsidies to German colonists so that they could dominate their Polish neighbours (Landau and Tomaszewski 1985: 16). Exactly the same process took place in the German–Danish border region from the beginning of the First World War. Here, the patriotic credit institution the National Safeguard (*Landeværnet*) was established in 1913, as a protection against German colonialism (Fink 1999). In both cases, the formation of social capital by means of a co-operative form of organization served as an important survival strategy, not unlike the strategies applied under nineteenth century rampant capitalism.

In the Russian part of Poland mainly consumer co-operatives developed, both in urban and rural areas. Southern Poland had a higher concentration of savings and credit co-operatives, due to the influence of Austrian rule where, for example, the Raiffeisen credit system was highly developed (World Bank 1990).

In particular, a dynamic development within the Polish co-operatives took place from 1918 to 1939 (Landau and Tomaszewski 1985: 76). As in Denmark, dairy co-operatives became a common form of peasant co-operation. Although not developed with such complexity as in Denmark, their main role was also to organize the supply of dairy products to the urban market (OECD 1995). Similar to the development in Denmark, Polish co-operative banks supplied farmers with credit. Thus, before the Second World War, Poland had approximately 1,600 co-operative banks, which provided savings and credit services for agricultural and household use (Hunek 1994).

Another illustrative example of the fruitful inter-war growth within the Polish co-operative movement is the aforementioned Union of Consumer Co-operatives, *Spolem*. Before the First World War, this union had 274 consumer co-operatives with 40,000 members, but by the beginning of the Second Word War, this number had increased to 1776, 87 per cent of which were located in villages, with approximately 400,000 members (Lerski 1996: 562). Furthermore, after 1918, when Poland had regained its sovereignty and unity, the regional differences gradually became less significant as regionally developed co-operative models extended into other regions, and a coherent movement gradually evolved. As a result, most of the 20 basic types of co-operative were associated at the central level in nine auditing unions and 24 different trading and financing organizations. (For more details, see World Bank 1990.) By 1938, Poland had about 14,000 viable co-operatives united in various auditing unions (ibid.). Outside these unions, there were several thousand weaker and generally short-lived societies.

Although different from the Danish ones, various supportive co-operatives also existed in Poland. During the communist period, private farmers co-operated under the framework of 'peasant self-help co-operatives' (*samopomoc chlopska*). This type of co-operative had a more third-party enforcement character, since it had its roots back in 1948 when a number of agricultural and marketing co-operatives were merged into the 'peasant self-help supply and marketing co-operatives' (Hunek 1994).

The main function of this type of co-operative was to supply private farms with agricultural inputs, in particular to market agricultural products from private farms, to process some agricultural products for mainly local needs, and to supply the rural population with consumer commodities. The peasant self-help supply and marketing co-operatives held a dominant position in purchasing the majority of agricultural products from private farms, and also performed other services, such as running catering businesses (OECD 1995). Thus, the economic activities of these co-operatives were divided into three main groups: production, wholesale and retail trade, and purchase of products. The wholesale and retail trade activities were most important to these co-operatives, which operated over 70,000 retail stores as well as warehouses and purchase centres. In 1988, there were 1,912 peasant self-help co-operatives, with 3.5 million members, and employing 434,000 people (World Bank 1990).

The other important type of Polish co-operatives was known as 'agricultural circles'. Their objective was similar to the peasant self-help supply and marketing co-operatives, but their distinguishing feature was that they functioned as 'machinery pools', and were also known by this name. The service they offered to private farms included ploughing, chemical applications, transportation, construction of buildings and the repair of agricultural machinery (OECD 1995). In 1988 there were in total about 2,000 agricultural circles. Usually one circle served farmers in one *gmina* (a local government administration unit). Depending whether the *gmina* was located in a rural area or not, there were usually 10–200 farmers per circle (oral communication with J. Idczak, University of Poznan, Poland, September 2001).

In sum, the two case studies show that voluntary agricultural co-operatives in Denmark and Poland from the nineteenth century to the beginning of the Second World War were not established by a circle of philanthropists, or even by the landlords for the purpose of benefiting the working farmers. In contrast, these organizations grew bottom up, as local and regional peasant responses to economic threats from other social classes or from abroad. Once established, they paved the way for inclusive and lubricated co-operative relations among peasants, that is, productive social capital implying reciprocity, trust and civic engagement.

Even today, the Danish co-operative movement is wholly voluntary, receiving no subsidies from the state. Co-operatives are independent of one another and spring into existence when farmers find it necessary. Although the state does not directly interfere in the co-operatives, it promotes the general co-operative idea. In contrast, the Polish co-operative movement, which was almost completely destroyed during the socialist regime after the Second World War, has found it difficult to regain power after 1989. One possible explanation for this contemporary status quo will be discussed below.

3.2.   MEASURING SOCIAL CAPITAL IN DENMARK AND POLAND

3.2.1.   Measurement

With regard to measurement, Putnam (1993a) proposes a simple operational proxy for social capital, namely the density of voluntary organizations of any type. As will be remembered, by comparing the North and the South of Italy he concludes that the density of voluntary organizations is much higher in the North than in the South. This difference should then explain why economic performance is much higher in the former than in the latter.

Putnam states that the reason for this difference in density is the level of hierarchy. The North and South started on divergent paths in the eleventh century when the South was subject to a hierarchical Norman kingdom in 1100. This type of society reduces the amount of trust in leaders. Ordinary people and leaders are not interacting socially and do not build up social capital. So the South experienced the Hobbesian outcome of amoral familism, clientelism, lawlessness, ineffective government and economic stagnation (ibid.). The solution would then be to scale down the role of hierarchical state intervention to avoid this 'southern deadlock' and thereby leave room for horizontally structured voluntary organizations.

As will be remembered, sociological research shows that both kinship relations in the form of strong ties and non-kinship relations in the form of weak ties are important elements in the building of social capital (for example, see Granovetter 1973). The strong ties are necessary for internal solidarity within the community; the weak ties lead to linkages to extra-community networks (Flora 1998: 483; Hofferth and Iceland 1998).

Several empirical examples may be mentioned here. In Romania, it is common for people to participate in wide networks with manifold functions. Here friends, relatives and neighbours – more than having a mere social function – are supposed to help one another with advice and services as well as acting as an economic safeguard. In Romania the rates of interest of private loans are extremely high – something which is clearly strengthening this tendency towards an informal economy. A case of the strength of ties of kinship, that is, 'strong ties', can be found in Russian Karelia, where 'networks of kinship and friends help many who are in the poorest situation, providing them with food, clothes and other necessities' (Kortelainen 1997: 33). Another recent example is the kinship-based alliances in Kazakhstan. These informal networks experienced enormous growth after the fall of the Soviet Union (see Odgaard and Simonsen 1998).

However, in the following we omit the measure of networks, trying to compensate by showing the historical formation of important co-operative networks in both countries, that is, by use of qualitative data primarily.Instead, we focus on three other theoretical approaches to measure social capital, namely: membership of voluntary organizations; trust; and civic participation (Paldam 2000).

To investigate the level of social capital in different countries, Paldam and Svendsen (2004) have produced a questionnaire to identify these three aspects of social capital. Let us now turn to the empirical results from Denmark (1,206 respondents, year 2000) and Poland (1,004 respondents, year 2002) (ibid.).

First, with regard to membership in voluntary organizations, Putnam (1993a) suggested that this proxy could be used for social capital. In this book, the agricultural co-operative proxy measures the voluntarism aspect. To a similar end, Putnam used the density of organizational membership in the Italian case. As well as it will be remembered that he found that on average a person in northern Italy was a member of far more organizations than a person in the South and, moreover, that this difference should explain the striking difference in economic wealth between the North and the South.

The results from this measure are listed in Table 3.1, which shows that the average Dane is a member of 12 times more voluntary organizations (1.7) than the average Pole (0.14). Also, roughly one in four of all Danes is not a member of any voluntary organization at all compared to five in six of all Poles.

Table 3.1 Membership of voluntary organizations, Denmark and Poland

Membership (no. of organizations)	Denmark (%)	Poland (%)
0	23.4	88.0
1	29.1	10.5
2	21.8	1.1
3	13.3	0.5
4	6.8	–
5	3.3	–
6	1.3	–
7	0.7	–
8	0.2	–
9 and more	0.2	–
Average	1.72	0.14

Source: Reproduced from Chloupkova et al. (2003: 247) with permission.

Second, general trust among citizens and trust in formal organizations can be measured. With regard to general trust among citizens, people were asked whether they trust other people in general. The result is that Danes trust other Danes three and a half times more than Poles trust other Poles (73.9 per cent compared to 20.1 per cent), see Table 3.2.

Table 3.2 Standard generalized trust, Denmark and Poland

Frequencies in %	Denmark	Poland
Can trust	73.9	20.1
Can't be too careful	21.3	79.9
Don't know	4.8	– *

Source: Reproduced from Chloupkova et al. (2003: 247) with permission.
*Data are missing.

However, even more significant appearthe results for corruption and general trust in formal institutions, see Table 3.3. The results are presented as an average of citizens' trust in four types of formal institutions, namely: the legal system, the police, administration and government. In comparison, Danes trust these four institutions ten times more than the Poles do (20.8 per cent and 2.1 per cent respectively, for 'a great deal').

Table 3.3. Trust in institutions, Denmark and Poland (%)

	A great deal	Quite a lot	Not very much	None at all	Don't know
Denmark					
Legal system	29.5	55.2	6.7	2.4	6.2
Police	34.6	59.5	3.1	1.3	1.6
Administration	9.0	63.2	18.3	3.4	6.1
Government	10.2	58.5	21.7	3.5	6.1
Average	20.8	59.1	12.4	2.7	5.0
Poland					
Legal system	1.3	37.4	35.6	15.4	10.4
Police	3.9	53.4	24.9	9.6	8.3
Administration	1.1	40.7	31.6	15.7	10.9
Government	2.2	36.7	33.0	14.8	13.4
Average	2.1	42.1	31.3	13.9	10.7

Source: Reproduced from Chloupkova et al. (2003: 247) with permission.

Civic participation, such as involvement in elections, contacting the press over societal problems, charity work and so on is the third attribute of social capital. In a range of 13 sub-questions covering different 'civic actions', the respondent was asked whether he/she had engaged in this particular civic action within the last three years. Table 3.4 simply displays the average number of 'yes' and 'no' answers, expressed in percentages. As shown, Danes participate in twice as many civic actions as the Poles do (34.7 per cent and 17.1 per cent, respectively).

Table 3.4 Civic participation, Denmark and Poland (%)

	Denmark	Poland
Yes	34.7	17.1
No	65.1	82.6
Don't know	0.2	0.3

Source: Reproduced from Chloupkova et al. (2003: 248) with permission.

3.2.2.   Destroying Social Capital

Considering the current economic conditions in CEEC, it would be desirable if the level of social capital were higher and farmers would trust one another more and thereby reap the gains of co-operation (Chloupkova and Bjørnskov 2002a). However, the bad experiences incurred during the previous regime act as a mental block, as indicated by our analysis. Thus, the re-installed democratic regime and free-market economies in CEEC have a tendency towards passive reliance on the state (Chloupkova and Bjørnskov 2002b).

A main objective of communist rule in Poland was to replace the capitalist with the new socialist. During the Second World War, practically the whole co-operative movement in the country, with the exception of consumer co-operatives, was abolished by the occupiers (The World Bank 1990).

A period of somewhat more independent rebuilding of the co-operatives damaged in the war ended as early as 1948. At this time, the introduction of a socialist economy implied that the natural evolution of the co-operative movement was interrupted.

The socialist reconstruction of agriculture was proclaimed at the Central Committee meeting in July 1948 by trade and industry minister Hilary Minc. Having promoted the idea of large-scale nationalization of the Polish economy since 1945 (Landau and Tomaszewski 1985: 205), he now imagined a fruitful mixture of modernized state farms driven by enthusiastic co-operatives: 'Within the socio-economic system of a people's democracy farm co-operatives are the simplest and easiest way, within the grasp of a common peasant, to develop a new system of large-scale economy, capable of utilising all the benefits of modern technology and agricultural knowledge' (ibid.: 193).

The programme of agricultural reconstruction was started in autumn 1948. In reality, this meant an enforced collectivization. However, the Polish collectivization did not imply liquidation of farmers, threat of physical violence and expulsion, as had been the case in the Soviet Union under Stalin between 1929 and 1936. Instead, it involved a variety of economic reprisals directed against the private farmers, who, at this time, owned 77 per cent of the agricultural land. Thus, a compulsory saving system was introduced in order to hit medium-sized and better-off farms. By 1949, the first attempts to exert administrative pressure on private farmers had begun (ibid.: 193–4). Furthermore, private farmers were obliged to sign contracts in advance, specifying the amount of produce they would sell to the state and accept the prices that would be set by the state. This meant that although they were considered as private farmers, they were not allowed to exploit the properties of a free market (Chloupkova 2002a and b). At the same time, state co-operatives were favoured by receiving state subsidies as well as tax reductions (Landau and Tomaszewski 1985: 194). Consequently, and despite continuous peasant opposition to collectivization, the number of state co-operatives grew rapidly, to approximately 10,000 collectives by 1955 (Nelson 1983: 176).

In this process, the voluntary peasant-owned, co-operative farms were subordinated to the central economic plan and their independence limited (ibid.: 206). These amounted to 4 per cent of the agricultural land, while the state farms amounted to 19 per cent (European Commission 1998).

Overall, the communist regime restricted voluntary co-operation, just as they restricted religious freedom, in order to avoid any rise of potential political opposition. In this way, they deliberately destroyed valuable social capital within the voluntary sector. The co-operative (collective) farms, which existed during the communist regime in Poland as well as in other CEEC, were not based on any principles of voluntarism, but were an extended hand from the state. Membership in the secondary and tertiary co-operative organizations was obligatory. For example, this was revealed in 1956 when the more liberal policies of Władysław Gomułka led to the abolition of obligatory membership. Immediately, farmers withdrew en masse, and the number of collectives was reduced to less than 2,000 (Nelson 1983: 176).

Thus, although most Polish farmers were involved more or less reluctantly in the state co-operative structure, small-scale private farming persisted even during the communist period. As documented above, the co-operative farms, essentially 'collective farms', which 'appeared' as ordered by the communist government, never covered a large area of Polish agricultural land. For this reason, Polish agriculture today continues to be dominated by small, subsistence-oriented farms. In practice, they carried out the orders of the central authorities. Their productivity was somewhat comparable to that of state-owned farms, but was usually slightly higher as a few aspects of private ownership were maintained. These co-operative (collective) farms assumed a monopolistic/monopsonistic role in the provision of inputs, purchase and processing of agricultural products, deposit and credit activities in rural areas, and provision of marketing and other services, as well as housing. Collective farms also had a social element, as they played a major role in training and education, in organizing events in local communities, and in creating new jobs and rehabilitation for the disabled.

Generally, co-operative unions provided the links between the planning authorities and primary co-operatives by operating wholesale and processing enterprises (World Bank 1990). Thus co-operatives of various kinds were assigned special tasks within the national economy. This resulted in a near split of the consumer movement into an urban movement and rural peasant self-help co-operatives. The introduction of the command system into the co-operatives was destructive to self-governing functions and led to a lack of involvement of the members, thereby reducing the level of social capital (ibid.). The socialist regime violated the abiding principles of co-operatives in a number of ways: the imperative of meeting central-planning objectives effectively eliminated the right of co-operatives to make their own decisions, to potentially leave the co-operative, or to choose their own leaders. The 'leader' was an assigned 'apparatchik' from the communist party.

As co-operative (collective) farms grew in size, the feelings of responsibility diminished, and members adopted a wage-worker mentality in their relationship to the enterprise and its property. It soon became evident to most people that the state farming system was inefficient, involving corruption, fictitious figures, and 'the general ignoring of cost accounting principles by farm operators, an attitude that was abetted by the regular provision of subsidies to cover losses' (Nelson 1983: 178).

There were political and ideological reasons why the real, democratic Polish co-operative structures were so easily abolished between 1947 and 1956. For communists, co-operatives were the tool for transforming the whole society, while negating the market. On the assumption that co-operatives work for society as a whole, all the advantages that a co-operative member had previously obtained, such as the dividend, priority rates, priority in using the co-operative services, and so on, were revoked. Furthermore, the co-operatives lost their voluntary character, and became more like a state enterprise (Maliszewski 1995).

By 1956, there were no more credit, housing, dairy, supply and distribution co-operatives, the last being replaced by the peasant self-help co-operatives (*samopomoc chlopska*) (ibid.). In the years from 1956 to 1957, the co-operative idea was somewhat revived in Poland, although it was a more or less semi-co-operative movement, as the value of democratic management was tolerated only as a panacea for the bureaucratic state economy (ibid.). From 1958, the co-operative sector became centralized, and local co-operatives were replaced by giant complexes, where membership was obligatory (ibid.).

With the abolition of true co-operatives, the communist regime created collective farms (and called them 'co-operatives' or 'co-operative farms'). Compared to many CEEC, Poland was fortunate in that collective farms did not involve a great proportion of the Polish communist agricultural sector (Chloupkova 2002a). These collective (co-operative) farms were not based on any principles, as we know them from the pre-communist co-operative movement, thus eliminating the important social control mechanism. Therefore, during the communist period in Poland, there existed a range of state subordinated 'co-operatives', usually with a monopolistic market position (membership was explicitly obligatory), whose stated goal was to cater to the interests of private farmers as well as collective farms. Table 3.5

illustrates the operation of state-controlled cooperatives during the communist regime.

Table 3.5 Polish rural co-operative movement (1988)

Type	Number	Members	Employees	Significance
Supply and marketing	1,912	3,531,500	434,570	59% of marketing of agricultural products
Dairy co-operatives	323	1,199,400	112,793	95% of milk processed
Horticultural co-operatives	140	372,600	55,519	50% of fruit and vegetable
Agricultural production co-operatives	2,086	177,000	2,700	2.8% of arable land
Savings and credit	1,663	2,566,100	31,290	18.5% of population's savings
Agricultural circles	2,006	113,200	154,447	Important share in mechanization service
Total	8,130	7,959,800	791,319	

Source: Reproduced from Chloupkova et al. (2003: 250) with permission (see ICA, 1993).

Despite the communist doctrine proclaiming a collectivist vision of society (and thus perhaps creation of social capital), the socialist ideology led to a society that was entirely fragmented. Thus, the cohesive/cementing role of social capital, acting as a primary drive in the pre-communist co-operative movement, was replaced by third-party enforcement (centrally directed orders from the communist government). Since (a) membership was not voluntary, (b) there was no democratic control, based on one person, one vote (was subject to central planning), (c) members were dispossessed of any property in favour of the collective farm, and (d) members' influence on the collective farm operation was rather limited (for example, the owners of land could not take any decisions regarding their land), this led to the destruction of social capital. A further reason for this was the above-mentioned ban on forming associations, and the worker's total dependency on the workplace, indeed, on the state. In this way, the level of social capital deteriorated over time under the totalitarian regime, and its replacement under the renewed democratic system is not an easy or a 'short-term' project.

Since 1989, as a consequence of the restoration of the democratic regime and the free market economy, agricultural circles have gradually fallen out of favour. Nowadays, every farmer owns a tractor, even though, considering the small plot of land they own, it might not be efficient. This leads to machinery overinvestment, although the machinery equipment used is usually old, technically outdated and inefficient. The inherited low level of social capital from the communist regime explains the continued reluctance to co-operate among Polish farmers today.

Considering the small and fragmented structure of private farms in Poland, purchase of common machinery would be justified as an efficient means of co-operation. Polish sources do not explicitly mention social capital. Rather, they argue that the relatively weak development of producer organization is rooted in the fact that the development of producer groups and organizations requires a longer time for farmers to be exposed to the appropriate market stimuli (SAEPR/FAPA 2000). Polish agricultural circles could clearly benefit from assistance in adapting the German concept of agricultural machine sharing to Polish conditions (FAO 1994). Similarly, bilateral co-operation with West European co-operative societies is viewed as potentially useful in assisting the renaissance of the Polish agricultural movement. Thus, because of the lack of social capital among other reasons, the renaissance of the co-operative movement in Poland has been delayed.

3.3.   SUMMARY

Social capital, measured as the level of trust among people, may be regarded as a new production factor alongside the traditional ones of human and physical capital. With appropriate levels of social capital, monitoring and transaction costs can be reduced and thus economic growth stimulated.

By linking social capital to rural development and comparing the cases of agricultural co-operative movements in Denmark and Poland, we first identified the possible roots of social capital accumulation suggesting that it developed through a lengthy process in both countries during the nineteenth century.

We highlighted the well-developed cooperative movement in both Denmark and Poland, prior to the Second World War. Most of the farmers' operations were based on both specific and generalized trust. Politically speaking, in both countries in the inter-war period a full range of political parties (left and right), and thus also market stimuli, existed and supported the idea of cooperation. The underlying objective of this political support was the fight for influence in the cooperative movement.

As Denmark, after the Second World War, followed a democratic path of economic development, the cooperative movement was not proscribed and it continued to play a crucial role in the success of agriculture. The Danish cooperative movement created a 'strong pillar' for various framing activities. Thus, a range of horizontal and vertical links between people satisfying their different needs in particular social groups existed in democratic societies.

Unlike Denmark, Poland was obliged to follow a totalitarian doctrine. First fascists, then communists, tried to fight the cooperative idea, and then to infiltrate and subordinate it. Since cooperative movements play a crucial role in building a capitalistic and democratic society, it is no surprise that it was one of the first targets of the communist government.

Therefore, these voluntary organizations in Poland were brought under the control of the party and people became accustomed to obeying orders rather than making their own decisions, at the same time destroying the stock of social capital.

Next, we turned to the actual measurement of the social capital levels in present-day Denmark and Poland, which indicated that the level of social capital is significantly higher in Denmark than in Poland. We suggested that the reason for this disparity is due to the fact that the original accumulation of social capital in Poland was destroyed by the communist regime. Our empirical findings seemed to confirm this hypothesis, as the average Dane is a member of 12 times more voluntary organizations than the average Pole. Being a member of a voluntary organization gives Danes, in addition to achieving the purpose of organization, what we call a 'platform' for social mingling and the exchange of other information (see also Chapters 4 and 7).

Likewise, one could argue that the massive state intervention in the Polish economy under communism established heavy bureaucratic systems monopolizing the right to approve all actions in society. Arbitrary use of central power intimidated the citizens and taught them to trust no one. Also, it created opportunities for corruption among bureaucrats, party officials and state monopolies, reducing the citizens' trust in formal institutions. This hypothesis was also confirmed by our empirical findings.

With regard to trust among citizens, Danes trust one another three and a half times more than Poles trust other Poles, and Danes would in general trust the four most important formal institutions (legal system, police, administration, and government) 'a great deal' ten times more than Poles do. Finally, similar to the case for membership of voluntary organizations, we would expect more civic participation and entrepreneurship in a capitalist country than in a communist one, where entrepreneurs were persecuted as a potential threat to the system due to their capability of organizing resistance. Accordingly, we found that Danes participate in twice as many civic actions as do the Poles.

As demonstrated, cooperatives have both an economic and a civic component, which make them a good example to shed light on the formation and destruction of social capital. Thus it can be argued that the capitalistic democracies are in general superior to the communist dictatorships in facilitating and accumulating social capital. Overall, the cases of cooperative movements in Denmark and Poland suggested that social capital was accumulated to the same extent and along the same lines in both countries in the nineteenth century.

However, we suggest that two different political systems during the twentieth century led to different levels of social capital and diverging paths for civic society. Capitalism maintained and perhaps increased social capital, whereas communism destroyed it. The lack of social capital in CEEC could therefore be one explanation for the rather disappointing economic results and hardships of transition so far. In conclusion, more research has to be undertaken to validate these suggestions.

NOTE

1. Chapter 3 relies heavily on Chloupkova et al. (2003). We thank co-author Jarka Chloupkova for generously allowing us to use parts of her work.

4. Bridging Social Capital and Entrepreneurship in Rural Denmark

4.1.   INTRODUCTION

During the nineteenth century, a broad tradition of civic organization was established in the Danish rural districts. From the beginning of the century, this organization was led by energetic entrepreneurs and institutionalized in the form of associations, so numerous in the last part of the century that the period was known as *Foreningstiden*, 'the time of associations'.

We observe how this surprisingly strong and idealistic commitment to the common good involved the formation of civic movements and, hence, the building up of valuable and non-excludable capital. Thus, the accumulation of physical capital developed from the establishment of shared economic and cultural buildings or, in our terminology, 'platforms' securing the mix of various groups; cultural capital in the form of common norms and common identity; and, most significantly, social capital as an informal institutionalization of bridging social capital smoothing or lubricating co-operative relations.

Such economically and culturally fruitful civic enthusiasm we also find in other Western countries at that time. Especially, in the United States, civic life developed through the nineteenth-century, reaching a peak during 1850-1900 (Putnam 2000), that is, in exactly the same period, when major civic movements took place in Denmark. Thus, Putnam illustrates the widespread 'Toquevillean' civic virtues of early nineteenth-century Americans by recounting the instance of the founding of a community lyceum in New Bedford, Massachusetts, in 1829. The founder, Thomas Greene, formulated the purpose of such a lyceum in the following, instructive way:

> We come from all divisions, ranks and classes of society to teach and to be taught in our turn. While we mingle together in these pursuits, we shall learn to know each other more intimately; we shall remove many of the prejudices which ignorance or partial aquaintance with each other had fostered . . . In the parties and sects into which we are divided, we sometimes learn to love our brother at the expense of him whom we do not in so many respects regard as a brother . . . We may return to our homes and firesides [from the lyceum] with kindlier feelings

toward one another, because we have learned to know one another better. (Cited in Putnam 2000: 23)

As will soon become evident, such ideas summarize many of the main themes in this book. However, the main question in this chapter still remains: why *do* these civic-minded entrepreneurs – these 'Thomas Greene's' – emerge and organize local groups in the form of associations, thus contributing to voluntary collective good provision and the creation of bridging social capital?

As argued in Chapter 2, bridging social capital is derived from regular face-to-face, co-operative relations among larger groups in local areas, as the outcome of close human relations based on balanced reciprocity – something that is clearly facilitated by decentralization. It is precisely such relations, we argue, that were rooted in civic traditions, which – dating back to a civic society that emerged in the late eighteenth century – developed in rural Denmark during the second part of the nineteenth century. Furthermore, we argue that open and widespread co-operation is initiated by writing down formal 'rules of the game', which can be sanctioned effectively. This suggestion seems to be confirmed by empirical evidence from entrepreneurial activity in rural Denmark, 1800–1900. During this period, written rules in the form of the formal founding statutes of co-operative associations enhanced informal peasant co-operation and stocks of beneficial social capital of an inclusive nature, that is, bridging social capital. As an outcome of this process, entrepreneurs voluntarily organized larger groups, which provided collective goods locally, thus contributing to economic growth in formerly poor, rural areas.

Furthermore, we argue that it was the formal organizational structure behind these associations in the form of the written rules of the game that, acting as a kind of 'kick-starter', led to extended networks and, ultimately, to beneficial capital building. Right up to the 1960s, this process again gave rise to generations of entrepreneurs continuously establishing and maintaining 'networks of associations' at local, regional and national levels. In this way, when first established and institutionalized due to certain, organizational principles, securing predictability and the possibility of sanctions, bridging social capital was rapidly accumulated in all Danish rural districts, fostering local entrepreneurs who would guarantee group action and the provision of collective goods.

An understanding of the growth of new and more recent forms of bridging social capital is reinforced with reference to a major wave of sports hall building in Denmark, following the general increase in leisure time. The implications for voluntariness and public support are discussed in this perspective.

4.2.   EARLY BRIDGING SOCIAL CAPITAL

Studying the historical material carefully, it becomes evident that the political system has a strong impact on social capital building within specific time–space contexts. Thus, the political set-up and its formal institutions clearly constitute the overall framework for formations of different levels of 'civicness' involving different levels of generalized trust and distrust among a population and, ultimately, for accumulations of bridging/bonding social capital. A notable example here is the communist Eastern European countries before 1989 compared to, for example, the Scandinavian welfare states based on capitalism, political pluralism and democracy, deeply rooted in unbroken rich, civic traditions. However, is it possible in our main study object, rural Denmark, to detect a shift of political set-up leading to civic traditions and (bridging) social capital building? In the following, we argue that it is certainly possible.

4.2.1.   The Rise of a Civic Society

About 1750, feudal Denmark was marked by economic stagnation due to serious shortcomings in the overall political–economic system. Therefore, inspired by the new liberal ideas coming from Enlightenment Western Europe, the Danish monarch and his officials began to search for new alternative ways of enhancing economic growth.

As a direct result of this, land reforms entailing wide-ranging consequences for political institutional and physical organization were effectuated during the last decades of the eighteenth century, motivating and, partly, also enforcing peasants to buy their own land. This necessitated the well-known abolition of the Adscript of June 1788, severing the formerly strong and unequal economic ties between feudal landlords and peasants. In this way, the central administration tried to create strong incentives for common peasants to increase personal profits, to the general benefit of the Danish state. Thus, the purpose of this law, introducing what should turn out to be an extremely successful economic strategy, was summarized as the consolidation of the 'general prosperity' of the state by securing the 'rights of our dear and faithful subjects belonging to the peasantry, in particular their personal freedom' (Law of Abolition of the Adscript of June 1788, in Hansgaard 1981: 194). Characteristically, on a famous monument – the so-called 'Monument of Freedom' (Frihedsstøtten) raised in Copenhagen about ten years after to celebrate the abolition and, in a more fundamental way, the transition from feudalism to liberalism and capitalism – it was written that the main purpose of the abolition had been to ensure the 'freedom of citizens', the 'thirst for knowledge', and 'desire of diligence' (Feldbæk 1988: 12–13).

However, such new liberal and physiocratic ideas not only reached the monarch and his closest employees, they were also adopted by other parts of the more educated population in the major towns and cities. As a consequence, the 'thirst for knowledge' was aroused, leading to the establishment of a large number of so-called clubs at the end of the century, particularly in Copenhagen. In these clubs – the model of which had been imported from England – the Danish intelligentsia could discuss the new revolutionary ideas, undisturbed and in pleasant surroundings.

A contemporary author and historian of literature, Rasmus Nyerup, wrote in 1800:

> These clubs have brought about a major change in social intercourse in particular among the middle classes . . . These are closed societies having their own laws and arrangements, which, for a fixed yearly subscription from each member, rent out rooms, provide for reading and billiard tables, arrange concerts, balls and assemblies, and where a man, no matter which evening he chooses, can always be certain to meet acquaintances. (Nyerup, cited in Balle-Petersen 1976: 46, our translation)

All this new civic enthusiasm, which formerly had been totally forbidden by Danish monarchs, led to the formation of a gradually more extended 'net of communication' (Leisner 1988: 37), mainly including learned scholars belonging to a still more powerful citizenry. These new networks spread rapidly during the 1790s and, due to newly established, non-government-controlled scientific, reading and philanthropic societies, scientific journals, and so on, they were able to disseminate the ideas of contemporary Enlightenment Western Europe to a large part of the Danish population. Thus, largely exclusive networks in the clubs seemed to be transformed into strongly inclusive networks at the meso and macro levels, leading to open democratic debate, mutual confidence between groups, civic traditions and, in the long run, to political–economic conditions promoting the accumulation of beneficial bridging social capital.

Thus, during the first part of the nineteenth century, the English-inspired clubs – being platforms for the accumulation of a, prevailingly, mild and non-aggressive form of bonding social capital – gradually died out, leaving space for the establishment of a multitude of voluntary associations within a still growing and still more viable civic society. As will be clear from the following sections, such associations in particular became popular among the large group of formerly adscript serfs, but now independent farmers.

4.2.2.   Associations, Entrepreneurs, and the Accumulation of Social Capital

It was not only the increasing number of associations, rooted in eighteenth century club life in the cities that facilitated the emergence of a strong, rural civic society in Denmark. It was also the diversity of their functions. Thus, knowledge and organizational training were transmitted through economic and cultural associations ranging from insurance associations, savings banks, production associations, agronomist and political associations to youth associations, gymnastic clubs, rifle clubs and temperance societies – all of them closely related to shared buildings financed and raised by the local communities themselves, such as free schools, community high schools, free churches, teacher training colleges, agricultural colleges, religious meeting-houses and drill-halls. Ultimately, this process led to an extremely active, rural population, taking care of local and regional political, economic and cultural functions and thus – without any state interference – gradually improving their own living conditions, which at the beginning of the nineteenth century had been extremely poor.

At the local level, the historical sources indicate that such civic initiative was primarily due to the activities of certain individuals engaged, it seems, in every single associational innovation in their communities. Obviously, these charismatic entrepreneurs or *ildsjæle* – literally 'souls of fire', that is, public-spirited citizens – acted from a blend of economic, idealistic and purely personal motives, often not realizing that their strong commitment was a public good, ultimately leading to common benefits for all the members of the local society – both economically and culturally. As we shall see, an excellent example here is the men behind the Danish co-operative movement.

Moreover, the historical evidence makes it clear that from the 1840s most of these local entrepreneurs developed into organizers of local as well as regional *networks of associations*, that is, specific 'associational milieus' consisting of a variety of associations sharing the same political and/or religious ideology and, typically, with an overlapping membership. The regular face-to-face interaction resulting from such a network of associations – voluntarily established and maintained by local entrepreneurs – led to a general strengthening of mutual trust and common norms in the rural districts, thus lubricating society.

However, due to major innovations in organization, association building rapidly increased and finally culminated in the establishment of a Danish co-operative movement from the mid-1860s. In this way, association building turned into social capital building, fostering entrepreneurship and the provision of collective goods. Thus, bridging social capital, possibly *the* most crucial production factor, led to improved material as well as non-material living conditions in the countryside. These collective, that is, *non-excludable*, goods were provided by local entrepreneurs (*ildsjæle*), whose personal, economic net gains were clearly negative, compared to both the amount of time and energy spent, and, especially, the benefits they provided their communities in the form of strengthening shared norms and, ultimately, enhancing economic growth. This is in accordance with James Coleman, who – as will be remembered – talks about 'underinvestment in social capital' due to the fact that 'the actor or actors who generate social capital ordinarily capture only a small part of its benefits' (1988a: 119; see also 1988b: 389, 1990: 317ff.).

4.2.3.   Early Philanthropic Entrepreneurs

As described earlier, from about 1780 a feudal Denmark based on a subsistence economy was gradually transformed into a liberalistic society based on a modern monetary economy. Agricultural reforms had made it profitable for landlords to allocate land to peasants, who moved in great numbers from the villages to their new homes. Thus, the reforms promoted a demographic transition that had already been initiated in the eighteenth century.

The need to finance such large-scale enclosure of land and the subsequent demographic transformation immediately led to serious cash-flow problems. Thus, the poor liquidity among the peasants meant that the state as well as landlords, merchants and private persons had to guarantee the sums needed. However, as expressed by a famous Danish historian, the peasants were often exploited by professional moneylenders, charging 'ruinous interest' (Hertel 1917: 18).

Consequently, both landlords and peasants increasingly sought new forms of economic co-operation in the rural districts in order to secure economic and social stability. The kingdom's first credit and savings bank was established in 1810 by Count F.A. Holstein, who, strongly influenced by German philanthropy, adopted the idea from Prussia (ibid.: 19). Of an equally moralistic character were the rural district savings banks, established during the 1820s, which invited the ordinary rural population to protect themselves from personal misfortune through lifelong money saving. During the 1840s, there was an increase in the number of savings banks and private joint stock companies, offering the peasants low interest loans. Even cheaper, however, were the loans offered by the new credit associations from about 1850. The latter introduced the idea of shared economic responsibility in the rural districts, an organizational strategy which was to become one of the cornerstones in the founding statutes of the co-operative dairies in the second half of the century.

During the first part of the nineteenth century, then, the finance market was less dominated by the state and by the philanthropic and liberal-thinking landlords, thus making way for financial institutes owned by the peasants themselves. Especially during the 1850s and 1860s, with the foundation of a great number of local agricultural savings banks, this trend became clear. Thus, the rural financial institutes and similar peasant-owned institutions such as health, cattle and fire insurance associations should be seen as a basic element in the process of self-organization, leading to an increase in economic and political independence among the rural population (Bjørn 1982: 97).

The competition between rural and urban savings banks should be seen in this light. So we see that, at the micro level, the majority of the peasants who had been the leading figures behind the first savings banks, situated in the provincial towns, now left the bank committees to establish new local, rural savings banks, called 'parish savings banks' (Blinkenberg Nielsen 1950: 11) (see Figure 4.1). Thus, these local parish entrepreneurs (the *ildsjæle*), by taking an active part in the conflict between rural and urban Denmark, promoted a decentralized co-operative structure in the countryside.

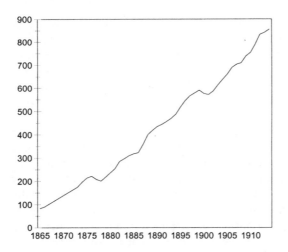

Source: Blinkenberg Nielsen 1950: 172–3.

Figure 4.1 Parish savings banks (Denmark), 1865–1914

4.2.4. The Danish Co-operative Dairy Movement

4.2.4.1. Introduction

An instructive example of the emergence of a reserve or stock of strongly inclusive, bridging social capital is the co-operative movement, which emerged in the mid-nineteenth century (Svendsen and Svendsen 2000, 2001). Here it is the organizational structure or the *written rules of the game*, which lay behind the network-based co-operation so decisive for the creation of reserves of positive or negative social capital.

This seems to confirm Mancur Olson's idea that high quality of formal institutions is important for predictable behaviour, common norms and widespread co-operation among a population. This idea was also reflected in new institutional economics, for example, Douglass North (1990) argued that 'rules of the game', that is, formal institutions, are fundamental for economic growth. However, our case studies clearly demonstrate that potentially productive, informal exchange in the form of a social capital goes hand in hand with formal institutions – 'written rules of the game' – which secures predictability of exchange, co-operation across group cleavages and the possibility of sanction. In other words, high-quality formal and informal institutions are an important tool for accumulating bridging social capital. An illuminating example of the dynamic interplay between formal and informal institutions is Elinor Ostrom's studies of social capital and collective action, which highlight crucial aspects of the interplay.

In this chapter, when measuring how social capital is built, we shall use Putnam's approach and focus on participation in voluntary organizations, with the establishment of a co-operative dairy movement in rural Denmark at the end of the nineteenth century as an example. When explaining the destruction of social capital, we shall focus on the declining number of co-operative dairies, which began about 1960 and escalated during the following decade. Because of this drastic reduction in the number of local dairies due to economies of scale, we hypothesize that this is the main reason why bridging social capital fragmentized and partly transformed into exclusive, bonding types of social capital, often harmful to society (Chapter 5).

4.2.4.2. How social capital was created: 'written rules of the game'

When feudalism gradually had been wiped out by land reforms about 1800, this led to the creation of a whole new class of family farmers owning their own land. The struggle for a better life in the countryside seemed to stagnate during an economic crisis in the 1870s. International corn prices slumped, and the small, corn-producing, Danish farmers in particular found themselves in a hopeless economic situation (Bjørn 1982: 17–19).

Generally, the shift to exporting secondary agricultural produce instead of grain due to the new demands of the world market led to an increase in the production of animal produce. But in 1879, Germany imposed a duty on all livestock coming from Denmark, and the export of cattle was halved the following year (ibid.: 48). The loss of the German market gave rise to the so-called 'home dairies', where neighbours collaborated in the production of butter.

As a counter-reaction, the early philanthropic associations described earlier were to form the basis of a regular co-operative movement within Danish agriculture – a movement which quickly evolved during the second half of the nineteenth century. In this period, the peasants established a multitude of co-operative associations, ranging from co-operative wholesale societies from 1866, to co-operative dairies from 1882, co-operative fodder and fertilizer purchasing associations from 1883, and co-operative meat packing plants from 1887.

The decisive innovation consisted in the specific organizational structure of these associations, strongly promoting co-operative networks of an inclusive nature and thus the accumulation of beneficial social capital. As we shall see, right from the beginning this organizational structure was institutionalized in the standard founding statutes of the co-operative association.

The idea originated in England. In 1844, in Rochdale near Manchester, a group of weavers founded the first co-operative wholesale society in the world, that is, a sales and purchasing company owned by the members themselves. Nearly 20 years later, two friends living in the village of Møgeltønder in the southern part of the Jutland peninsula – F.F. Ulrik, a doctor, and H.C. Sonne, a priest – discussed the Rochdale principles. Ulrik had been familiar with these ideas for some time and now he evoked passionate interest from Sonne (Ravnholt 1943: 30). In various ways, these philanthropically minded men were trying to alleviate the conditions of the poorest part of the population by establishing a wide range of charitable organizations and institutions in the area (Dollerup 1966: 34ff.).

However, after the defeat by Prussia in 1864 and the consequent loss of the southern part of Jutland, Ulrik and Sonne, being ardent patriots, were forced to leave the region, though they continued their entrepreneurial activities in close co-operation with other kindred spirits. So, in Copenhagen, Ulrik set up a building association for shipyard workers in 1865, while Sonne established the first Danish wholesale society in the small borough of Thisted in 1866.

The great success of this first wholesale society in Denmark was due to Sonne's vast insight into the original organizational principles used in the English co-operative wholesale movement – a knowledge he had obtained partly during several study tours, and partly by reading all the English literature about the subject he could get hold of. All this is documented in a book Sonne wrote in 1867, the year after he had founded his wholesale society (see also Dollerup 1966: 50). Drawing on practical experience of the wholesale society in Thisted, he propagated the 'laws from Rochdale', that is, the founding statutes he himself had successfully implemented in a Danish local community (Sonne 1867: 4ff.). Thus, inspired by key principles such as allocation of profits according to the amount of purchases made by the members (§2 and §6), shared economic responsibility (§3), open membership (§4) and democratic decision making (§5), the *purpose* of the wholesale society in Thisted (§1) is 'in perfect accordance with the Rochdale laws to establish a foundation by subscriptions voluntarily paid by the members, in order to allow them to purchase more profitably the necessities of life' (ibid.: 5). However, this programme expressed only the 'means' whereby one could achieve the 'true' objective (ibid.). Sonne continues:

> If this is overlooked, our attention is easily attracted to the economic and purely material side and we lose sight of the true depth and great significance; no, the goal is to elevate what in the civic sense is the lower ranking, dependent and pressured segment of the population to a higher moral, intellectual and social level and thereby to a more honourable place in society. (ibid.: 5; our translation)

If the founding statutes did not fully lead to this idealist goal – at least, not in Sonne's lifetime – nevertheless, they *did* offer an organizational structure that would increase the material welfare of the poor majority of the population, not least in the countryside, where the peasants followed Sonne's advice and formed their own wholesale societies to protect themselves against economic exploitation. Thus, and especially from the mid-1880s, the number of wholesale associations rapidly increased to about 850 by the turn of the century and – quite a remarkable feat in an international context – the vast majority were established in local rural communities (see Figure 4.2).

However, even more importantly, the founding statutes of Sonne's co-operative wholesale society were to be widely applied within the agricultural sector, introducing important formal institutions in the form of self-enforced written rules of the game that would strongly enhance co-operation and the building of bridging social capital among farmers as well. In the following, we shall look more closely at that sector within the co-operative movement that had the strongest socio-economic impact on farmers' everyday life: the co-operative dairy movement.

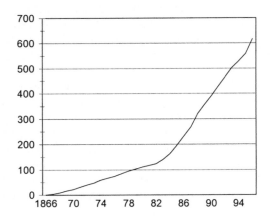

Source: Christensen 1985: 200.

Figure 4.2 Wholesale societies (Denmark), 1866–1900

4.2.4.3. 'Written rules of the game' within the dairy sector

The culmination of the co-operative movement can be said to be the establishment of numerous dairy co-operatives in the last two decades of the nineteenth century. As was the case with the purchasing co-operatives, an important explanation for the success of the co-operative dairies was the organizational statutes in the form of written rules of the game. These formal rules came to constitute legally binding promises, which would facilitate co-operation between the large farmers and smallholders, a co-operation which until then had been totally inconceivable. In addition, the written rules of the game entailed the possibility of sanctions against any members who attempted to cheat. Thus, network-based co-operation of an inclusive nature was promoted within economic life, with the resulting accumulation of productive, bridging social capital.

Not surprisingly, then, it was particularly within the co-operative dairy movement from 1882 that the co-operatively based form of organization formulated by Sonne in 1867 (*andelskontrakten*) was further elaborated, juristically as well as in practice, to fit the norms and culture of the rural population. It was in the village of Hjedding near Varde, in the western part of Jutland, that a group of entrepreneurial farmers founded the first co-operative dairy. In his memoirs, dating from 1901, one of the main promoters of the project, farmer Niels Kristensen, writes about the initial discussions:

> During the negotiations, a general sentiment evolved expressing a preference for collecting milk instead of the butter . . . To be able to prepare the milk in one

place, it was necessary to build a dairy. This, however, gave rise to another problem, since some of the farmers had no wish to build a dairy with others, while they agreed to selling their milk to the dairy. Thus, without anybody realizing, the negotiations moved in the direction of the realization of what was later to become a widespread and magnificent co-operative ideal: that everybody who joined the dairy should be allocated profits on the basis of the amount of milk he delivered. (Kristensen cited in Manøe Hansen 1972: 13, our translation)

Immediately after this meeting, some of the peasants collaborated to write the contract of the association. Overall, their articles reflect all the ideas of Sonne and the English wholesale society movement, stressing principles such as allocation of profits in proportion to the amount of milk delivered by the members, shared economic responsibility, open membership, and, not least, democratic decision making, which here was further specified as 'one man, one vote' at the yearly general assembly, where all major decisions regarding the dairy should be taken (for more details, see Svendsen and Svendsen 2000: 76). During the next two months, the dairy in Hjedding was built, under the leadership of the committee members themselves (Kristensen, cited in Manøe Hansen 1972: 16–17), and in June 1882, dairy production started.

Less than 10 years after this event, the 'Hjedding model' had spread to all corners of the country (see Figure 4.3). Looking at the figures, the economic success appears evident. In 1890, one-third of all farmers delivered milk to one of the 700 or so co-operative dairies. Consequently, Danish butter exports increased from 12.5 million kilograms in 1880 to about 90 million by the beginning of the new century, while the export of milk increased from 200 litres to about 600,000 litres in the same period (Bjørn 1982: 21, 552, 561).

This development took place *in spite* of the Danish government. Until the end of the decade, the government – being conservative and anti-socialist – did nothing to encourage the foundation of co-operative dairies. In fact, both the state and the agricultural organizations were often 'downright negative' in their relation to the dairies (ibid.: 80). But the movement was out of their control. The rural population joined voluntarily and the number of co-operative dairies increased rapidly. People put up their own money as start capital, raised loans from their own local financial institutes, asked for and paid for technical advice and so on. In short, they acted independently of the state, using their own resources. Thus we see that the co-operative dairies were not the result of central administration (see ibid.: 119).

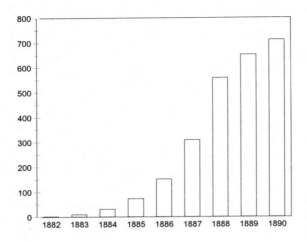

Source: Bjørn 1982: 85.

Figure 4.3 Co-operative dairies (Denmark), 1882–90

These resources, scarce though they were in the countryside at the beginning of the 1880s, sprang out of mutual confidence and mutual trust between members of the local society. To know one another well was clearly a precondition for people joining in any shared, economic adventure, especially such a risky one:

> Because the number of participants of a co-operative dairy was limited by the small size of the local area, one may presume that these people knew one another very well, and the joint and several liability, therefore, seems to have been the appropriate way to resolve common, economic tasks. (Ibid.: 96, our translation)

This phenomenon is reflected in Coleman's term 'closure'. As will be remembered, this means beneficial social capital building facilitated by most people knowing one another in a neighbourhood, including parents knowing their children's friends as well as *their* parents. Such chains of 'I know x, who knows y, who knows z . . . who knows me' enhance social control, rapid spread of information, generalized trust (*I* trust her, because *you* trust her, and I trust *you*) and similar collective goods. People who meet regularly face to face will most probably find each other trustworthy.

But why did all these generally trustworthy peasants engage in such activities? What purposes and interests did they share? And what common benefits did they achieve?

Apart from people knowing and trusting one another, a precondition for the success of the co-operative dairy was a common economic interest, promoted in the four standard paragraphs of the articles of such an organization (see Rørdam 1983: 27–34).

First, the idea of open membership was to invite everybody to join the local co-operative dairy (*andelsmejeri*), regardless of either political/religious conviction or economic ability. An important outcome of such a 'we welcome all' strategy was that the local *andelsmejeri* acted as a social meeting place or, in our terminology, a 'platform' securing a mix of different groups (see also Chapters 4 and 7).

Second, this inclusiveness was supplemented, and reinforced, by democratic decision making. Everybody, high and low, was equal.

Third, people shared an economic responsibility for their dairy, supplying start capital, and all bearing the responsibility of loans for buildings, equipment and so on. Thus, people were jointly and severally liable for the risks of loss and were, therefore, also forced to co-operate in spite of political, religious or social conflicts – a crucial factor (compare Bjørn 1982: 95–6).

Fourth, the profit was not shared in a socialist way: it was repaid to the members in proportion to the amount of milk delivered by each individual during a certain period of time. In other words, each member could harvest the fruits of his/her labour. This satisfied the larger farmers and enabled them to accept that voting within the co-operative association would take place on a one-man one-vote basis, rather than according to the number of head of cattle owned by each.

In this way the democratic, socio-economic elements – at that time interpreted by some as 'socialist influence' – were outweighed by the profit-making part of the whole business. The members actually earned money! Rationalizations and, due to social capital, the maximum utilization of new technologies (physical capital) and professionalization (human capital) increased the total profit from 20 to 25 per cent on average, compared to the home dairies (ibid.: 116).

Remarkably, these rules of the game which, adapted to and embedded in a specific culture, seem to increase the profits of physical, human and social capitals, have many similarities to the work of Ostrom and her findings on social capital and collective action (see Ostrom 1992, 1994; Ostrom et al. 1994).

Citing a famous passage from Coleman's works which, again, is echoing Durkheim's key notion of the collective being more than the sum of the individual beings, Ostrom (1994: 528) sees social capital as a new production factor that makes it possible for people, through joint effort, to achieve something that in the absence of social capital would not be possible or, in other words, things they would not have managed to achieve on their own. Thus, applying the case study of self-organized common-pool irrigation resources among farmers she shows that regular face-to-face communication, common economic interests, social control, efficient sanctions against free riders, and trust are fundamental elements in a viable, long-term 'contract' among groups of farmers (ibid.: 532ff.). Thus, self-enforced rules promoting strategies of inclusion, that is, clearly stated rules known and openly discussed in the public sphere and deeply embedded in reciprocity and common norms, seem to trigger (or 'kick-start') the building of beneficial bridging social capital.

Therefore, following Ostrom, investment in formal institutions means investment in an organizational framework that fosters stocks of bridging social capital – something that should be seen as just as important as investments in physical capital, in some cases even *more* important (as many development projects in third-world countries clearly reveal). Thus, Ostrom concludes that 'if external agents of change do not take into account the delicate balance of interests [among farmers] embedded in social capital, when investments in physical capital are undertaken efforts to improve productivity can have the opposite effect' (ibid.: 559). Again, this tells us that we must not underestimate the importance of the production factor *social* capital, even if we cannot see it, touch it, or measure it in the same strict, classical economic way, as is the case with the more traditional forms of capital.

4.2.4.4.   Entrepreneurship and the building of bridging social capital

The success of the co-operative dairies originated in the formal organizational structure behind the co-operation, that is, in the founding statutes of the model dairy of Hjedding. As we shall see in the following, such a long-term, reciprocity-based 'co-operative contract' (*andelskontrakten*) formed the organizational framework that helped to foster durable informal institutions in the form of bridging social capital. *Andelskontrakten* functioned to mediate between conflicting groups, thus securing a predictable and stable pattern of human interaction. However, founded on informal reciprocal relations – essentially, *un*written rules of the game – it also allowed for spontaneity in the form of rational or, more precisely, *raissonable* socio-economic strategies among actors.

First, all over the country, *andelskontrakten* involved an extraordinary compromise between two, conflicting groups: the well-to-do farmers and the smallholders. This compromise was based on the farmers' common economic interests institutionalized in the socio-economic principles of the co-operative association. In this way, the contract facilitated the formation of positive social capital (of an inclusive nature) or, in Putnam's formulation, *bridging social capital* encompassing 'people across diverse social cleavages' – an invisible, intangible but none the less extremely important form of capital, which in the long run would enhance economic growth in rural Denmark.

Using the Hjedding model as a concrete tool, the two groups – the well-to-do farmers and the smallholders – now began to co-operate on equal terms. The Hjedding model made such 'impossible' co-operation possible, precisely by stressing the shared, economic interest of all farmers. So we understand why §1 of the founding statutes from Hjedding underlined this shared interest by focusing on cash payment to the members in proportion to the amount of milk delivered by each individual during a certain period of time:

> The profit obtained from sale [of cheese and butter] is distributed among the members in proportion to the amount of milk each has delivered, minus the running expenses of the dairy. The profit from the sale of butter is distributed monthly, whereas the profit from the sale of cheese is distributed once a year. Every day, buttermilk and whey is delivered back to the members, in proportion to the amount of milk each member has delivered. (§1 of the founding statutes of Hjedding, Manøe Hansen 1972: 33, our translation)

In particular, this paragraph satisfied the well-to-do farmers. Moreover, in order to satisfy the smallholders as well, the statutes secured democratic decision making (§12). Thus the farmers voted 'according to heads and not according to cows' (with the exception of 10–15 per cent of all co-operative dairies, which voted 'according to cows and not according to heads', compare Bjørn 1982: 95). Everybody, whether high or low, was equal.

Written rules secured the formation of bridging social capital. This involved clear rules of the game, securing a formalization of co-operation, which included the possibility of sanctioning those members who violated the rules agreed upon by all (§9). Thus, any farmer who diluted the milk by adding water, used wrong fodder for his cows, or in any other way tried to cheat the others, would run the risk of exclusion:

> The milk must be delivered to the dairy in a pure and non-adulterated condition. Milk from sick cows must not be delivered . . . If it can be documented that the milk delivered by a supplier has been adulterated, either by addition of water or other mixtures, or if foamy milk is delivered, if the milk of sick cows has been added, or if the pails are dirty – in such cases, the supplier is excluded from the association and will be fined an amount of [etc.]. (Manøe Hansen 1972: 34, our translation)

Second, as farmers became accustomed to following the clear, written rules of the game, the formalized framework for co-operation became 'naturalized', that is, diffused into informal exchange as well. Thus, co-operation according to the rules of the game, implying collective good provision, became a natural way of acting, a normal behaviour that the peasants took for granted. The rules were internalized in people, that is, they became internalized culture or, in the words of Bourdieu, predisposed dispositions in the form of a habitus.

In this bottom-up process, the farmers financed their dairies themselves, making use of the local, parish savings banks, just as they paid for all professional assistance needed if they were unable to accomplish these various tasks themselves – just as formerly had been the case with the wholesale companies (Bjørn 1982: 100, see also Paldam and Svendsen 2000).

The first outcome of entrepreneurial activities and the accumulation of stocks of bridging social capital was a significant increase in economic growth in former poor, rural areas. The second, as has already been indicated, was a general lubrication of mutual relations within the local communities, including cultural life.

It is in this light that we shall investigate the formation of a multitude of cultural institutions during the second half of the nineteenth century, such as community high schools, village halls and drill halls – all of them enhancing the accumulation of various forms of capital in rural Denmark other than physical and economic, such as human capital (see Figure 4.4).

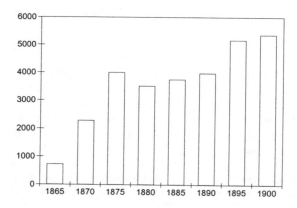

Source: Rørdam 1983.

Figure 4.4 Number of pupils in rural community high schools (Denmark), 1865–1900

This again strengthened the 'recruitment' of new generations of local entrepreneurs, providing collective goods and, at the same time, continuing the process of building beneficial bridging social capital. This can be illustrated as shown in Figure 4.5.

The figure shows that this development was – in line with Ostrom's ideas – initiated by innovations in organizational structure (rules of the game), acting as a kick-starter for the formation of networks of associations and stocks of beneficial social capital, that is, bridging social capital encouraging local entrepreneurs all over the country to provide collective, non-excludable goods. Consequently, this development not only profited the single, local community but also the whole nation. As suggested in Figure 4.5, this again contributed to the accumulation of social capital and the recruitment of new generations of entrepreneurs and so on.

We see that strong common, economic impulses, mediating between political, religious and social differences, first of all constitute the core of this kind of co-operation. People in the countryside simply became richer and richer during this period in spite of the international economic crisis.

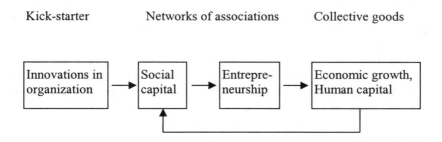

Figure 4.5   The building of beneficial (bridging) social capital

We have already shown that economic profit as well as democracy and trust appear to be crucial in the process of bridging social capital building, and lead to the formation of social capital, to its 'cytogenesis' so to speak. This is in line with Sen's (1999) ideas of basic freedoms as the main factor for economic growth.

But bridging social capital building involves another step: the spread of socio-economic networks or 'mytosis'. How was the idea and practice of co-operative dairies to be disseminated to the entire country? In order to understand this we have to supplement the three core elements – profit, democracy and trust – with that of entrepreneurship. Most importantly, the entrepreneurs had to be reliable: 'a word is a word' (*et ord er et ord*), as the old Danish saying goes. The element of entrepreneurship is, thus, closely connected to the element of trust.

At a *micro* level, the single local entrepreneur had to be regarded as a highly trustworthy person in every aspect, if he was to succeed with his dairy project. The choice would fall on the local schoolteacher, known by everybody, on a respected and well-to-do farmer or on a dairy technical autodidact, who had already proven his worth by contributing to the foundation of several dairies in other parts of the country. In short, the members wanted their leaders to be 'experienced men, inspiring confidence, whose participation was found to be valuable or even necessary for the foundation of the dairy' (Bjørn 1982: 104, our translation).

The local schoolteacher, especially active in the first years, only seldom acted on the basis of pure philanthropic, or socialist, motives. He wanted to profit economically. Normally, the community gave him a small piece of land, a so-called 'school-acre'. In order to supplement poor wages and thereby be able to provide for an often very large family, he had to be very resourceful in cultivating this piece of land. Furthermore, this intensive form of horticulture involved the raising of domestic animals, including cows. Thus, the teacher himself became a milk supplier, thereby enlarging his source of income, not to speak of the fees paid in connection with the writing of association articles for the society, and contributing his technical know-how (ibid.: 108).

The well-to-do farmer, who increasingly tended to take over the role as entrepreneur, had a special economic interest in the local dairy. First of all he had many cows and was, therefore, able to increase his profit. But often he was simply 'head hunted' by smaller entrepreneurs with less social, political and economic prestige, because he was seen as a man of honour, often with the power to gain access to the local savings bank and exercise major influence on the bank's board of directors.

This kind of head hunting was soon to become common practice at the *meso* level – that is, at a level where *groups* of entrepreneurs communicate and co-operate. So all these local consultants, experts and highly reputable men were invited to different corners of the country to talk about the revolutionary innovation, *andelsmejeriet*, the vast majority of them proposing strictly economic arguments (ibid.: 72). Moreover, after the talk these men were often invited to participate in the foundation of a new dairy in the local area in question because of their history of successful enterprises. So, from functioning solely as single, local entrepreneurs, they joined entrepreneurial groups at the regional level, thus enlarging the common good of their activity to include other communities.

The entrepreneurs, by first facilitating co-operation, trust and economic growth at a local, micro level and thence to a regional, meso level, were soon also to extend this particular stock of bridging social capital to a national, *macro* level.

Social capital spreading to a national level, then, first resulted in the promotion of the co-operative idea, and many dairies were built. Second, the foundation of a dairy followed exactly the same pattern no matter where it took place (ibid.). And third, but not least important: promotion and agitation metamorphosed into communication.

A common national interest was stimulated, as well as a debate. Towards the end of the 1880s, newspapers and agricultural magazines, formerly ignoring the matter, began to show interest, now criticizing, now defending the model. Educational institutions became an intermediary of the co-operational idea – and in 1889 even the government finally decided to recognize the movement by offering the co-operative dairies free technical support (ibid.: 80).

By means of entrepreneurship the co-operative dairy movement, *andelsmejeribevægelsen*, thus went through the 'mytosis' process. The model of co-operation embedded in a specific local network was exported to other localities and even to other countries. (For example, the Danish co-operative movement has strongly influenced the co-operative movements in Norway and Sweden.) Thus, the communication net gradually spread. Interregional relations based on mutual trust were created, uniting rural Denmark through strong socio-economic ties. Bridging social capital was accumulated, benefiting not only the individual and the local community but also the nation as a whole.

We have now seen that the process of social capital building in rural Denmark in the first place was caused by economic impulses in connection with two other elements, democracy and trust. This constitutes the initial part of the process, the cytogenesis of social capital. This is followed by the second part of the process, the spreading out of networks (or mytosis) through entrepreneurial agitation, promotion and exportation of a specific model of organization.

Such complexity is also noted by Putnam (1993b), who, in an article about democracy, makes the almost biblical remark that 'those who have social capital tend to accumulate more'. 'Stocks of social capital', that is, the civic traditions of a society defined as its, through history, accumulated sum of trust, norms and networks, thus form the basis of further accumulation of social capital (ibid.).

In fact, in our Danish case it becomes evident that the *political system* (capitalism) and, hence, the subsequent establishment of civic traditions generated the revolution, and the subsequent evolution. Thus, there is no doubt that the earlier land reforms – marking the final transition from feudalism to capitalism – created the overall 'structural framework' for the development (Bjørn 1988: 368). Also important for the movement were the Danish *folkehøjskoler*, community high schools, which, since the 1840s, had been important channels for the spread of knowledge to the rural population (see also Korsgaard 1997, for a more detailed analysis).

There is no doubt, though, that once the organizational model had been established, it formed an almost physical, socio-economic structure that satisfied not only economic purposes, but also social as well as personal ones.

Thus, the Danish co-operative movement, *Andelsbevægelsen*, should be regarded as a socio-economic phenomenon, whose social and economic factors are inextricably interwoven. Here, we witness a specific co-operative 'spirit' or *Weltanschauung*, enhancing 'closure' and allowing neighbours, tied together by strong socio-economic relations of trust, to communicate, exchange visits and services and help one another – in short, to participate in one another's lives.

4.3.   RECENT BRIDGING SOCIAL CAPITAL: THE CASE OF SPORTS HALLS

As we have learned from history, building 'lubricating' social capital and, thus, invisible but highly effectual bridges between individuals and groups seems to be closely linked to major civic movements that are, almost by definition, strongly inclusive and 'outward looking' networks (Putnam 2000: 22). As will be remembered, Putnam himself sees the American civic rights movement of the 1960s as one of the most important bridging social capital projects in American history. Likewise, the Danish co-operative movement should be seen as one of the most important bridging social capital building projects in rural Denmark during the latter part of the nineteenth and the former part of the twentieth century – and, most probably, *the* most important. However, in Danish rural history, civic movements seem to prevail, and it is possible to find examples of other builders of strongly beneficial stocks of social capital. This includes a regular 'sports movement', which reached its peak in the 1960s and 1970s.

In the following, we shall argue that in Denmark, the development of a 'sports hall movement' from 1960 to 1980 was a new cultural movement analogous to the 'village hall movement' one hundred years earlier. However, whereas the village hall movement in the decades before 1900 became enmeshed in political ideology and, consequently, developed into an increasingly 'inward looking' (ibid.: 22), exclusive and *bonding* network, the Danish youth movement from 1900 and its successor, the sports hall movement, appeared politically neutral and strongly inclusive.

4.3.1.   The Post-war 'Leisure Society'

Right from the beginning in the early 1950s, the formation of a growing sports movement was closely linked to what was called 'the leisure problem' by some country people, often those belonging to the older generations. Concerned adults and parents would say that the leisure problem made it difficult to persuade young people to stay in rural areas as they became more and more oriented towards the cities, both culturally and occupationally. Thus, where the driving force behind the development within the pattern of economic co-operation was changes in international market conditions, the driving force within the cultural area was seen to be the steady increase in leisure time, especially for young people (see, for example *Hb* 1958: 141; *DU* 1959: 72; *DUI* 1967: 208ff.).

From the middle of the 1960s, the organizational answer to these structural changes had been to merge local youth associations with each other or to merge youth associations with athletic associations (for example, *DU* 1964: 188). The big question was then how the centralization of cultural associational life would manifest itself in the buildings.

Since the 1920s, there had been a debate about the decline of community centres within the youth and village hall associations. Among the rural population, it was discussed whether it was too late to modernize the old village halls or whether the rise of a 'leisure society' demanded investment in modern cultural centres. However, the old and often decayed village halls could not provide room enough for all the new athletic activities. Therefore, local people started to organize new meeting places in the form of cultural common buildings such as leisure and cultural centres, sports halls and swimming pools.

In other words, there was a general recognition that a physical centre, a *place*, was needed in order to urge different people and different groups to join and mix – a general recognition that such a *platform* would generate trust and lubricate co-operative relations. This corresponds to recurring ideas that architecture and physical planning have a vital impact on human sociability and psychology, such as Ebenezer Howard's (1898) vision of 'garden cities' around 1900, or a contemporary 'New Urbanism' in the United States promoting an 'architecture of community' instead of an urban sprawl (Katz and Scully 1993).

Among the youth leaders in rural Denmark around 1960, it was recognized that the heyday of giving talks was over – a tendency confirmed by the many attempts to create interest in amateur theatricals and film shows. Consequently, most people knew that the increased leisure time among the youth demanded new and different leisure-time facilities.

Meanwhile the state played a crucial role by producing a report on cultural centres (1966). The aim was to establish a more formalized financial support of the new 'leisure society'. As such, the committee for cultural affairs received a mandate to undertake a closer delimitation of the type of cultural activity that was thought to be attached to the leisure-time activities already receiving public support and to elaborate a proposal concerning a fair subsidy scheme (Ministeriet for Kulturelle Anliggender 1966: 5).

Henceforth, youth associations fell from favour and became '[organs] where old men perform acts of courtesy to one another' as one youth leader remarked in harsh self-criticism (*DU* 1952: 421). Rather, the athletic associations now took the lead and 'The decade of the great sports halls was about to begin' (*DUI* 1967: 207).

4.3.2.   The Great Sports Hall Building Era

The new sports halls, which primarily were built to facilitate the formerly heretical urban sports, were greeted as the 'modern village halls'. This manifestation of the cultural urbanization of the rural district population meant that athletic associations began to outflank the traditional youth clubs in the countryside.

Articles from the journal of the so-called 'Danish youth movement' that was founded about 1900 (*Dansk Ungdom og Idræt*: Danish Youth and Sport, which from 1967 had replaced *Danish Youth*: Dansk Ungdom), demonstrate how local people would voluntarily co-operate to build sports halls, often incorporating public swimming baths. This 'fantastic building of sports halls' from the middle of the 1960s to 1980 was only possible due to the common initiative of and wide support from local citizens and entrepreneurs, including both natives and newcomers from the urban areas (*DUI* 1967: 300). As such, the networks behind this building of shared physical capital should be seen as strongly inclusive, that is, bridging social capital.

Numerous examples document its bridging effects. For example, in connection with the building of the Durup sports hall in Salling, Jutland (opened in 1968): 'most of the citizens in the municipality participated one way or another' (*DUI* 1968: 534, our translation). Much like the mytosis process of the co-operative associations in the late nineteenth century, the idea was rapidly spread due to pressure from local entrepreneurs and general consent among the locals that: 'So ein Ding müssen wir auch haben' (we must have one of those, too). Or, as one of the entrepreneurs behind the Durup sports hall comments more laconically: 'sports halls are now being built all over the country and one may say that it is odd that it did not happen earlier on considering the climate we have here in Denmark' (ibid.: 534, our translation).

A new athletic centre close to Holbæk in Zealand, which was opened in 1969, received 'colossal support in terms of voluntary labour force from the local area' and the purpose of the initiative had been 'to replace the two local village halls' (*DUI* 1972: 654, our translation). All age groups were represented: 'the youngest go to school and the oldest are close to eighty years old. Farmers, artisans, teachers and many other branches of trade participated – also those who took care of the coffee!' (ibid., our translation).

Even the 2,700 inhabitants on the small island of Fanø wanted their own sports hall in 1970. As in other places, a group of entrepreneurs from local athletic associations took the initiative and were the driving force (*DUI* 1971: 314ff.). The result was not only visible capital embodied as a useful common hall. Also, positive social capital was created due to improved co-operation and open inclusive social networks. For example, the sports hall building in the parish of Vallekilde-Hørve in Zealand had given rise to 'good fellowship and pleasant conversation' (*DUI* 1972: 655, our translation). Likewise, in Spjald close to Ringkøbing in Jutland, a new sports hall had been built in 1966 'by virtue of a unique unity in the local region' (ibid.: 984, our translation).

The articles in the influential journal *Dansk Ungdom og Idræt* give strong evidence in favour of the inclusive character of social networks. Arguably this is because of the tradition of neutrality in political and religious matters in Danish athletic associations.

Even though athletics was by far the dominating activity, the main idea of a sports hall, or a cultural or leisure centre was to create a meeting place for *everyone* in the new leisure society, not least for children and youngsters including the 'latch-key children' (*DUI* 1973: 341). Thus, the main idea and the purpose was to carry out social engineering by building physical capital in the form of a visible meeting place – a *platform* – to enable different people to meet and mix, thus producing trust, social control, reciprocity or, in sum, invisible bridging social capital with real tangible effects.

This theoretical assumption is widely documented in the empirical material. For example, the Herlufmagle sports hall north of Næstved in Funen (opened 1971), was introduced as: 'a leisure centre where everyone that feels like it can come and engage in the interests that absorb them'. Similarly, the leisure centre in Vallekilde-Hørve was a place 'where everyone could come no matter what age and interests' (*DUI* 1972: 677, 654, our translation). In Spjald, Jutland, the motivation behind a huge sports hall/swimming bath complex was to 'create a centre that really could frame the leisure time!' (ibid.: 489, our translation).

Another example is the Fredericia sports hall in Jutland (opened in 1969), where the rising interest for indoor athletics was overwhelming:

In the post-war period, there was a record-breaking participation of both women and men in the three local handball clubs. Handball also attracted the public. The two local gymnastic clubs did not have enough room and, like other sports associations with a rapidly increasing membership, had to move around from one place to another. . . Often, sports teams had to train at midnight. . . . Thus, the building of modern sports halls became a milestone for indoor sports by stimulating existing sports as well as introducing new disciplines. Like a volcano, athletic life exploded with new possibilities and new initiatives. (Honeré 1994: 19, 35, 59, our translation)

The sports hall builders were clearly affected by these thoughts of planning from a social perspective. One of the leading entrepreneurs, teacher Per Knudsen from Thisted in Jutland, stated: 'Imagine, if the leisure centres could become meeting places for all kinds of people' (ibid.: 650, our translation). Knudsen continued:

The main purpose is to serve as a place of refuge for people across all societal barriers, to give them the possibility for social contact and opportunities for self-expression by creating the framework for athletic/artistic activities and for free discussions in an informal gathering. (Ibid.: 650, our translation)

Similarly, Knud H. Aagesen, a vet from Horsens in Jutland, wrote of the necessity for planning the establishment of facilities such as kindergartens, playgrounds, modern youth clubs, sports halls, schools and so on as a basis for promoting well-being and continued: 'If these facilities do not exist, we make people live like television hermits without the sense of community. Then, the basis for democracy will vanish' (*DUI* 1971: 793, our translation). Consequently, the *physical planning* of sports hall facilities could, among other modern facilities, satisfy the longing for a unified leisure forum, a desirable place to be. It was even hoped that these 'modern village halls' from the 1970s would realize 'the harmonious human being' (*DUI* 1972: 652, our translation).

Another great entrepreneur expressed the same line of thought, namely priest Sejr Fink from Hover north of Vejle in Jutland. This 'sportspriest', who since the mid-1960s had already strongly advocated the building of more sports halls, thought that, as had been the case in the earlier youth, lecture and gymnastics clubs, the sports halls should function as the new gathering place where a sense of community could be fostered. Thus, human tragedies caused by alcohol and drug abuse, which were strongly feared around 1970, could be avoided (ibid.: 662). Another priest, Lene Johansen from Nordborg in Southern Jutland, spoke about 'fighting the threat of the closed rooms' (ibid.: 672, our translation). In Nors, North of Thisted in Jutland, it was feared that drug addicts in the notorious *Frøslevlejren* (a social experiment, a 'free city', just like Christiania in Copenhagen) would tempt and ruin the youngsters and therefore local endeavours were aimed at building facilities so that they had a place to go to (ibid.: 678).

Overall, the building of modern sports halls developed into just as big a feat as that of village halls, high schools and co-operative institutions from the second half of the nineteenth century. Therefore, this development can be described as the 'sports hall movement'. This working process called for comprehensive and unpaid labour efforts by extraordinary active entrepreneurs. The sports hall buildings were not part of any ideological crusade but rather represented a desire among local people to have their own facilities. Just as local people wanted their own store, dairy and village hall back in the nineteenth century, so local people wanted, in the period around 1970, their own sports halls.

What drove, and what still drives, the entrepreneurs behind such voluntary associations? Which motives do we find among the leading entrepreneurs themselves, for example those who devoted their time and energy to the Fredericia sports hall and tirelessly not only contributed to the building of the hall but also took part in expanding and improving it? Here are some comments from the entrepreneurs themselves: 'I just walk around the halls to see what's going on'; 'I like to go to the swimming bath and see the children when they crawl up as high as they can – and jump'; 'It is wonderful to see the children's joy'; 'You feel that you have contributed in giving your fellow citizens the possibility of a better life'; 'We have helped to give the youth and the coming generations a good start in life' (Honoré 1994: 61, our translation). The director of the Fredericia Sports Hall, Henry Jepsen, commented in 1976:

> I like the atmosphere in the sports hall where I spent many enjoyable hours. I take pleasure from the delight and eagerness that young people, especially, exhibit. If I were not a great idealist, I would probably not have continued because you really have to be interested in the problems you are dealing with. (Ibid.: 59, our translation)

Thus, there seems to be a private pleasure (or utility) to be derived from acting as an entrepreneur, which is strong enough to result in a positive net gain for the entrepreneur mobilizing a group for collective action such as the building of sports halls (see also Bjørnskov 2003, on the linkage between social capital and happiness).

The presence of entrepreneurs and the very building of sports halls and accumulation of visible capital can be perceived as the necessary precondition for the creation of networks and cultural identity, that is, invisible and non-material social and cultural capital. The fruits from this altruistic contribution are continuously transmitted to new generations as a valuable stock of bridging social capital. Here, a fertile civil life in open and inclusive networks formed the basis of a remarkable voluntary initiative.

4.3.3.   Between Voluntariness and Public Support

Danish athletic organizations have, just like the farmer's organizations after 1900, found themselves caught in a dilemma between an economic and regulatory dependence on the state and, at the same time, wanting to preserve distinctive features such as self-regulation and the principle of voluntariness.

Around 1970, there was still skepticism towards outside sponsors similar to that within farmer's organizations up until the 1950s. This scepticism was reflected in a number of articles defending the principle of voluntariness and the necessity of staying economically independent of the public sector.

In *Dansk Ungdom og Idræt*, critics argued that a one-sided public support policy could lead to the 'death of associations' and that the state, by 'buying up' voluntary associations, would be guilty of 'an incomprehensible undermining of the voluntary sports and youth work in Denmark' (*DUI* 1971: 5, 1973: 94, our translation). This critique was honed by the editor Arne G. Larsen, who wrote:

> It is no good believing that the state should pay for any kind of entertainment in our leisure time. . . . Any argument about the necessity of subsidies concerning teacher and leader salaries can be rejected out of hand by reference to our Ministry of Social Affairs, which under certain criteria, offers social security where needed. (*DUI* 1973: 254, our translation)

The sports hall buildings are an excellent example of the major shift from a principle of voluntariness to one of public support. In the rural areas, people were traditionally unstinting in the matter of voluntary work and money collection. However, through the 1960s, it was no longer considered shameful to receive public support such as direct subsidies, state loans, receipts from the state football pools and so on.

The increasingly positive attitude in favour of public support is illustrated in a characteristic statement by Arne G. Larsen. In 1972 he writes that: 'leisure time . . . in the modern society is a joint matter and it is up to politicians to deal with it' (*DUI* 1972: 706, our translation). Sixteen years later in 1988, it was announced that 'the era of the unpaid leader will soon be over' (*DUI* 1988, no. 12: 6, our translation).

A general acceptance of public support can also be traced in the information on new regulations and support schemes, which gradually became a standard part of the chief journal *Dansk Ungdom og Idræt* (Danish Youth and Athletics) from the 1970s, which changed from being a discussion forum for popular sports to a political channel for influencing and announcing public support (*DUI* 1997, no. 7: 44).

The amount of public support has continued to expand since the mid-1960s, mainly due to successful lobbying by the professional sports interest organizations such as The Danish National Confederation of Gymnastics and Sports (DGI), Team Denmark (an organization promoting the Danish sports elite), The Danish National Confederation of Enterprise Sports (DFIF) and The Danish National Confederation of Sports (DIF). Today, these organizations receive about €100 million annually of the total €5 billion public support allocated to sports in Denmark (Danmarks Idræts-Forbund 2001). The private foundation, 'DGI-byen' (the 'DGI city', i.e. a large building belonging to the abovementioned The Danish National Confederation of Gymnastics and Sports), with its annual budget of €5 billion has its head office behind the main railway station in Copenhagen, and this stands as a physical monument to the subsidized sports era in Denmark (DGI-byen 2002).

4.3.4.   From Duty to Right

Gradually, economic independence has been abandoned within sports halls, cultural centres, youth clubs and so on, especially since 1975. Overall, cultural life has not just undergone structural changes, it has become fully dependent on subsidies even in the rural areas. Members of the older generation within the active associational sphere have seen this development as a matter of regret because it breaks radically with the previous tradition based on economic independence and voluntary work. As such, too many economic subsidies from the state can be seen as a hindrance to bridging social capital building and, maybe, even a means to fragmentize it into bonding social capital. One representative entrepreneur, Arly Olsen, a former leader and initiator of a large sports hall complex in Stevns, made these comments about the municipality taking on more and more economic responsibility for building and maintaining cultural common facilities:

From the starting point in 1957, when the plans for a sports hall were displayed, and until today [1998], we have witnessed a continuous development whereby citizens have increasingly taken it for granted that public finances should subsidize cultural and athletic facilities, which cannot directly be regarded as essential. First and foremost, the Stevns sports hall [opened in 1967] became a reality because it was mainly the result of [local 'hands-on' effort] and based on collected voluntary subscriptions. When the swimming pool was completed in 1974, it was soon paid for with the help of public funding and in the case of the Erikstrup hall in 1980, for example, a theatre with stage and dressing-rooms was built, as if by magic, without private initiative and support, at a price of 10 million DDK. For those who experienced the 'Stevns celebrations' [supporters' parties for the Stevns sports hall] at the end of the 1950s and the social cohesion that gave us a sports hall, it can be rather sad to watch life in the 1990s, where we leave it all to the public sector and we are concerned with only ourselves. (Olsen 1998: 82, our translation)

The distinctive self-financing in the early stage of sports halls building relied on high-powered fund-raising activities. The Agerskov sports hall in Southern Jutland, for example, was from the beginning financed without any public support except that the municipality donated a piece of land (*Vk*, 8 May 1973). The strategy of economic independence also showed up in the eagerness to finance the building by a whole range of support measures such as fund-raising parties, bingo and lottery, obtaining sponsorships from local firms and so on. The idea was that the sports hall should support itself economically. The leaders, all volunteers, knew that it would be hard, especially in the first years, but worthwhile, because 'it would be the most healthy solution and it would please everyone who has had a share in building the sports hall' (*Vk*, 2 December 1974, our translation). After the sports activities had started, the leadership commented that: 'the interest in renting the sports hall has already proved to be overwhelming, probably because so many local people have contributed to the project and, by experience, you know that you look after what you have created yourself' (ibid., our translation).

In a similar vein, the famous Danish author, Lise Nørgaard, characteristically wrote in an article about contemporary amateur theatres that a cultural urbanization had caused a decisive shift from the duty of self-regulation and economic dependence to the right of receiving public subsidies:

If I can trust my own ears, the Minister of Culture said the other day that 120 million DKK have been given, among other things, to happy amateur actors who aspire to perform in the theatre. Isn't it strange that this hobby has always flourished by itself without the state taking money from the bottomless pit where our tax money is poured? In the old days – that is before people needed public subsidies for everything they did – amateur dramatics was performed in all rural districts. Now, these amateur groups have changed in character demanding subsidies even when the quality of their performance is at the amateur level. They have had the notion that it is the fault of society/Ministry of Culture that they cannot make a living from being on stage and solving the world situation with their loud voices. Nobody did them a favour by telling them that they would be much better off taking an ordinary job and then cultivating their passion for theatre as a hobby in their leisure time. Unfortunately, from the political quarter, it is becoming more and more common to give people money rather than telling them where to go, thereby helping them in the long run. . . . How far should we go? Are we also to expect cultural subsidies for . . . Trivial Pursuit, backgammon or chess? (*DUI* 1990, no. 6: 12, our translation)

Thus, the elimination of private civil institutions as a result of state intervention over the last 30 years can, in relation to bridging social capital, be viewed as a backlash for voluntary associational work and entrepreneurs. Nevertheless, we observe that the principles of duty and voluntariness still exert an important effect today in the Danish welfare society, which relies on societal members to pursue the common good in a relatively unselfish way, that is, based on socialization and voluntariness rather than formal law and compulsion.

4.4.   SUMMARY

This chapter has analysed the building of beneficial bridging social capital in rural Denmark since the beginning of the nineteenth century. It was structured in two main sections: the first traced bridging social capital building within the well-known Danish co-operative movement before the Second World War, while the second traced a more recent stock of bridging social capital localized within the sports hall movement in rural Denmark during the 1960s and 1970s.

The question we raised was: why do entrepreneurs emerge and organize larger groups in local areas, thus contributing to voluntary collective good provision and the creation of bridging social capital, beneficial to society? This question was important because voluntary collective good provision in a local area enhances economic growth and alleviates poverty. We argued that there is a gap in economic literature. If the individual economic gain from providing a collective good is negative, it does not pay an individual to act and organize. Nevertheless, larger groups actually *do* organize in local areas even though the individual net gain is clearly negative. This paradox cannot be explained in strict economic terms.

Thus, in an attempt to fill this gap in literature, we offered another solution to this paradox, namely the presence of social incentives called 'social capital' – an important production factor which, we argue, has been the missing link in traditional classical economic capital theories. Regular face-to-face interaction presumably encouraged co-operative relations among larger groups in local areas. Such relations, we argued, would be initiated (kick-started) by innovations in organizational structure in the form of clear, written rules of the game. This formalization of co-operation included the imposition of sanctions, most prominently exclusion from the group, on those members who violated the rules.

This theoretical suggestion seemed to be confirmed by empirical evidence from rural Denmark since the late nineteenth century. We presented an example of the rise of positive or beneficial social capital (bridging social capital) in the emergence of strongly inclusive peasant networks organized within the co-operative movement during the second half of the nineteenth century. Clearly, these networks were deeply rooted in the early economic associations formed by newly independent peasants in the first part of that century – that is, fully voluntary and self-enforced associations dating back to the initial emergence of a civic society in urban Denmark during the last decades of the eighteenth century.

How was bridging social capital built during this period? First of all, we found that the initial establishment of networks – what we called the 'cytogenesis' of bridging social capital – is contingent upon the existence of the three key elements: democracy, trust and the equal possibility of making profit. Here it was observed that written rules in the form of the standardized founding statutes of co-operative associations enhanced (kick-started) peasant co-operation and thus gave rise to stocks of highly productive, bridging social capital. As an outcome of this process, entrepreneurs provided collective goods, contributing to economic growth and education in formerly poor, rural areas.

It was precisely these written rules of the game that facilitated self-organization of rural districts, a self-organization that entailed a rapid accumulation of bridging social capital and consequently of other forms of capital, and which ultimately achieved great socially beneficial significance. Gradually, as farmers became accustomed to following the written rules of the game, the formalized framework for co-operation became 'naturalized', that is, diffused into informal exchange as well. In this way, co-operation according to the rules of the game, implying collective good provision secured by agreed-upon sanctions, became a natural way of behaving, that is, which the peasants no longer questioned.

Thereby, the rules were internalized, that is, turned into informal and *un*written rules, allowing the actors to engage in socio-economic strategies. In other words, they were turned into a specific 'habitus', which again would further speed up the accumulation of bridging social capital and promote the recruitment of future generations of local entrepreneurs. In this way, a healthy circle of bridging social capital building was secured, which was in line with Professor Ostrom's findings in social capital studies of farmers' common-pool irrigation systems.

Second, the spread of networks – or, in our terminology, the 'mytosis' of bridging social capital – is contingent upon entrepreneurship on a regional and national level.

These two stages in the cycle form what we have called 'bridging social capital building'. The common goods achieved in this way consisted of a significant increase in productivity from the beginning of the 1880s. This occurred in a broader context of increased communication between people, at a local, regional and national level, in spite of international economic crises and the governmental scepticism towards the co-operative dairies.

Also more recent stocks of bridging social capital can be detected in rural Denmark. Therefore, we next presented a case study belonging to the twentieth century but which still today, in the new millennium, has a great impact on rural life: the sports halls movement of the 1960s and 1970s. Originating in, and gradually replacing, the youth movement from 1900 and onwards, the sports hall movement involved strongly inclusive, bridging networks – much like what had been the case with the local and regional networks within the co-operative movement from the mid-1860s to the mid-1960s. Thus, the 'fantastic building of sports halls' from the middle of the 1960s to 1980 was only possible due to the common initiative of high-powered entrepreneurs, including people born locally and, not least, newcomers. Together, these country people did an enormous amount of voluntary work during these two decades.

However, the sports associations behind the new sports halls rather quickly became dependent on state subsidies, which in more radical cases seemed to destroy entrepreneurship by diminishing people's pleasure in spontaneously and voluntarily doing good things for their fellow citizens, or their enjoyment in striving towards a pet project of their own. In other words, these people would no longer feel that they participated in indispensable, local co-operation for 'our' hall and, hence, they would no longer feel a sense of responsibility and their enthusiasm would quickly wane. Therefore, we hypothesized that too many public subsidies tend to destroy stocks of bridging social capital.

At a more general level, the two cases of bridging social capital building showed us that, because the only sanction mechanism in voluntary groups is that of social ostracism, the setting for these effective social sanction mechanisms must be maintained. As such, voluntary groups should not be formally institutionalized and the size of such well-functioning voluntary groups should not be increased. Otherwise, the disciplining effect of repeated face-to-face interaction will be reduced.

5. Bonding Social Capital and Centralization: The Post-war Danish Co-operative Movement

5.1. INTRODUCTION

An often used cliché is that 'culture is made of sterner stuff', that is, culture implies continuity and functions as a natural link between people in the past and people in the present. In an attempt to trace this cultural continuity, researchers in Denmark have focused on culture as derived from rural areas and the voluntary co-operative movement. Consequently, researchers have tried to trace the present culture back to its roots in the second half of the nineteenth century (see Chapter 4).

Surprisingly, life in the rural districts has been ignored in the post-war period in spite of the drastic socio-economic changes that took place here from 1950 to 1970. It is as though a modern industrial society does not need to deal with agrarian culture, values and life because the present rural population is no longer regarded as a culture bearer. The very phrase 'agrarian culture' is no longer used.

Thus, during the 1960s, Denmark's leading experts within economics, political science and statistics used stringent scientific methods consistent with the focus on economic growth, as documented in the leading agricultural journals of the time. The case study of the post-war co-operative movement shows that these people were eager and impatient to make the developmental leap, in line with the main idea among Western modernistic thinking academics, who – much like the medieval Christian crusaders – wanted to disseminate 'The' development all over the world. However, by the end of the 1960s, other experts such as ethnologists and anthropologists were landed with the often hopeless task of alleviating the more destructive consequences of the development (about which, it was – and still is – said, 'it is impossible to strive against'), for example, by ameliorating the one-sided ethnocentric character of foreign aid projects. Also, in Denmark, sociologists were enlisted to defend cultural corner-stones and the human aspects of the individual against a macro development that was basically out of human control.

In the 1960 the still numerous smallholders feared that they would become superfluous in the developmental race. Characteristically, in terms of the cultural dimension, they appealed to sociologists, who were also applying statistical methods in the continuing fight for expert assistance. The leaders of the smallholders tried to stress that there was a lack of understanding about the importance of social research, both among the leading employees in organizations and among politicians (*Hh* 1965, no. 11: 2). In fact, in our opinion, what these leaders were really saying was: 'Listen, people, you are forgetting the factor of *social* capital'. Thus, both ethnographic and historical data (for example, Solvang 1984, 1999) show that, from about 1900 to about 1970, the smallholders can be seen as the most numerous and vociferous group of 'social capitalists' in rural areas, networking at formal as well as informal levels and, thus, lubricating civic life in the villages.

The agricultural journals clearly show that statistics totally dominated the debate in the 1960s. This was not least the case within the dairy sector. Even if dairy statistics were not considered final proof, they were regarded as the main contribution for understanding the economic effects of rationalization (*Ab* 1961: 1205). As such, a limited provision of economic data became the dominant paradigm behind centralization and the mergers within the co-operative movement in general (ibid.: 1149; *DL* 1962: 65). However, what was not quantified in these statistics, was the value of local entrepreneurship and voluntary co-operation. The absence of the positive economic externality of bridging social capital in those cost–benefit analyses, as argued below, means that too much centralization will occur. The value of a missing social capital *should have been quantified as well* and then added to the benefits of decentralization, but the more traditionalistic and 'anti-development' element of the rural population did not know of this concept back then or how to link it to economics.

First, we shall briefly analyse an important case of early bonding social capital about 1900, resulting from religious conflicts; then we shall trace how an underestimated, if not completely ignored asset, bridging social capital, may erode in practice due to market centralization processes. Then we shall discuss the main arguments for and against centralization and focus on the cultural changes in the rural districts from 1950 to 1970, implying the transformation of beneficial bridging to harmful bonding social capital. Finally, we shall focus on Danish dairy production as an important and illustrative example of market centralization that has general implications for social capital discussions in future western democracies.

Overall, we argue that the cultural effects on the stock of bridging social capital following centralization were ignored and that too much centralization occurred when such destruction of bridging social capital was not taken into account in private market decisions.

5.2.   EARLY BONDING SOCIAL CAPITAL: RELIGIOUS CONFLICTS

As we saw in Chapter 4, important stocks of bridging social capital were accumulated within the Danish co-operative movement and closely related movements during the late nineteenth century, not least within the co-operative dairy movement. However, during the 1890s and in many rural areas, we detect a counter-reaction within the co-operative movement, due to religious conflicts between two major groups among peasants, the 'Home Mission' people and the so-called 'Grundtvigians'.

These conflicts lead to a partial fragmentation of the stock of open co-operative networks established during the last decades of the nineteenth century. Note that this bridging social capital in rural Denmark was deeply rooted in early nineteenth century economic associations, which in their turn were rooted in civic fervour dating back to the rise of a new civic society in the late eighteenth century. However, in a large number of local communities, these strong civic traditions did not hinder a surprisingly sudden shift from inclusive types of social capital to exclusive and often harmful, bonding types. And all of a sudden the balance sheet was inverted: from prevailingly bridging to excessively bonding. From this we learn, how fragile a collective good bridging social capital is. It's here today. It might disappear tomorrow. How could it happen?

The sources indicate that it happened due to symbolic violence,that is, both tacitly and in words. Thus, group isolation and lack of co-operation between the two conflicting parties involved the transformation of bridging to excessive bonding social capital of an exclusive nature in many rural parishes. As a consequence, in those parts of the country where conflicts ran out of control, economic success was quickly turned into economic decline. Here, a lack of co-operation between the two groups finally resulted in a dividing of physical capital in the form of shared economic buildings, such as co-operative dairies and co-operative warehouses, as well as formerly shared cultural buildings, such as churches and village halls.

Such religious fundamentalism was rooted in several religious revivals that took place during the 1830s and 1840s. One outcome was the emergence of two religious movements, which took shape from the mid-1860s: the Home Mission or the 'holy' (*hellige*) on the one hand and the more mundane Grundtvigians, referred to as the 'children of the world' by the Mission, on the other.

Gradually, during the 1870s and 1880s, and especially in the western part of rural Denmark, these two groups formed their own separate, cultural institutions from their own economic resources and without state involvement. These institutions ranged from private schools, agricultural colleges, community and Home Mission high schools, churches and so on. Moreover, the two groups had their own associations, serving a broad range of functions: the Grundtvigians joined a multitude of youth associations, gymnastic clubs, rifle clubs, lecture and reading societies, choral societies, temperance societies, political associations and so on; the Home Mission had their own biblical societies, temperance societies and charitable associations, and their children met in Sunday schools and various youth associations.

Consequently, in some rural parishes two rival networks emerged, recruiting their members from the same local community and, in particular, among their own children. Gradually, this led to *excessive* bonding social capital, clearly upsetting the balance between stocks of bridging and bonding social capital in the rural parishes.

The increasing overlapping of members, internally, within the two networks is well documented, as well as the emergence of regular network organizers, that is, local, regional as well as national *ildsjæle* or 'public-spirited' individuals respected as charismatic people of stature among their own community members while despised by the others (Balle-Petersen 1976, 1977; Haue 1977; Lauridsen 1986; Svendsen 2001). Thus, about 1900, previously strongly inclusive associations dating back to the first part of the century, including the co-operative associations, were increasingly monopolized by such religious entrepreneurs, making them conform to their ideology.

The two groups became increasingly estranged, constructing and eventually institutionalizing their own traditions, norms and identities, that is, they were in binary opposition in the structuralist sense of the word. This ultimately led to a decisive split between the two groups, that is, psychological distance turned into physical distance, revealed in the division of cultural activities and, gradually, also in economic co-operation.

The religious community extended into material life and there was a form of moral economy or economic solidarity, which manifested itself in the trading and exchange of services among members within the community. Thus, the decisive factor in the choice of where to buy their groceries was not special offers or the proximity of to the grocery, but rather 'whom you met in the Mission House on Sunday evenings' (Lauridsen 1980: 25).

The ultimate result of economic and cultural life gradually becoming fully monopolized by the two competing groups, was that shared buildings were also divided, thus allowing the formation of *separate stocks of capital* – in other words, there was a duplication of facilities. In practice, during the 1870–1900 period, this resulted in a peculiar kind of material rearmament, with the building of approximately 1,600 Grundtvigian meeting-houses in the countryside, as well as 900 Mission Houses – the latter for the most part concentrated in the Western part of Jutland (Balle-Petersen 1976: 44).

Moreover, during the 1890s, such materialization of group identity in space clearly escalated into what can be regarded as a regular symbolic war, marking the final realization of distinct, exclusive stocks of capital, that is, group monopolized stocks of cultural, social and physical capital, interrelated in a consistent way within the overall framework of specific ideologies.

So, geographical space was divided oppositionally. Thus, in the villages of Kirkeby and Bøvlingbjerg, the religious bastions of the two groups – the meeting-house and the Mission House – were situated on each side of the main street, while in the village of Vrå, they were placed at opposite ends of the village. Similarly a considerable number of ideological buildings were also structured in 'oppositional pairs', including free schools, high schools, free churches, teacher training colleges, agricultural colleges, and so on. Thus, bonding social capital took visible form in the buildings in a most dramatic way, materializing a socio-mental charter in space and thus, physically, turning the co-operative village, *andelslandsbyen*, into a non-cooperative one.

The most radical outcome of such a process of group identification through group isolation can be seen within the co-operative dairy movement during the 1890s, when the Home Mission established its own 'Sunday resting dairies'. All the 'holy' members withdrew from the one parish co-operative dairy – formerly supported by all peasants regardless of political and religious convictions – in order to found their own Sunday resting dairy. Thus, at great economic and human cost and with purely religious-ideological motives, a competing dairy would be opened. Not surprisingly, in small rural areas this often had catastrophic economic consequences for all the dairy farmers. Dall, a farmer in the village of Skanderup in the southern part of Jutland, painfully recalls:

> It was important to the holy farmers to have the dairy come to a complete standstill on Sundays; but the population could not agree upon this, and as a result they divided. Consequently, a new dairy was built, though many farmers had serious concerns in doing so. This happened during a bad period for agriculture, and money was short. Running two dairies instead of one was more expensive. A [Home Mission] man said: 'Well, clearly we cannot work on Sundays. Nor can we make our farming pay with a decrease in output. We have been used to having our interest on the dairy profits paid out in the settling month of December, that is, the additional payment, and there will be no more profit from now on. Nor can we violate the commands of God. Our friends move in that direction, they leave it to God to determine their future. So do I. (Our translation from Balle-Petersen 1977: 93)

So, within the co-operative movement at the turn of the century, strategies of isolation by means of exclusion became common practice among the religious communities in some parts of the country. Consequently, formerly inclusive stocks of capital embedded in bridging social capital in these rural parishes became stocks of capital of an exclusive nature, ultimately leading to the institutionalization of communities within communities, manifested in the buildings. However, more seriously, the balance between bridging and bonding social capital was disturbed after the Second World War, due to conflicts between localists and centralists and, ultimately, centralization partly enforced by the national agricultural leaders.

5.3.   THE POST-WAR DANISH CO-OPERATIVE MOVEMENT

5.3.1.   Arguments in Favour of Centralization

The trend towards large-scale operations in agriculture can be traced back to the changes in social capital that took place at the beginning of the nineteenth century with the rise of new corporatist actors. The leading entrepreneurs behind the new co-operatives initiated powerful networks without local anchoring, that is, 'local disembeddedness'. These new networks within the economic sphere of associational life could be said to create a special stock of, primarily bonding, social capital at the macro level. Here, the entrepreneurial leaders received, in the terminology of Bourdieu, the status of 'mandated agents' (Bourdieu 1986: 251). In other words, power was gradually delegated from the networks at the micro and meso levels – which were intact before the mid-1960s – to networks at the macro level.

The result of such a 'concentration of social capital' (ibid.) was, first, that the co-operative networks came to represent the agricultural sector to the corresponding state corporate actors. Second, these interest group activities, which were significantly increased from 1960, were accompanied by a strong expansion of the macro networks at the expense of the networks at the meso and micro levels, which were eventually done away with by the central administration (Svendsen, 2000). Overall, this took place within what Coleman (1988b: 390ff.) has called a 'decline in embeddedness' in the Western world due to 'the drift toward the corporation and the state'. Thus, the working force was centralized in the cities, and power was mandated upwards to the national leaders of a small number of extremely strong state and professional corporations. This involved a dramatic loss of social capital in the local communities, including local institutions and, not least, in the families.

The idea that too much centralization leads to local losses in social capital is in line with Vincent Ostrom's remarks on self-management among American workers:

The worker self-management that I know occurs within the collegiality of the small enterprise; and the small enterprise gives access to resources and opportunities that could not otherwise be made available by exclusive reference to large enterprises. The 500 largest firms in the American economy are not the place to look for patterns of worker self-management. You can find much greater manifestations of worker self-management on family farms and in the hundreds of thousands of other enterprises that provide an essential part of the infrastructure of the American economy and American society more generally. It is in this context that most Americans accrue their personal experience with self-government and with worker self-management. (Ostrom 1985: 12)

In rural Denmark, such corporate tendencies leading to 'mandated agents' and 'concentration of social capital' can be detected from about 1900 and, hence, through the first part of the twentieth century, deeply affecting civic society. However, as we shall see, in rural Denmark the culmination came in the 1960s.

5.3.1.1.   Early propaganda
Studying the volumes of Danish agricultural journals in the decades around the First World War, one is astonished by the harshness and implacability surrounding the debate about centralization versus self-government within the Co-operative Movement. However, from the end of the 1950s, a new and apparently quite efficient 'both/and' argument was launched by the new generation of co-operative leaders. The idea was that the two principles were compatible and that the classical principle of self-government could be preserved.

At the co-operative congress in 1959, Nyboe Andersen, one of the most influential leaders within the movement, stated that the present situation differed from the beginning of the co-operative movement in three ways (*Ab* 1959: 264). First, the associations had become formalized and the original co-operative spirit had vanished, resulting in more passive members. Second, the associations had grown bigger, implying that the co-operative movement needed educated specialists as leaders. Third, the tasks could no longer be accomplished at the local level:

The tasks are at a level that requires national accomplishments, and often their character is so complicated that the ordinary member of a local co-operative society has a hard time assessing the problems and realizing that the identification of solutions makes a demand on him, thus choosing the easy solution of passivity. (Ibid., our translation)

According to the new logic of co-operatives, the lack of locally based self-governance could be compensated by continually bombarding members with information so as to 'activate the single members to such an extent that democracy would prevail' (*Ab* 1963: 1280; *Hh* 1960, no. 14: 3; our translation). Because the informational work that traditionally came from the community high schools had stagnated around 1960, Nyboe Andersen suggested that the co-operative movement should hire professional public relations (PR) experts and then compete with other media such as television (*Ab* 1959: 266). These experts could supplement the official co-operative journals by showing the movement in a good light (ibid.).

New PR activities were needed because this would convince the local shop stewards of the necessity to '[adapt] the organizational framework to modern requirements'. Nyboe Andersen then added that the local associations, following good Danish tradition, should maintain their independence, for example, economic responsibility should lie entirely with the local co-operative committee (ibid.: 268). Self-governance was the feature that distinguished the co-operative from the private firm (ibid.): 'Among top leaders in the agricultural organizations, there was general agreement that the rationalization should not destroy the decentralized structure in the co-operative movement. One wished, as it were, to "…build on the established order", (*Ab* 1960: 609, our translation)

Thus, the social capital in the countryside was officially supported in the shape of a well-functioning associational life rather than solely focusing on the economic gain from mergers. Consequently, the result of the early centralization debate was not widespread mergers. In contrast, it was generally argued that the individual farmer should specialize in order to save the 'family farm' and thereby the independent farmer as the basic unit in modern farming.

Nyboe Andersen justified this attitude in 1961: 'great human values are at stake. No one disputes that the independent farmer represents a valuable way of life and it would be a significant loss for society if only a small part of the population could sustain life in this way' (*Ab* 1961: 793, our translation). Even the president of the Agricultural Council of Denmark, Anders Andersen, who was known as an aggressive promoter of centralization, said that mergers leading to landed estates were undesirable and that the development would not force small farmers out of the market. Rather, those who could not keep up with the development would be those who failed to specialize in production (*Ab* 1964: 722).

A concrete result of these early discussions was, as suggested by Nyboe Andersen, that PR experts were hired in the co-operative movement in connection with the establishment of the Public Relations Service Institution of Danish Agriculture (Landbrugets Oplysnings- og Kursusvirksomhed: LOK) in 1964 (*Hh* 1960, no. 3: 5). Through the 1960s, the LOK argued that more information was needed to create understanding for the modern co-operative movement and to stimulate debate and participation among ordinary members.

5.3.1.2.   Recent propaganda and the paradigm of economics

On one hand, the LOK consultants argued in favour of large production units while on the other, they tried to activate passive members locally which, admittedly, was a result of centralization and the undermining of the self-governmental principle (for example, *Ab* 1962: 281). The LOK leader and chief of section in the Agricultural Council, Mogens Munch, stated in an article:

> Education, information, societal contact, member contact, teaching, education, training, refresher courses, personnel policy, rationalization, efficiency, development, adaptation, conferencing, co-operation, co-ordination and meetings seem to be current concepts for Danish agriculture. (*DL* 1967: 237, our translation)

Such a point of view, combined with policy recommendations concerning neutralization of detrimental effects following the development, dominated the numerous books published by the LOK, written by highly educated and academically trained experts. The propaganda for centralization was undertaken within the different sectors of the co-operative movement such as dairy, slaughter and wholesale.

Nevertheless, the majority of ordinary members ignored the propaganda. The result was that members voted against closure, in contrast to the recommendations from the central leaders and experts. The central administration discussed what to do with these unenlightened members, who often belonged to the older generation. In fact, explicit comparisons were made with developing countries where such reactionary elements also impeded progress and 'natural development'. Some even argued that the Danish rural population – like that in America – lagged behind the more civilized urban population so that the relation between town and country directly reflected that between developed and developing countries (see *Ab* 1963: 3).

Robert C. Cook addressed this issue in 1963 with reference to the poor black farm-workers in the southern states of America:

> With regard to income and upbringing, the rural population is typically far behind the urban population. This inherited difference threatens the rural youth now when our complicated and technological society demands more skills acquired through a more extended education. (*UfL* 1963: 733, our translation)

From the mid-1960s, the advocates of centralization became increasingly impatient. At the same time, centralization was also recommended by experts in international organizations, for example the International Co-operative Alliance (ICA), which was strongly in favour of a unity movement directed by highly educated specialists (*Ab* 1965: 1186 and 1368).

In Denmark, the sensitive discussion on voting rules (see below), gradually became a part of the political agenda as the vision of one dairy company, one cooperative society, one slaughter society, one chemicals and feed company and so on progressed from the idea phase to the planning and implementation phases.

From 1965, it was decided at the central level to use propaganda as a means of modifying the rules in line with modern requirements (ibid.: 341). This project had the support of LOK and Axelborg, the latter being established in 1965 as: 'the first agricultural propaganda centre of its kind' (ibid.: 579). Herewith one had to abandon the both/and argument that implied historical continuity. For example, in 1965 the editor of *Andelsbladet*, Clemens Pedersen, published an article called: 'Preserving the old system is no solution but self-destruction'. The article reflects the new dominating trend in the debate that structural development would have to take place at the expense of democracy:

> The tendencies to merge and to concentrate local co-operatives will mean that many of them will disappear. These tendencies are, however, strongly motivated by an economic necessity, so that other considerations of local popular interest cannot be taken into account. It would be extremely dangerous and harmful if wider circles of members let themselves be led by the spokesmen of such popular movements. Well, they may often be genuine enough. But they are always steeped in ignorance or lack the will to understand things, some even expressing straight black reaction. (ibid.: 176, our translation)

Thus, it became politically correct among the leading officials in the co-operative movement to talk about 'enlightened solidarity', meaning that the ordinary members could be declared incapable of managing their own property. The experts knew best and as such they had to take the leading role; the end justified the means. Anders Andersen defended this point of view. So did other 'hawks' such as the chairman of the dairies, Christian Speggers and manager Johannes Dons Christensen. In his article, 'We have to lead the development', Christensen wrote:

> It is not enough that we work hard in our position to maintain the established order. We [the leaders] must be ready to take the lead when searching for new paths – and also when it comes to persuading the members to follow these new paths, which the leaders have realized the necessity of before the members themselves . . . This holds in particular when leaders and committees have presented plans that they found good, but which were rejected by the members through resistance or passivity. The fact that proposals are rejected does not give the leaders any excuse for shelving their plans and concentrating only on the day-to-day work. Bring out the plans again, assess and revise them perhaps – then the leaders must start again to convince shop stewards and members that they were right. (ibid.: 1302, our translation)

5.3.2.   Resistance to Centralization

A large part of the rural population was to a great extent unable to stand up for themselves in the public debate. In consequence, they were excluded from defining reality and thereby from practice through 'constitutive naming' (see Chapter 6). Concurrently with the rising dominance of academic concepts rooted in Latin through the 1960s, the countrypeople became alienated and therefore only reluctantly expressed their views in public. Everyday language had disappeared from the public sphere and it was no surprise that most of the public resistance against centralization stemmed not from the ordinary rural population itself but from academics outside the co-operative movement.

5.3.2.1.   Community high schools

Characteristically, the early resistance against centralization was voiced by two theologists who argued in favour of human values in contrast to a societal organization based on financial centralization. These were the principal of Askov community high school, Knud Hansen, and Johannes Engberg, a teacher at Baaring community high school. The latter was the most important defender of cultural life in the rural parish, expressed through numerous articles in *Højskolebladet*.

In an article from 1955, 'The trade organizations and society', Engberg complained about the minority status that the Danish population had been brought to through political ignorance among voters in general (*DU* 1955: 18, 28). His point was that interest groups following the union model – autocratically controlled by leaders and other experts – had achieved a disproportionate share of power in society. The organizations, which previously had mobilized citizens and had been a social asset, now used this power and became a threat to individuals, who increasingly felt that 'society is a machine that takes its own course and is not subject to outside influence from individuals' (ibid.: 18, our translation). As an example, Engberg mentioned the co-operative movement:

> It has often been claimed that the co-operative undertakings represent the economy governed by the people in contrast to private capitalism. In this respect, however, the co-operative undertakings do not differ from other business. Also they have in most cases become impersonal capital concentrations, which in reality are managed by the directors and business managers and not the owners, that is, the members of the co-operative society. I wonder if not even the leaders of smaller firms, dairy managers and cooperative store managers would willingly admit that special knowledge is required to run a small co-operative nowadays, and that business is most successful if the committee and the general assembly interfere as little as possible with the dispositions of the leader. (Ibid.: 22, our translation)

In the same year, Knud Hansen spoke from a philosophical viewpoint of the lack of human dignity in the modern world. The solution in Denmark could be a new form of *social liberalism* within the co-operative movement, which, as a tool for reorganizing the relationship between humankind and technology, could lead to humans once again ruling technology and not the other way round (ibid.: 16).

In 1967, another community high school teacher, Thomas Rørdam, warned about the price to be paid when centralized technocracy and rational economics prevailed at the expense of democracy in the agricultural societies:

> The larger a co-operative association becomes, the greater the distance between the single member and the leadership. Many members feel that it is none of their business. They feel, whether rightly or not, just as incapable and almost indifferent about their own business as the anonymous army of small shareholders in a big company. Local and direct democracy is endangered. It has to give ground under the demand for a centralized ruling system of experts follows. Already in the FDB [the Union of Danish Co-operative Wholesale Societies], for example, the voting rule is now based on the specific turnover in the firm rather than the traditional co-operative rule of 'one man, one vote'. The old democratic co-operative ideas lose ground when they collide with rational development. (DUI 1967: 401, our translation)

The editorial board of *Andelsbladet* expressed concern that such thoughts from a highly respected person like Rørdam should spread to other community high school teachers and eventually to the students. In a leading article titled 'Does the co-operative movement ignore the community high school?', the critique by Rørdam was claimed to be reactionary and outdated (*Ab* 1967: 785). Nevertheless, Rørdam seriously questioned the both/and argument – centralization and democracy through information campaigns – which many members would not relinquish in their efforts to maintain the special features of the co-operative movement. Also, he anticipated the formation of monopolies within the dairy, slaughter and wholesale sectors (ibid.: 838).

5.3.2.2.   Bonding social capital within the co-operative movement

The majority of the rural population remained remarkably silent during the centralization debate, even as the time-honoured co-operative principles fell one by one. Nevertheless, two men within the movement openly defended the two classical co-operative principles of democratic self-governance and open membership, namely the leader of the smallholders, Peter Jørgensen, and farmer Laurs Laursen.

Jørgensen criticized the liquidation of the direct democracy principle and open membership based on equal treatment of all members. In particular, the new principle about voting according to 'cows' tails', i.e. according to the number of cows owned by each farmer in contrast to one member one vote, was a discriminative act that strained the co-operative mind itself (*Ab* 1962: 832; *Hh* 1964, no. 3: 2ff.). It was a broken relationship of trust, Jørgensen continued, because 'the smallholders have felt and still feel obliged to the co-operative movement but in return they expect that the co-operative movement should also feel obliged to them'. In protest, the smallholders could form their own organization and by that 'act in their own self-interest' (*Ab* 1961: 793, our translation).

Thus, by the mid-1960s, the smallholders experienced a shift towards unbalanced reciprocity among rural social groups, as well as – in terms of (tacit as well as verbal) symbolic violence (see Chapter 6) – a breach of confidence leading to mutual distrust and lack of co-operation.

This situation, where different interest groups start fighting each other and so impose economic losses on each other, can be related to 'bonding social capital' (see Chapter 2), because the fragmentation of economic exchange – reinforced by symbolic violence – is followed by isolation and cultural alienation between the agricultural groups in question. Other agricultural groups also feared that they would become losers under the proposed reforms, especially small farmers and local leaders, who increasingly criticized the policy laid out by the central leadership.

Farmer Laurs Laursen also opposed the suggested reforms, which would benefit the big agricultural producers. He argued:

> The co-operative movement is a large-scale construction for small producers where each member keeps his/her independence and full rights to decide freely in all matters on his/her own responsibility and risk, which automatically means maximizing the interest in day-to-day work and striving to achieve even greater insight. (*Ab* 1962: 174, our translation)

Many notables within the co-operative movement openly gave their full support to Laursen. For example, a dominant entrepreneur within the dairy sector, Johannes Jensen, although in favour of rationalization, did not think that it was necessary to 'deviate from the tried and tested democratic voting rules to introduce Prussian-type principles whereby a single member's opinion can be ignored in a highly unworthy manner' (ibid.: 175, our translation).

Heated discussions followed within the co-operative movement. Laurs Laursen continued to argue against reform, suggesting that it had not been convincingly proved that standardized large units were more profitable. In contrast, the smaller units had proved to be profitable this far (ibid.). Most crucially, however, one should not 'throw out the baby with the bathwater':

> There are also other values in life than narrow efficiency. Even if a survey found that efficiency in production would rise if all producers between 18 and 67 years

were put in prison, one would still decline with thanks such progress in productivity. The price would be too high. (Ibid., our translation)

By this, Laursen drew attention to what we have called social capital. The stock of social capital would be reduced if local social networks were ignored, and this counterproductive effect would also need to be taken into account when deciding whether or not to centralize production. Laursen also questioned the removal of local, voluntary delegates. What would all the local committee members do when the big mergers occurred? Laursen suggested somewhat flippantly that they could form a glee club. Nevertheless, he continued, centralization would be a huge misfortune in terms of the loss of many responsible committee members (*Ab* 1964: 92).

Thus, Laursen feared that dynamic local entrepreneurs, and thereby self-government, would die out at the local level. He maintained that the quality of the present staff would deteriorate when they were employed as servants on regular pay under a hierarchical leadership that does not know the members or the local conditions. Therefore, a wider economic approach was needed where factors other than the purely financial ones were acknowledged as valuable for co-operation:

> I wonder why our most elevated leaders do not think that the right of self-determination in local associations has any value in what regards public life, human lives – culturally and also economically by the way. Something that is not worth two pennies and therefore can be ignored. (Ibid.: 1212, our translation)

Overall, in line with our social capital approach, Laursen concluded that what is gained in one way (by centralization) may be lost in another (ibid.: 1213). Others argued that the co-operative movement in its traditional form 'brings human beings to the fore and thrusts materialism into the background' (*Ab* 1965: 1102, our translation).

5.3.3.   Centralization of Production

All accessible sources suggest that from the establishment of the first one at Hjedding in 1882, the dairies dominated rural society. These small local became enterprises were centres of power until they were closed down during the 1960s.

5.3.3.1.   The dairies as a social meeting place before 1960
Local dairies were typically the largest workplaces and a crucial economic engine (Bjørn 1997; Rasmussen 1982). Often, the establishment of a local dairy led to further settlements, which were a magnet for other firms and shops. The economic and symbolic importance of these local dairies was

underlined by the fact that new settlements around them were often referred to as 'dairy towns' (Hansen and Rasmussen 1995: 18).

A specific outcome of this economic co-operation was direct collective good provision such as an organized fight against cattle diseases, harmful insects and so on. Likewise, members in the co-operative movement also formed insurance associations (Rasmussen 1982: 258). In addition, the dairies offered a whole range of services, for example, economic support to breeding societies and prizes for cattle shows. They functioned as wholesale societies and loan firms for the members and gave contributions to charitable organizations and, occasionally, industrial ventures (ibid.: 259).

Other services included telephone facilities, and the dairy offices could be used for private meetings or lectures (Hansen and Rasmussen 1995: 18). For example, breeding societies held their meetings in the dairies; and agricultural advisers, vets and so on were invited to give informative talks concerning agricultural issues. The machinery in the dairy was also used for other purposes, especially energy-consuming services such as electricity production or potato boiling. In several places, the dairies produced hot water for public baths, thereby performing an important health role in local society (Rasmussen 1982: 259; also see Chapter 2 for the economic net gain from such collective good provision).

Overall, the dairy was, like the village hall, a *social meeting place*, used for many purposes dependent on the needs of the local population and traditions of co-operation. It was the backbone of voluntary local self-organization – for example, the school, the church, shops, slaughterhouses, electricity and water supplies, cold stores; it was the essential prop for local social networks and as such a platform for generating social capital. Ethnologist Nina Fabricius comments that all these agricultural institutions contained a 'societal glue' which, among other things, expressed itself as a constant social interaction, namely, the 'comings and goings between local people' for the solution of local co-operative problems (Fabricius 1991: 80).

In this connection, it is interesting to observe the diverse range of socio-economic functions undertaken by the dairy in everyday life, which were crucial in building locally based stocks of social capital. For example, the milk carriers formed a link between suppliers by passing on news. Even more importantly, the suppliers on one 'milk route' took it in turns to meet at each other's house once a month to receive their dairy money. Also, dairy managers and dairymen were extremely active in social activities.

5.3.3.2.   Entrepreneurs within the dairy sector

The entrepreneurial role of the dairy managers was indisputable. This new social class co-operated closely with the farmers and, just as in the case of the fishermen, it became established during the 1920s and 1930s (Vestergaard 1991).

Typically, the well-functioning co-operation was due to the fact that 70 per cent of the dairy managers came from rural areas themselves. Often, many other economic associations benefited from the relationship of trust between dairy managers and farmers, because the dairy manager would normally take on a number of voluntary and unpaid positions, for example as treasurer in the local sick benefit association or as chair of the cooperative society. On the other hand, the dairy manager seldom took an active part in the cultural associational life (Rasmussen 1982).

One illustrative example is dairy manager Kristen Kristensen Tange. He was born and grew up on a farm but as a youngster he was already fascinated by the miracles of industrialization. Thus, Tange remembers the enthusiasm he had felt in 1880, as a 15 years old boy, when seeing a modern dairy for the first time:

> It was the cream separator that I watched with most excitement and wonder: it was rich in hidden secrets as it stood there with its polished skim milk spouts and drainpipe finished off in red. That was what it was all about, as if everything else should help and serve it, the machine that had created this fantastic new development within the dairy sector. These thoughts could easily excite admiration and respect in a young man's mind. It was a great day when I first saw the whole machinery running, it was almost like being in a sacred place, where one should take off one's shoes . . . Indeed, it was something very big to be a part of this business, if only one could be allowed to do so! (Tange 1965: 19, our translation)

Ever since, it was with this intense feeling, Tange performed the work which 'gave everyday life the value of a deep and fixed job satisfaction' (ibid.: 55, our translation). Likewise, as dairy manager, Tange would not give up his many extra activities in spite of the scepticism among members of the co-operative society. For example, he worked voluntarily and unpaid as a gym master, an editor of the progress association and a leader/teacher in an evening school: 'My open, willing participation in current popular and political movements always created opposition against me among members of the co-operative society and this presented a persistent threat to my position as dairy manager' (ibid.: 56, our translation). This work, he continued, 'absorbed me and was to me something very profitable that filled my mind with a great joy. It was more the being together than the teaching in itself which gave these evenings their value' (ibid.: 57, our translation). Just as in the case of the sports hall building (see Chapter 4), the pleasure derived from unpaid work is in itself a driving motivation (see also Frey and Stutzer 2002, on the linkage between happiness and economics).

The jubilee celebrations also indicate the close relationship that existed between farmers and the dairy until 1960, when the centralization process started. For example, a dairy manager at the Lindencrone dairy, Holger Thomassen, comments:

> In 1956 the dairy celebrated its 50 year jubilee with great festivities. There was a triumphal arch at the dairy and the milk carrier wagons were decorated. Different activities were launched during the day. In the evening there was a party for invited guests and co-operative members. There were so many speeches that it was a long time before dancing could begin. We all felt very glad about our small dairy and some thought that it would continue to function for many years. (Thomassen 1999: 130, our translation)

Such enthusiasm displayed by Tange and other entrepreneurs in the dairy sector was a result of the vast possibilities for self-organization. In this way, these entrepreneurs, involved in unpaid activities that benefited society as a whole, became creators of new working relations and societal glue, that is, the positive externality of (bridging) social capital.

5.3.3.3.   Rationalization within the dairy sector

In July 1937, a commission was established to investigate 'the economic and technical conditions for possible expansions of production and employment plus savings of foreign raw materials' (Produktions- og Raastofkommissionen 1949: 1). This commission submitted its report on the rationalization of dairies in April 1938. Because of the war, the report (no. B 24, *Rationalisering af Mejerier*) was first published at the request of the prime minister's department in 1949 when the question of merging once more topped the political agenda.

That report introduced the biggest wave of mergers and market centralization in the history of Denmark, with the closing down of local dairies. Thus, from 1930 to 1999 the number of dairies was reduced from nearly 1,400 to less than 25, that is, a closure of roughly *98 per cent* of the total number of dairies that existed in 1930! Note that the total number of dairies dropped from 1,127 in 1962 to 280 in 1971, that is, 75 per cent of all local dairies were closed down *within a single decade* (see Figure 5.1.).

The 1949 report explicitly stated that the motivation for suggesting rationalization within the dairy sector was that small-scale production was less economical than large-scale production. According to the report, the solution was to establish large centralized dairies while shutting down the small ones: 'There is no doubt that large dairies are better capable of implementing the needed technological innovations that can ensure the best quality products' (ibid.).

In January 1963, a dairy adviser from the so-called Dairy Office in Aarhus, Torkil Mathiassen, suggested that one single dairy association rather than 1000, 500 or 100 associations should be established (Vedholm 1995: 20–21). Mathiassen succeeded in convincing the leadership of the dairy federation

(*Fællesorganisationen*) that limited mergers were insufficient. Furthermore, it would be easier to obtain subsidies for one national merger, since the state was poised to intervene in the internal matters of the dairy sector (Buksti 1982: 366). Thereby, the leaders' fight for only one company, 'Mejeriselskabet Danmark' (MD), was launched.

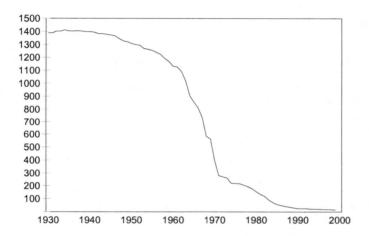

Source: Danish Dairy Statistics

Figure 5.1 Number of dairies (Denmark), 1930–99

The propaganda for full centralization and only one company within the dairy co-operative movement was basically rooted in the idea of a global development race. In the centralization debate, influential arguments were that 'other countries have overtaken Danish dairy production', 'the current methods of working are outdated', 'the Danish dairy industry must rationalize to keep its position among the leading countries', 'the dairy sector is lagging behind' (*Ab* 1962: 113, 125, 303, 958, 1963: 1045).

That the time-honoured dairy co-operative would be lagging behind in the near future was a worrying argument. Often, such bogeys in *Andelsbladet*, for example, were supplemented by photos of poor people and primitive dairies in developing countries such as Africa and India (*Ab* 1962: 958). Thus, the dairy culture was seen as a barometer marking the degree of economic development, and the risk was that the dairy sector would lose its position if it did not rationalize its mode of production. The fear of involution (degeneration) led to a general consensus among top leaders and editors that a full merger was the only option that ensured survival under the 'law of development'.

Like the aforementioned Laursen and Jørgen, other dissenters spoke openly out against the central propaganda. For example, a farmer from Rebild, Peder Christensen, questioned, whether the central leadership in a big merger was capable of preserving the renowned Danish co-operative movement, which had been laboriously built 'bottom up' by ordinary farmers (ibid.). He argued:

> [I]t will be no good if the development results in a situation where a central leadership consists of 20–30 people. They would be so occupied by meetings, first in one central board of directors, then in another, first in one committee and then in another, that they would not have time to take care of local matters and create contacts there. (*Ab* 1965: 45, our translation)

Even if the leaders sent out experts to local areas to assist the management when implementing decisions, the problem was that local representatives would no longer be a part of these decision-making processes. These representatives were the entrepreneurs, Christensen continued, typically gifted men of vision, who because of their extensive voluntary work for the common good were the leading forces in local co-operative business. By replacing local entrepreneurs with outside experts, there was a risk that the connection with the producers would be lost (ibid.).

Likewise, in 1964, the earlier mentioned Laurs Laursen issued a warning to

> the co-operative members who are exposed to intense propaganda these days from delegate consultants who promise them big advantages . . . if they will vote yes and so declare themselves incapable of managing their own affairs in their own associations . . . However, in my humble opinion, the proposed reform can lead to huge economic and cultural losses, and there will be little left of the founding principles in the co-operative movement but its name. (*Mt* 1964: 682, our translation)

'Dear Laurs Laursen', replied his fellow dissenter Grønborg, 'you hit the bull's eye! We agree – agree that the cultural loss is so big, so bitter to recall' (ibid.: 683).

Finally, a representative and nostalgic comment from the 'backward-looking' sceptics was made by a dairy manager from Thyholm, Hvidbjerg, in 1964:

> I wonder why no one has critically reviewed the recent development; I cannot believe that all the members of the co-operative movement think that it is a good and healthy development, so why not discuss the question in our members' journals? It is as if everybody agrees that the development is moving in the right direction and that there is no other alternative. I guess that one sign of this change is when a dairy or dairy manager celebrates jubilees or birthdays on which a round

number is reached, then it is announced: 'No festivities' or 'I am not in that day'. (ibid.: 939)

5.3.3.4. Traditional versus modern farmers

From the beginning of the 1960s, the powerful macro networks between top leaders became an increasing threat to the locally based stocks of social capital. Of course, local people fought for the jobs in local dairies and co-operative stores but also for their local roots and identities. As such, the fight against decentralization was viewed as a cultural clash between the modernists, that is, those with a modern evolutionary worldview (the law of development), and the traditionalists, that is, those with old-fashioned local preferences. Therefore, the aim of the modernists was to eliminate the culture of local loyalists, especially within the tradition-bound dairy sector because the traditional identity here was perceived as a barrier to economic development.

The idea that traditionalism belonged to primitive and backward people was strongly promoted by the leaders. The big problem for the central leadership and members in favour of centralization was that a change in the statutes required a qualified majority. This meant that a decision about closing down an association needed a two-thirds or even three-quarters majority.

The main argument from the modernist leaders in the raging public debate was that the voting rule of qualified majority was undemocratic. Any minority should give up their right to control the majority because the fatal decision about qualified majority stems from a time when its dramatic importance in a situation like the current one was not foreseen (*Ab* 1963: 282). Furthermore, modernists claimed that the most important issue is never the formal rules but rather a common understanding of the problem. So if a majority support a decision, the minority should allow the proposal to pass in order to let the majority decide the leadership and the direction: 'the minority has the right to slow down the development now and then but it never has the right to use this power beyond the purpose of ensuring that the minority is heard!' (*Ab* 1964: 869, our translation). This self-contradiction originates from the both/and argument identified above. On the one hand, modernists wanted to preserve a well-informed co-operative democracy. On the other, those members who, in spite of information campaigns, used their democratic right to vote 'no' at the general meeting, should not slow down development and by that endanger common economic goals. In other words, the leaders wanted to get rid of slow and outdated decision procedures (*Ab* 1966: 1307). The co-operative movement could not afford the luxury of waiting, since development elsewhere, for example in the United States, had already made giant strides (ibid.). Thus, one had to fight the ignorance of farmers entrenched in a remote and false romantic movement by constantly emphasizing the provable inevitability of structural rationalization and concentration (ibid.: 940).

One specific and representative example of this both/and approach is the ballots concerning a merger of five slaughterhouses in Vendsyssel in April 1965. These events were covered in detail by *Andelsbladet*, and the editorial board was amazed by the passive and reluctant attitude behaviour of members. The journal compared the situation to the information service established in Greenland where such 'irrational' animosity against development was also observed. Similar to the less-developed Greenlanders, such members could also be identified in the Danish co-operative movement. The common economic advantage from a fusion was evident and was the only question that mattered (*Ab* 1965: 473). The problem was that most of the 11,400 members of the five slaughterhouses stayed at home, and only about 700 members participated in the general meeting where 423 were for and 248 against the merger (ibid.).

In the same paradoxical way as in Greenland, *Andelsbladet* presumed that the absent members were actually in favour of the merger because the meticulous groundbreaking work by the leadership must have had an effect. The reality was simply that most members could not leave their farm work in the spring:

> The opposite interpretation that the absent members are opponents of the proposal is not likely. One must rather assume that they – just like the speakers at the general meeting – in principle support the centralization proposal even though they might have wanted some minor details changed. Really determined opponents would have left their harrow and sowing machine to go to the general meeting and protest. However, we do not believe that they exist. (ibid., our translation)

Silence obviously equated with consent in this case. The 94 per cent absence of members was not considered a serious problem – it was all a question of more information and then new ballots (ibid.: 474). The new ballots were held three months after, immediately following a massive information campaign. On this occasion, 1,313 out of the 11,400 turned up and the result was 707 for and 606 against the proposal. *Andelsbladet* observed that 606 'no' votes must not stop development. Waiting until the members themselves took the initiative and organized an alternative proposal was completely out of the question – the leadership did not think that there was time enough for that. Rather, the anti-progressive members in the pedantic local co-operative democracy should be converted from a reactionary to a progressive viewpoint through information. *Andelsbladet* concluded that if all members had fully understood their own interests and the content of the proposal, then they would have voted 'yes', and that the matter is more urgent than the 606 no-voters think (*Ab* 1965: 918).

But the local members continued to resist the increasing pressure from their national leaders. Thus, in December 1967 the merger was rejected once again, giving rise to a leader in *Andelsbladet* entitled: 'Minority abuse' (*Ab* 1967: 1249). In March 1969, one of the leaders claimed that they were being forced to carry out the structural changes (*Ab* 1969: 281). However, in this particular case, the members refused to follow the advice from their leaders, agricultural experts, consultants, PR officers and so on.

However, the persecution of local 'no' voters was widespread. Within the dairy sector, for example, statements from prominent local dairy managers were a constant thorn in the flesh of the leaders. In particular, they were subjected to political pressure from a small number of impatient and aggressive dissenters who set up the Joint Organization of Farmers (*Landbrugernes Fællesorganisation*: LFO). The LFO supported local initiatives against centralization to defy the leaders and their officials; see, for example, this statement from 1967:

> From the leadership of the dairy organizations, mergers and the establishment of a single firm are promoted via professional employees with price indexed wages. If the co-operative members do not bring them into line at the first general meeting where many convincing arguments from consultants are given but where questions about the economic gain for each farmer are not answered, a new and extraordinary general meeting is held, and if the leadership does not succeed the second time, it will try again a third time. We shall begin to feel the strain, we farmers. Even before it is all settled, the leadership has started establishing itself with new offices, new buildings, new directors, assistant directors, administration and so on. (*Ls* 1967: 151, our translation)

Another illustrative example of the fight against 'no' voters is found in connection with a planned dairy merger in Randers, in 1963. Here, the local dairy leaders had publicly stated that they did not want to participate in the plan for rationalization but rather try to serve the producers better by working independently as they have done so far (*Ab* 1963: 1066). The prompt reaction from the editorial board of *Andelsbladet* was that such a short-sighted and reactionary attitude among local dairy managers was unacceptable when the plan had been worked out by the experts of their own organization (ibid.).

5.3.3.5. Centralization and the rise of Mejeriselskabet Danmark (MD)

In spite of the general scepticism among members, the leadership continued its fight for full merger into one dairy company, namely 'Mejeriselskabet Danmark' (MD). Soft and invisible values of culture and local feelings could not match the 'hard' and visible facts of economics. What would come first, *Andelsbladet* asked in 1970, a single dairy company in Denmark or a single dairy company in Sweden (*Ab* 1970: 118)?

A tough negotiation process had taken its toll. The central leadership found itself up against local leaders who were less supportive of full centralization because they were committed to locally based dairy associations (*Ab* 1969: 414). Also, negotiators from four local dairy associations in Jutland that wanted to merge into MD, had sudden misgivings when it came to the crunch (ibid.: 260). It is clear from a statement made in 1969 that they believed that one should first concentrate on a separate merger of these four associations, rather than attempting a full merger into the MD (*Mt* 1969: 50).

A propaganda campaign was launched by the central leadership, first and foremost in *Andelsbladet* where phrases such as 'irresponsible not to continue', 'continued full support', 'continue, not shelve', 'in the interests of dairy producers', 'firm backing to the goal of Mejeriselskabet Danmark' and so on were repeated again and again. At the same time, similar mergers within other co-operative sectors such as wholesale, chemicals and animal feed, and slaughterhouses, were discussed. These sectors should also be strengthened by delegating the business side to 'a few, very strong and competent leaders' (ibid.: 777). This and other quotations demonstrate the blind faith in strong leaders around 1970 leading to a peculiar situation where the opinions expressed outside the top circles did not count. Such feelings of superiority among top leaders were apparent when they were agitating in favour of a single dairy company, the MD. For example, a leading article in *Andelsbladet* stated that the merger plan 'cannot be shelved as a few helpful voices in the press have expressed, as long as the idea is right. And it is right!' (ibid.: 367, our translation)

The message in *Andelsbladet* was particularly aimed at rebellious local dairy managers who kept delaying the development. For the same reason, there was a continuing fight with the 'no'-voting 'minority dictatorship' at the local general meetings where the question about merging into the MD was put to the vote time after time (for example, *Ab* 1970: 1143, 1161). Also, chief editor Poul Toft-Nielsen in *Landsbladet* agitated for what was called 'the crucial trust in the leaders' within the top circles of leaders and experts (*Ab* 1969: 1113). Toft-Nielsen puts it this way:

> The secret of success for a grand new course is: does one have the right leaders? It is not a big, impersonal fabulous monster like a co-operative movement that would create something new. It is the people who are leading the way to create something. Therefore, I do not understand the words that continue to be voiced in the dairy sector: it is something one should create from the bottom. There has to be someone who initiates something, and this is typically the men at the top. If the farmers do not understand by now that someone from the top has to take the initiative and put things together, I do not think that the Danish dairy stands any chance. (Ibid.: 341, our translation)

Some leaders even went so far in their centralization efforts that, in the same way as some agricultural organizations did in the 1930s, they suggested a full merger of all the co-operative sectors into one state-financed unit. *Andelsbladet* found this idea 'valuable' and continued that the whole project should not start from the bottom up, of course, but rather should be seen as a promotion of the total economic result (ibid.: 1210). Here, in 1969, there was evidence of much relief among the editorial board in *Andelsbladet* and the majority of its contributors. By planning the great mergers within the co-operative movement, a 'giant step' had been taken, while the realization of them meant that the leadership was at last keeping abreast of developments (*Ab* 1965: 1). However, though most people were, by then, generally captured by the optimism of economic development, some were still worried about the future of the co-operative movement. For example, a survey by economist Gunnar Viby Mogensen on the social consequences of structural changes showed that widespread dissatisfaction with the diminished influence in local co-operative associations existed, among both elderly and young people (Mogensen 1970; *Ab* 1970: 1183ff.). Also, within the private business sector, two other economists, Kaj Lindberg and Jørgen Paldam, discussed similar hierarchical problems within the large impersonal firms (Lindberg and Paldam 1954: 120).

After the great mergers within the co-operative movement was finally guaranteed, the leading article commenting on this in *Andelsbladet* in 1970 appeared under the heading: 'Then they [the co-operative sectors] were not behind the development after all' (*Ab* 1970: 69). In other words, the Danish Co-operative Movement had finally succeeded in cathing up with *The* development. Within the dairy sector, the merger was formally signed in June 1970 and from 1 October 1970, the giant MD (later MD Foods and Arla Foods) could commence activities.

5.4.   SUMMARY

In this chapter, we observed how beneficial bridging social capital, accumulated by energetic entrepreneurs before the Second World War, was transformed into harmful bonding social capital after the war.

The chapter was structured in two main sections. Following the Introduction, we first briefly analysed the nineteenth-century religious conflicts leading to bonding social capital in rural Denmark. Next, we traced the destruction of bridging social capital within the post-war co-operative movement.

We traced the counter-reaction within the co-operative movement from about 1890, ultimately leading to particularistic trust and harmful bonding social capital in a number of rural parishes, especially in the western part of Denmark. This was due to religious conflicts between two major groups among farmers, the Home Mission followers and the Grundtvigians. Such a transformation of bridging to excessive bonding social capital materialized physically in the form of a duplication of meeting places in economic as well as cultural life – that is, in those platforms that formerly had secured regular face-to-face contact between different groups and, thus, bridging social capital building. Most seriously, this led to the establishment of superfluous Home Mission co-operative dairies involving serious economic backlashes for all farmers.

We then presented empirical evidence suggesting that while the old Danish saying 'A word is a word' used to be valid in the countryside, the level of trust decreased when agricultural production was centralized after the Second World War. This occurred most dramatically within the famous co-operative dairy sector, where local parish dairies – previously the fabric of bridging social capital – were shut down en masse during the 1960s.

However, this formerly rich peasant community life seems to have collapsed gradually when these small local dairies were shut down. We drew attention to the fact that any loss in bridging social capital must be deducted from the economic gain following economies of scale (for example, market centralization of dairy production). We suggested that alternative possibilities should be considered, taking the production factor of inclusive and 'lubricating' bridging social capital into account, because it is uncertain whether the net gain is positive or whether another way of organizing production – and maintaining the high level of bridging social capital – would significantly have increased economic growth further.

As demonstrated, an important incentive for the radical shift in co-operative organization during the 1960s was changes in the discourses of rurality, promoted by agricultural leaders and experts. Likewise, in Chapter 6 we shall see how from the beginning of the 1970s, this modernist, Fordist paradigm was already being seriously challenged by an urban, non-agricultural paradigm, and what impact this had on the stocks of social capital in rural Denmark.

6. Bonding Social Capital and Theory Effects: The Danish Village Society Movement

6.1. INTRODUCTION

This chapter deals with another important case of the formation of bonding social capital in Denmark after the Second World War. Here, the main purpose is to analyse the background for the close linkage between bonding social capital and discoursive elements ('discourses of rurality', involving propagandistic effects, that is, 'theorization' effects). Thus, it appears that serious culture clashes in the public debate among representatives of various conflicting groups strongly accentuate the psychological distance between groups and individuals, thus preparing the ground for group isolation and bonding social capital in practice. This linkage corresponds to our historical findings in the preceding chapters. We saw here how the principle of *distance*, reinforced by what Bourdieu (for example, 1977: 191) has called 'symbolic violence', that is, the hidden and tacit violence taking place in everyday life, or, in our extended understanding: symbolic violence expressed tacitly, *as well as* in spoken and written words. Thus, distance arguably lead to distrust and lack of co-operation and, ultimately, to the transformation of bridging social capital into bonding social capital, harmful to society. This in contrast to the principle of physical closeness or reciprocity linked to bridging social capital.

Therefore, we want to shed light on how, during the 1970s, the construction of a non-agriculturalist conceptual universe, primarily built by newcomers, was formed partly in overt opposition to dominant worldviews among the native rural population.

On the one hand, in these symbolic struggles, we point to a striking continuous absence of a term denoting a social production factor (social capital) that would link culture to economics. On the other hand, we highlight how discursive elements in the form of symbolic violence directed towards the exclusion of social groups tend to lead to psychological distance, distrust, group and individual isolation, lack of co-operation – in sum: to harmful bonding social capital. This corresponds to both our ethnographic case study

(Chapter 7), as well as to our historical findings where both physical distance (centralization of buildings and production implying physical distance between rural inhabitants), as well as psychological distance (severe conflicts between religious groups, between national and local/regional agricultural leaders, between modern and traditional farmers, between locals and newcomers) lead to generalized distrust, destroying formal and informal, non-excludable practices of reciprocity and mutual aid (that is, collective goods).

As in many other Western European countries in the decades following the Second World War (for example, Woods 1997), we shall be talking about two dominant discourses of rurality, namely early agriculturalist and later non-agriculturalist. The conflict between urban newcomers and farmers is a general trend in Western Europe, and it illustrates well the formation of exclusive networks and bonding social capital.

Although still important in Denmark, the agriculturalist discourse had its heyday in the 1960s, as we saw in Chapter 5. It belonged to a group of modern farmers who used a modernist–productionist terminology in the public debate. This terminology was mainly based on keywords that were taken from agricultural economics, such as development, structural changes, vertical integration, rationalization and centralization, that is, highly abstract academic terms imported from abroad.

Partly as a counter-reaction, a second discourse was established during the 1970s, involving severe clashes of symbolic violence – tacitly as well as verbally – between groups of rural natives and newcomers. As we shall see below, this 'family' of powerful words was applied and promoted by new non-agricultural elites in the villages. Similar to the agriculturalist vocabulary, the non-agriculturalist vision of rurality was expressed in academic terms, mainly borrowed from the social sciences, such as community, culture, natural development and active citizenship.

This chapter focuses specifically on the new conceptual creations that occurred at the end of the 1970s. At that time, the urban newcomers and returnees to the rural communities attempted to construct their own vocabulary in an effort to appropriate political power. In this struggle over words, they were led into battle by the nationwide association the National Confederation of Village Communities (*Landssammenslutningen af Landsbysamfund*, LAL). This organization was established in December 1976 and has during the subsequent decades continued to promote and further develop its characteristic discourse of rurality, based on certain ideological theories of the ideal way of living a rural life. Apart from newspaper articles, newsletters, agendas, reports and so on, this has been done through its own journal *Landsbyen* ('The Village').

As is evidenced by articles in *Landsbyen* in the 1977–78 period, the LAL became one of the most important founders of a new, powerful conceptual universe among the rural population. Therefore, we shall explain in detail the *genesis* of a consistent universe of ideas, theories and concepts of rurality among the LAL leading members by analysing articles in *Landsbyen* between 1977 and 1978 – a discourse of rurality that was quickly overtaken by members of many local citizens' associations in the villages, as well as by social scientists, state bureaucrats and local politicians. In this way, the non-agriculturalist formulations of rural identity and practice came to dominate the rural political debate in Denmark during the 1980s and 1990s, thereby challenging an agriculturalist terminology of an older date. At an overall level, and in the context of rapid changes in national economy, landscape and buildings, such a discursive shift mirrored the cultural transition of Denmark from a peasant society to an industrial, urbanized society.

Before we analyse the LAL rhetoric in *Landsbyen*, we shall briefly review the existing literature on discourses of rurality and their effects on rural identities and realities. This includes a review of the already mentioned two most dominant discourses of rurality in Denmark after the Second World War (the modernist–agriculturalist and non-agriculturalist). In particular, we shall focus on the formation of the non-agriculturalist discourse belonging to the rural newcomers of the 1970s. Next, we shall compare the practical impact of these two discourses of rurality in post-war rural Denmark.

Overall, the formation of bonding social capital in Denmark seems to be closely linked to theory effects stemming from the public debate and, hence, the implications for voluntary entrepreneurship and the creation/destruction of social capital (see also the fieldwork study in Chapter 7). Therefore, we shall close the chapter by summarizing our findings on the linkage between excessive bonding social capital and discursive elements in post-war rural Denmark, the latter not least involving symbolic violence.

6.2. DISCOURSES OF RURALITY AND THEORY EFFECTS

6.2.1. Naming and Theory Effects

In recent years, a growing number of rural studies have stressed the importance of discourses of rurality in the construction of new rural identities and realities (for example, Mormont 1987, 1990; Hoggart et al. 1995; Ray 1997, 1998; Woods 1997; Herbert-Cheshire 2000; Halfacree 2001; Woodward 2001; Halfacree et al. 2002; Svendsen 2002, 2003a).

This reflects a general trend within social science research, where the focus has been on classification, knowledge production and group identity. Thus, Bourdieu (1977: 178, 1990a: 134, 1990b: 134) has spoken of 'constitutive naming' and 'theory effect', Ian Hacking (1999: 80ff.) of 'elevator words' and 'nominalism', while Bruno Latour (1999: 69) has recently described knowledge as an 'operator', which communicates a given culturally-based viewpoint about the relationship between things and words.

As our case studies in rural Denmark will clearly demonstrate, knowledge and classification do not constitute neutral human tools. They express underlying power interests. As such, they will always operate as an integrated part in a social discourse, which has consequences in the here and now. In an explanation of the terms 'naming' and 'theory effect', Bourdieu puts it in this way:

> The categories of perception, the systems of classifications, that is, essentially, the words, the names which construct social reality as much as they express it, are the crucial stakes of political struggle, which is a struggle to impose the legitimate principle of vision and division . . . a struggle for the legitimate exercise of the theory effect. (Bourdieu 1985: 198, 217)

The words always communicate a specific view on an event, as denoted by the old Greek word *theorein*, which literally means 'to view', 'to contemplate' (as a spectator at a play, for example). However, it is evident that a certain way of viewing and communicating the events of the world, a *theoria*, also contributes to defining that world. In that sense, the introduction of new words has a direct impact on people's (legitimate) worldviews and, hence, on reality itself – as was the case with many of Marx's inventions, such as 'working class' and 'class struggle'. Such abstractions often appear in a definite form: *the* working class, *the* class struggle, *the* development, *the* structural changes and so on – a reification process that seems to confirm their transition from abstract academic concepts to legitimate 'real' things. Or, as Marx and Engels express it in a famous formulation in *The German Ideology*: 'Language is real, practical consciousness' (Marx and Engels [1848] 1947).

Within this logic and in a sociological perspective, Bourdieu (1990a: 54) states that 'politics is, essentially, a matter of words'. Consequently, groups and group identities can be seen as the outcome of words, that is, 'the instruments of the struggle for the definition of reality' (Bourdieu 1977: 170), in the form of symbolic struggles:

> Principles of division . . . function within and for the purposes of the struggle between social groups; in producing concepts, they produce groups, the very groups which produce the principles and the groups against which they are produced. What is at stake in the struggles about the meaning of the social world is power over the classificatory schemes and systems which are the bases of the representations of the groups and therefore of their mobilization and demobilization: the evocative power of an utterance which puts things in a different light. (Bourdieu 1989: 479)

Recent rural studies literature has examined 'theory effects' from various perspectives. For example, research on rural restructuring (for an overview, see Hoggart and Paniagua 2001), rural conflicts (Woods 1998), governmental rural development strategies (Herbert-Cheshire 2000) and powerful representations constructed and promoted by rural interest groups (Woods 1997; Woodward 1999) have implied a strong focus on discursive elements and their effect on rural identities and realities.

In particular, Michael Woods's (1997) interesting case study on twentieth century local politics in the rural county of Somerset, England, clearly reveals how power in a local community is discursively constructed (ibid.: 457). Very similar to the Danish cases presented in this chapter and in Chapter 5, we here witness the historical formation of competing discourses, which have had 'a real effect on the lives of local people' (ibid.: 472). So we see that, from the end of the First World War until the 1960s, an 'agricultural community discourse' dominated, enhancing narrow agricultural interests. However, from the middle of the 1970s, this discourse became increasingly challenged by an 'environmentalist discourse' (ibid.: 458) belonging to the still more numerous and powerful service class consisting of urban-thinking newcomers. In contrast to the indigenous people in the villages, these newcomers 'were not exposed to the traditional discourse of rurality, which regarded the countryside as a space of production, but developed alternative discourses, regarding the countryside as a space of consumption' (ibid.: 468).

Similarly, we shall see how, in rural Denmark, a discursively established rurality dominated by farmers' interests – that is, an agriculturalist discourse of rurality – gradually became more and more challenged by a non-agriculturalist discourse of rurality belonging to the newcomers.

6.2.2. The Agriculturalist Discourse of Rurality

Reading the Danish agricultural journals, magazines and newspapers of 1945–70, one is struck by the high frequency of abstract concepts (see Svendsen 2002). Not least, the impressive number of technical–academic words that include many combinations beginning with the word 'structural', such as structural change, structural development, structural problems. For example, as we saw earlier, this can be seen in the articles of one of the most influential agricultural journals during the 1950s and 1960s, *Andelsbladet*, issued by the Danish agricultural co-operative movement. The popularity and impact of this word *was* and *still is* enormous in a Western European country as Denmark – not only within agricultural economics, but within academic and political discourse as such. Thus, in the year 1970 the word 'structure' appeared in the main title of almost 25 per cent of all articles in *Andelsbladet*!

But where did these revolutionary 'structural changes' come from at the first place?

Evidently, the Danish term *strukturændringer* – that is, a direct translation of 'structural changes' like the German (*Agrarstrukturwandel*) or the French (*changement structurel*) – was imported from the United States after the Second World War, Thus, search on article databases reveals that the concept was developed for the first time in the *American Economic Review* in the late 1930s. For example, Alvin H. Hansen (1937: 131) wrote about 'deep-seated structural changes in economic institutions' after the First World War. In the same journal, Benjamin M. Anderson, Jr. (1940: 247) wrote about disturbances in global economy after 1929, due to 'structural changes'.

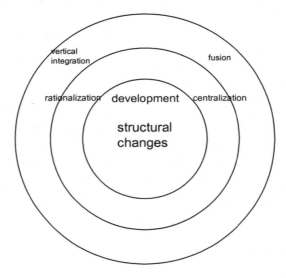

Note that the concepts closest to the centre are the most powerful and most often applied words.

Source: The authors.

Figure 6.1   The agriculturalist discourse of rurality, established during the 1960s

However, articles in the Danish agricultural journals of about 1960 reveal that the Danish farmers had difficulty understanding the new Latin terminology that at this time was being propagated by agricultural economists and other experts. As expressed in *Andelsbladet*, March 1962, 'Structural change, rationalization and adjustment . . . have become [the new] slogans. However, until now no-one has offered an exact definition of these words' (*Ab* 1962: 290, our translation).

Nonetheless, by the mid-1960s, Danish farmers were becoming familiar with the new terminology. The import, internalization and spread of a distinct discourse of rurality on the initiative of a group of energetic and modernist-minded agricultural leaders and experts gradually had an effect on the common farmers. This was the case among the members of a dairy association in the village of Agerskov. Unfamiliar with the prevailing concepts of the day, a referent here wrote in June 1963 that 'it was not the intention of the fussion [sic] to make immediately use of milk tank lorries' (Svendsen 2001: 47). Similarly, at the neighbouring dairy of Rangstrup, the referent wrote in October 1960 that a farmer, Anton Holm, 'wants ratsinalization [sic] of the dairies and held the view that the dairies were much too small: all sales had to, and ought to, be in fewer hands' (ibid.).

Were these people unable to spell correctly? Apparently not. Rather, the misspelling of 'fusion' and 'rationalization' was caused by their unfamiliarity with such academic words – a fact that has also been confirmed in interviews with two former members of the dairy association in Rangstrup.

In this way, the structural changes – a term expressing external global market conditions and, at the same time, implicitly promoting a modernist worldview – suddenly became reality for the rural population during the 1960s, just as real as the second-hand tractors that had been imported from the UK since the Second World War; or the fields, or the wheat in the fields. As we have seen within the co-operative dairy sector, the structural changes were 'proved' by the statistics, often referred to as 'the speech of the numbers' or, in sum, THE DEVELOPMENT. 'Nobody can resist the development', was the resigned conclusion of a still larger group of farmers.

However, to the great surprise of the agricultural elite, there was a group of farmers who would exhibit another, quite irrational behaviour when confronted with what the leaders and experts had called 'the laws of necessity', 'the laws of centralization', 'the speech of the numbers', 'the inevitable path leading to production of scale' and so on, that is, the effects of the structural changes and the development that, it was believed, were completely out of control. As we saw it within the co-operative movement, the leaders and experts categorized these heretics (often from the older generations) as 'harmful reactionaries', ridiculously 'nostalgic' or 'romantic' people or simply as 'primitive' and 'backward' – similar to the populations in the so-called underdeveloped countries. Thus, as we also saw in Chapter 5, as a result of symbolic violence and generational conflicts social capital was partly fragmentized and a majority of peasants were alienated from their national leaders.

So, finally, during the 1960s, it became profitable in all respects for the rural dwellers to be modernists, progressive, far-sighted and responsible, as was dictated by the prevailing discourse of rurality – a terminology which at the turn of the new century is still powerful in rural Denmark, as well as in other European countries, in particular among a still shrinking number of farmers.

6.2.3.   The Non-agriculturalist Discourse of Rurality

However, modernists also get outdated. So we see that, since the beginning of the 1970s, a new post-Fordist worldview has developed among the rural population. This worldview is propagated in the form of increasingly powerful concepts, expressing anti-modernist and anti-materialist values, such as life quality, local cultural traditions, political decentralization, and social well-being, often in explicit opposition to the agriculturalist paradigm (see Figure 6.2).

Note that the concepts closest to the centre are the most powerful and most often applied words

Source: The authors.

Figure 6.2   The non-agriculturalist discourse of rurality, established during the 1970s

As in the 1960s, the new rural concepts were imported from abroad and directly translated into Danish. Again, the terminology primarily consisted of

Anglo-Saxon academic words, such as local community, village community, the small community, ecological communities and so on. Crucial imports were also various combinations beginning with favourite words such as 'social' (social cohesion, social life, social welfare, social networks and so on). and 'natural' (natural environment, natural community, natural mode of life and so on).

However, whereas the modernist terminology had mostly been taken from 'hard' sciences, such as economics, statistics and political science, the new urbanized terminology primarily included concepts borrowed from 'soft' sciences, such as sociology, anthropology and history. In this context, the word 'structural' – denoting macroeconomic processes – gradually gave way to 'social' and 'natural'. Furthermore, and even more interesting in our context, constellations including the word 'social' were completely cleansed from connotations referring to 'evil' macroeconomics.

In the beginning of the 1970s, at a time when it had become popular for young urban dwellers to move to the countryside and live a more natural and social life, the conceptualization of this new worldview took place within newly established citizens' associations. As we shall see from 1977, these initiatives were coordinated by the nationwide association, the National Confederation of Village Communities (LAL).

6.3.   ESTABLISHMENT OF THE NATIONAL CONFEDERATION OF VILLAGE COMMUNITIES

The drastic decline in the number of local, business-oriented associations through the 1960s makes it increasingly irrelevant to speak of 'agricultural co-operatives' by the 1970s – a co-operative movement that from the second half of the nineteenth century had had an all-pervasive impact on economic and cultural life in rural Denmark (Svendsen and Svendsen 2000, 2001). In pure demographic terms as well, the rural districts were being drained of their inhabitants.

It was primarily the young farm workers who were made redundant, as was the case in many other Western European countries. Generally, the transition from agriculture to industry occurred relatively late in Denmark, in comparison to early industrialized countries such as England and the United States. Therefore, it was primarily during the 1960s and 1970s that significant numbers of Danish farmers were made redundant.

Consequently, during this period the rural dwellers were to a great degree transformed into labour reserves for the larger towns, where former farmers together with smallholders working part-time in agriculture, as well as many newcomers and returnees adapted to a commuter lifestyle.

6.3.1.   Construction of a New Rural Identity

From the early 1970s, however, there arose in many areas a new network of urban newcomer-dominated residents' and citizens' associations to fill the vacuum left by the rationalized economic co-operatives. The National Confederation of Village Communities (LAL) became an important coordinator and inspirational source for these networks. LAL saw its role as that of bringing new life into the eroding parish and village communities.

The LAL movement should be seen as one of the outcomes of a major trend in Denmark in the 1970s, namely the left-wing and environmentalist political ideology that predominated in the public sphere during this decade, and which was most radically promoted by Danish intellectuals. Thus, right from the start, the construction of a new, socialist-inspired rurality was conceived by academics, who had consciously chosen to move from the cities to small pretty villages in order to realize their vision of the ideal way of living. The dream of a new rural way of life was literally architect designed by these young intellectuals and former urban dwellers. Thus, after 1970, architects – together with sociologists and anthropologists, primarily – verbalized their dream of a new rural life in an amazing number of publications, including newspaper articles, rural political agendas and scientific articles, reports and books.[1]

A good example is architect and village newcomer Poul Bjerre, who early made important contributions to the non-agriculturalist discourse of rurality. Thus, in his book *Village Politics – State Politics* (Bjerre 1974), he spoke about a decentralized humanistic society in balance (*balancesamfund*). This ideal society could only be established in small village societies, in contrast to the both socially and physically polluted life in the big cities. Following Bjerre, this could be stated as a scientific fact, as it could be scientifically proven that human beings were born with a need of social values (*socialt værdibehov*). Moreover, this biological need could only be satisfied in the form of what Bjerre saw as a social, gregarian way of life in the villages.

In a more or less modified form, such rhetoric has been adopted and utilized during the late 1970s, 1980s and 1990s by leading LAL members. Thus, glorifying a traditional and 'naturally' social way of living in the countryside, Ole Glahn, a LAL chairman, has given the following characterization of the rural districts' 'third-world' status in relation to the urban areas:

> The village parish is relegated to delivering raw materials and labour to the towns, where secondary agricultural production now takes place in large units. A consequence of this development is that residents of the countryside can no longer get to know each other via the work they perform. In former times, many people worked together, for others or for themselves. It brought them closer together.

Formerly, many local workers had a host of local meeting places, all of which served a certain purpose the smithy, the garage, the carpenter's workshop, the bakery, the dairy, the butcher's, the doctor's and vet's surgeries, the grocer's, the co-operative store, the barber's, the hairdresser's, the cycle shop, the shoemaker's the saddle maker's, the parish council office, the school and the like. There are very few villages, which have more than 3–4 of these functions left. (Glahn 1985: 173–4)

Apart from the influence of left-wing academics, the form of argumentation of the members of the residents' and citizens' associations during the 1970s is to a great degree reminiscent of the trade unions of the workers' movement. Accordingly, these members sought to exercise direct influence on the local and regional political decision-making processes, especially via an influence on the 'local plans', that is, the public institutions' physical planning in the individual local areas. For example, in 2002 a former chairman of the residents' association in the village of Sandager on the island of Funen told one of the authors in an interview that he decided to establish the association in 1978, because he thought that the village at that time 'needed such an organ in order to make sure that the village residents could meet and discuss common issues'. However, this smallholder admitted that he had long been reluctant to take this step. The reason was that he did not like the various local councils, parish and citizens' associations, which had been established on Funen after 1970 on a 'negative foundation' and as 'demonstrations of protest' against the new, large-scale municipalities.

The associational networks the former chairman refers to, consisted mainly of young, well-educated newcomers from the cities. Here, the terminology gradually acquired a special ideological character. Primarily, this was due to the energetic efforts of the Confederation, which through its journal *Landsbyen* ('The Village'), and from 1990 its sister journal *Landsbynyt* ('Village News'), had exercised a significant influence on the rural dwellers' conceptual universe.

In the first issue of *Landsbyen*, in February 1977, the two objectives of the new association are revealed in its statutes: 'to support the work being done to re-establish, preserve and further develop the village communities and the environment and culture they represent', and 'to support the efforts to provide the citizens with local influence, local co-responsibility and local possibilities of co-operation' (*Lb* 1977, no. 1: 2, own translation). In other words, the LAL sought to promote local participation, which by far the greater part of the rural dwellers – newcomers as well as 'natives' – felt they had lost in the period from 1960 to the years following the 1970 reform in municipal administration, which reduced the number of self-administering municipalities from 1300 to 273 (see Mogensen et al. 1979: 255).

LAL's means of promoting local influence was to pursue what was called 'natural development' in the villages, that is, the idea of neither too much nor too little development, but rather a harmonious well-balanced development (see, for example, *Lb* 1977, no. 2: 10).

These basic themes were already highlighted in the very first sentences of the new journal *Landsbyen*:

> What does a resident in a village do when development has stagnated, where the school is to be closed down and when the parish becomes too small to support a priest, where the tradespeople are forced to close one by one and associational life stagnates and dies out? Or a village where development proceeds much too quickly and threatens to drown the original environment, where the municipal administration imposes their plans on the local inhabitants and does not consider that a life in a suburb with over 3000 inhabitants is perhaps not exactly what the residents had dreamed about? (*Lb* 1977, no. 1: 1, our translation)

This idea entailed a break with the modern-productionalist worldview, which had characterized an agrarian-dominated population in the 1950s and 1960s. There was now an open reaction against the idea that no one can fight 'structural changes' or 'the development', partly via expressions such as 'putting on the brakes' and 'changing the direction of the development'. However, the new rural inhabitants operated within the same evolutionary mindset, which achieved popularity after the Second World War within the agriculturalist 'structural development' discourse.

6.3.2.   The Entrepreneurs Behind the New Network

Who were the leading forces behind this identity-related, conceptual re-orientation out in the rural districts, and what did they want?

These new networks of passionate entrepreneurs in the villages consisted primarily of recent arrivals and returnees, especially the younger and middle-aged people who had lived for many years in the towns, where they had acquired an education. They had now become employed in the rural areas, mostly in the public sector and service professions.

Most prominent among these entrepreneurs – or 'activists' in the strictly literal meaning of the word – were those from teacher training colleges. Carsten Abild, the chairman of LAL's first board from 1977, was a 35-year-old teacher in the village of Bredstrup. He grew up in Bredstrup and after many years moved back to the village in 1975. Similarly, LAL's vice-chairman Ole Glahn, a 30-year-old instructor at a teacher training college, had returned to his natal village of Viskinge in 1974. The other board members also primarily consisted of relatively well-educated returnees. These people's mission was to change the situation in the rural areas by spreading information and experiences about life in the villages so as to mobilize the rural population. As such, it was nothing less than a 'popular movement' with roots far back in 'the traditional peasant culture', a 'local society movement'. This view is also reflected in the subtitle of the journal *Landsbyen: Tidsskrift for Landsbysamfundsbevægelsen* (The Village: Journal of the Village Society Movement).

Such a peasant or village culture, it was said, had its roots in agrarian history: in the old feudal village community up to about 1800 and especially in the village life during the classic era of the rural co-operative movement in the late 1800s.

The statements from LAL's chairman and vice-chairman nevertheless bear witness to the fact that the board members did not all agree that the popular movement should predominantly be a more political interest-group movement, or whether it should simply disseminate information about culture and living conditions in the villages. This situation is also reflected in the above-mentioned statement of the association's objectives.

Chairman Carsten Abild seems from the start to have represented LAL's moderate wing, which preferred co-operation and dialogue with local authorities, that is, a voluntary principle. In contrast, vice-chairman Ole Glahn represented a more aggressive, revolutionary faction, which sought to exert political pressure on public authorities, that is, a more extortionary principle.[2] As will be explained, the two factions came to represent, respectively, a rural cultural–historical wave (the Abild faction) and a 'red–green' wave (the Glahn faction).

Although there was not always agreement about the means to be utilized towards the outside, there was agreement regarding the main goal, namely, in the style of the Norwegian, populistic village movement, led by sociologist Ottar Brox, to preserve and to further develop the village communities (see, for example, *Lb* 1977, no. 10/11: 17). Similarly, there was agreement on the means to be used internally, within the individual villages. Here a mobilization of the village inhabitants would take place in the form of an effective information campaign based on an ambitious journal and the issuing of publications by its own publishing house, *Landsbyens Forlag* (The Village Publishing House).

Most importantly, however, the LAL entrepreneurs seem to have been in agreement about utilizing the same concepts within a cohesive terminology, which could disseminate the new messages. In contrast to the native rural inhabitants, these largely newcomers and returnees had made a conscious choice to move back to the countryside. For example, board member Ann-Dorte Rørby, who moved to the village of Jelling, commented that her migration to the countryside was 'exclusively with the goal of living in a village society' (*Lb* 1977, no. 1: 10). Yet now all these ex-urbanites had

become impatient about realizing their dreams of the natural life in the
countryside.

6.4.   THE DREAM OF AN ACTIVE NATURAL VILLAGE SOCIETY

It would seem that the very words – and here not least the more or less
abstract concepts, which dominate the public debate – have a great
significance for the extent to which different groups succeed in appropriating
political power. In other words, a group's aspirations for appropriating power
seem to be contingent upon the ability of its members to legitimate concepts
and arguments in the public debate.

As is clearly evidenced by the Danish case, the success of rural groups in
obtaining political power – and, hence, of acquiring both material as well as
non-material forms of capital – thus appears to derive from and be created by
the verbalization of these interests within unique dynamic, social processes in
time and space. In this way, it is through a struggle about words in the public
space that groups are able to promote and legitimate their own identity and
thereby, in a broad sense, serve their own interests. However, as we know
from previous case studies in this chapter, this often entails confrontation
strategies, symbolic violence and distrust between groups, ultimately leading
to bonding types of social capital.

6.4.1.   The LAL Terminology

The new dominant concepts as they appear in *Landsbyen* from 1977, can on
first sight seem overwhelming. The articles reveal a large vocabulary of
abstract and relatively heavy ideological concepts as well as a high frequency
of repetition of the individual concepts. A typical example is an eight-page
article from April 1977 about development in the village of Heltborg (*Lb*
1977, no. 3: 5–13). Here the word 'development' appears 14 times,
'community' 13 times, 'environment' 9 times, and 'active' 6 times. In
addition, we encounter value-loaded concepts such as 'technocrat', 'local
democracy', 'inequality', 'local community', and so on.

Beyond expressing a concrete strategy of actions to serve the rural
population, these concepts articulate some of the basic, more implicit values
behind the so-called 'village society movement', namely, the view of people
as social and equal beings who thrive best in small accessible village
communities. This view was reiterated by Carsten Abild in the inaugural issue
of *Landsbyen* in February 1977:

I see the creation of the National Confederation as a form of popular movement, which builds upon a knowledge that we are not satisfied just by living a materialistic way of life for ourselves. Instead, we should focus more on togetherness with others and creating satisfactorily intelligible societies where the individual can thrive. (*Lb* 1977, no. 1: 3, our translation)

This view was fully shared by vice-chairman Ole Glahn, who formulated this universal truth in even sharper terms: 'By a conscious change of the objective for social development, I believe that we can create a more humane existence. And this is connected to the idea that I view man as a social being who feels happiest in togetherness with other people' (ibid., our translation).

The idea of a 'natural society' in the village clearly took its point of departure from an opposing view of an unnatural and unhealthy life in the towns. Thus, city life was implicitly viewed as a negation of village life: urban life as a never-ending and egotistical pursuit of material goods, in contrast to the 'sustainable' village society, which rested on values such as 'independence', 'solidarity', 'local democracy', 'self-sufficiency', 'ecology', 'non-material values', and so on.

LAL came to operate with two classical concepts of culture: a pessimistic one based on an idea of evolution as involution or degeneration, and an optimistic idea of culture based upon evolution as a movement towards humanity's redemption, that is, the Christian idea of paradise. On the one hand, we find the unclean, infected culture of the towns, a culture alien to nature and therefore alienating; on the other hand, there is the 'rich cultural life' in the villages, that is, the pure, uncontaminated life, which links itself so close to nature that culture seems to meld with nature.

When new terms such as 'village environments' (contrasting with the 'concrete environments' of the big cities) were incorporated into LAL's rhetoric, it was therefore a view of the pure pristine, rural culture existing side by side and in harmony with nature (though paradoxically enough, even the concept of 'environment' had apparently been taken from the urban sociologists' studies of suburban life). Hence, in comparing life in the villages with that of the big cities, we read that:

The children and the youth in the villages are most often characterized by their rapid incorporation into the community. This means that the children learn to get on with one another and also that they find for themselves an active and meaningful place. In many villages, there also exists a rich cultural life marked by the community hall and the school, and by the close contact they have with one another. Furthermore, the villages are characterized by their close proximity in relation to nature, which *also* means that agriculture is the most significant occupation ... A large portion of the children and youth in the big cities are affected by concrete environments and 'TV culture' (a culture marked by passivity and lack of community). This makes violence and vandalism become a part of the harsh everyday life in the big city. Furthermore, the towns are marked by pollution and dangerous, unbearable traffic. (*Lb* 1977, no. 1: 5, our translation)

6.4.2.   The Active Village Society

Compared to the 1960s, the ideas of new village societies as they took form in the latter part of the 1970s distinguish themselves with their high ideals about equality, naturalness, sustainability and non-materialist cultural values.

The introduction of these concepts set the new movement apart from the agriculturalist discourse that had dominated totally until about 1970. After the Second World War, the farmers had adopted a productivist terminology from abroad, based on key concepts such as development, structural changes, rationalization, centralization and vertical integration. Moreover, since the late nineteenth century, the farmers' worldview had been strongly influenced by a major rural, agriculturalist movement, the Danish co-operative movement, consisting of a large number of consumer co-operatives, co-operative dairies, slaughterhouses, grain and fodder associations, and so on (see Chapters 3 and 4).

The 'natural, active society', which LAL promoted, should primarily arise from below, from the grassroots. As distinct from the 1960s, here it was a case of a 'local struggle' against the influence exerted by non-local representatives in the form of politicians and various experts, encapsulated in the concepts of the 'centralists', the 'bigwigs' or the 'armchair philosophers'.

Such expressions reveal the very generalized feeling of powerlessness among those living in the countryside, a feeling that their parish-based, rural self-government had gradually withered away since the end of the 1950s, culminating in the 1970 reform of municipal administration. First it was 'our' schools which disappeared, then 'our' dairies, shops and so on, and finally, the municipal administration office – a closure of village institutions that is still going on today, especially in the more marginal rural areas. This feeling of powerlessness was virtually ignored in the 1960s' debates about rural life, especially within the co-operative movement. Seen in this light, the village society movement established during the 1970s has been a logical counter-reaction. Yet the struggle against the non-local politicians and experts also reflects an attempt to spread a new moralistic message among the inhabitants of the rural areas, that is, new times – new moralisms.

As was the case prior to the First World War and in the 1960s, efforts were made to disseminate this message via several internally connected slogans, which on first sight appeared simple and easily understood, but which on closer inspection show themselves to be extremely diffuse: abstractions constructed on the basis of the concrete interests of a specific group. In the main organ for the dissemination of these slogans, *Landsbyen*, the text was supported by illustrations of a propagandistic type – just as in the 1960s, when centralization and rationalization campaigns were conducted in the journal of the co-operative farmers' movement, *Andelsbladet*, then promoting a new modernistic, agriculturalist worldview.

A terminology of the 1960s centred around the key concept 'structural changes' was supplemented with – and partly replaced by – a new legitimate worldview among the rural dwellers. Instead of the 'laws of development' and the neutral testimony of statistics – the 'speech of the numbers' (*tallenes tale*) – discussed by the agricultural experts and leaders during the 1960s, an urban-inspired discourse now prevailed, centred around 'the natural, active village society'.

It thus became natural to be active and unnatural to be passive. Although the LAL members generally distanced themselves from the experts, they nevertheless used experts who were sympathetic to LAL to support their arguments, a contradiction they clearly acknowledged in the first issue of *Landsbyen*. Apparently because most LAL members were themselves educated in the cities, they were clearly very conscious of the increased impact, which expert assistance could bring to the association in the struggle against the centralists, in particular the administrative authorities.

How could the experts provide support for all the arguments about the natural, active village society? And how could they sanction a view of part of the rural population as 'passive' or 'against nature'?

They could do so primarily by employing Marxist-inspired scientific terminology to support the predominant red–green wave, which lay at the roots of the LAL movement as it took form in the late 1970s. This ideological linking of ecology and socialism (or more precisely, egalitarianism) was attractive especially to the newcomers and returnees, who through their education in the towns had been trained to understand and utilize such an urban-style rhetoric.

It was not only the insiders who helped develop the red–green rhetoric within the Confederation. Outsiders such as the architect Poul Bjerre and novelist and former history student Ebbe Kløvedal Reich also helped to expand LAL's conceptual universe. Bjerre believed that LAL's 'main problem' was their inability – in contrast to the Marxist theoreticians – to distinguish and choose between 'real politics' and 'idea politics' and, in line with this, between a 'system adaptive' and a 'system transcending' line (*Lb* 1977, no. 10/11: 12). Bjerre writes:

> A worldwide politics of ideas is at the disposal of LAL. It is a case of a beginning world movement [the village movement] with system-transcending character. Will LAL join it? Or is it more profitable to harvest the short-term benefits of being realistically system-adapted? (*Lb* 1977, no. 10/11: 13, our translation)

Bjerre opted for an activist line on the basis of the theory rather than the adaptive strategy based on pragmatism and co-operation. In similar terms, other socialist academics argued that for 'our health', 'late capitalism' must necessarily yield to 'the collective unity', that is, the local village society (*Lb* 1977, no. 8: 3). In March 1978, sociologist Jon Sundbo sought to disseminate the same message by analysing 'the contradiction between the local community and the capitalist form of society' (*Lb* 1978, no. 2: 10, our translation).

Such concepts were largely imported from an international vocabulary, which was especially predominant in Western Europe at that time, not least in the Nordic university environments within the social sciences. However, the very idea of local community as a delimited, homogeneous unity, was a continuation of the ideas which had predominated in the Anglo-Saxon community research tradition of the 1920s and 1930s.

Endogenously, within the Danish rural population, passages from *Landsbyen* reveal the influence exerted by the red–green experts on the native rural population. Hence, a most trustworthy man from among the older generation of indigenous village inhabitants in the small village of Bjernede sought to use and to partly reformulate the new terminology. This man was smallholder Carl Wiese, who, attending the congress of consumers' co-operatives in 1965, had criticized the idea of dissolving the local associations and taking away the sense of responsibility from 'us little people out here in the countryside' (*Ab* 1965: 1501). In an article entitled 'We must change our attitude about life' (*Lb* 1977, no. 10/11: 9–10, our translation), Wiese lamented the demise of economic co-operation in the countryside, calling for 'new forms of community'. 'The collective way of life', declared the 70-year-old Wiese, who for more than 40 years had cultivated his tiny piece of land but was now embracing local history and local politics, 'is nothing new. My parents also talked about it, but if it is to function as a working community, the workplaces must be moved out here, where the labour force is'. The former chairman of the home handicrafts association and consumers' co-operative in Bjernede argued that the villagers' future depended on 'us changing our attitude, abandoning egotism and finding another measure of value for life than money'.

The expert statements were most clearly integrated into the rhetoric of the more radical Glahn faction. Here, one could observe the most wide-ranging desires for a 'dynamic and active village society' (*Lb* 1977, no. 10/11: 20). What until then could be called the 'active citizen paradigm' within LAL and related organizations, had begun to take form.

In the 1960s, local activists in the associations struggling against organizational centralism had often been condemned as harmful reactionaries (*bagstræbere*). From the mid- to late 1970s, the situation reversed itself: those who were neither active in associations nor local patriots risked being viewed as harmful reactionaries by the more 'progressive' LAL-inspired activists in the rural districts, the latter consisting primarily of red–green and/or traditionally-oriented newcomers and returnees, who often for many years had resided in the towns and cities.

The leading activists in the villages – the new guarantors of progress so to speak – therefore became those who, from within the residents' and citizens' associations, came forward to do battle with the external enemy, that is, the centrally oriented politicians and officials outside the local communities, whose almost absolutist domination, according to Carsten Abild, had been caused by several unfortunate factors such as the 'municipal reform, materialism, television isolation, subordination to experts and technocrats, politicians' misunderstood views of being master and not servant' and so on (*Lb* 1977, no. 3: 3). The new village heroes were those who actively participated in the village work and leisure communities.

Opposed to the village activists stood the new reactionaries, that is, the villagers who isolated themselves from the community; those who simply remained passive and resigned towards a development that no one could resist anyway. Thus, Glahn stated in 1978:

> The time has passed where each one can be content with his own affairs and soothe his underlying social needs by material acquisitions. The era of the car and the television as compensation for our emotional needs is coming to an end. We do not thrive on it, and it is too costly for society. We must therefore use our time in another, more sensible way, by being together with our fellow residents on projects for the common benefit. The flourishing of the citizens' associations, residents' associations, environmental groups, etc., are a precise expression that the human need for social togetherness centered around work and leisure cannot be suppressed. As an organization we must support this. (*Lb* 1978, no. 4: 8–9, our translation)

6.4.3.   Cultural and Physical Urbanization

The consequences of the ideological and conceptual urbanization of the rural districts, of which LAL has been the exponent, can be best summarized as a major change in cultural identity, a process conditioned by various internal and external factors, which takes place even today, and which has a real influence on the behavioural patterns of the rural populations.

In the era following the municipal reform, a rural identity thus seems to have gradually taken form under the terms set by the newcomers and returnees. Even the word 'local' took on a new significance after 1970, and the term 'local community' quickly became an emotional concept used both in political argumentation as well as in social science research (Korsgaard 1997: 431).

This change in identity was accompanied by a change in the patterns of co-operation. In *quantitative* terms, the change was reflected in the increasing number of associations dominated by the newcomers and returnees. On one hand there were more associations with an interest-group character, such as residents' and citizens' associations, parish associations, urban guilds, parish guilds, citizen guilds, village guilds, local councils, homeowner associations, various environmental associations, groups promoting 'general well-being' (*trivselsgrupper*) and so on. On the other hand, there emerged within cultural life various newcomer-dominated amateur theatre clubs, youth clubs, athletic associations and so on.

The change was also reflected in the *quality* of the associational activities, that is, in the new unique character of co-operative relations, a character distinctly marked by life in the towns, and the urban dwellers' dreams of a good life in the countryside.

The changes in identity and in patterns of co-operation have again had an influence on rural settlement patterns, which is partly reflected in the emergence of new community buildings such as culture centres, community halls and multi-function activity halls, and in new residential forms in the countryside such as subdivisions of single-family homes, hobby farming and low-income public housing projects.

This not yet completed process of change in rural dwellers' identity, rural practice and settlement can be viewed as both a cultural and physical (settlement-related) urbanization. If one chooses to view the process on the basis of the conceptual universe of the newcomers, however, a more precise label would be 'urban ruralizations', that is, the phenomenon whereby urban dwellers settle in the villages in order to legitimate and later fulfil their own views of the authentic country life, in idea and in practice, as well as purely physically, in the settlement.

However, the new 'localist' (*hjemstavn*) movement in the late twentieth century is characterized by its attraction to all groups. Hence, innumerable local museums and local historical associations have popped up in recent years, often with the support of both urban newcomers and native-born villagers. In contrast, it seems to be primarily the newcomers and returnees who have endowed the word 'development' with a new content. They insist on what has often been called the 'right to development', understood as the right to receive public funds in order to preserve and further the development of a village culture, which, without being assured of such natural development, runs the risk of dying out.

In this way, the change in cultural identity also entails a shift from *duty* to *right*, that is, a transition from a (pre-modernist) agriculturalist feeling of obligation to feed the rest of the population before Second World War to a now prevailing demand to *be* provided for. In this sphere as well, LAL contributed with more or less scientifically inspired terminology and arguments.

6.4.4.   Dying Cultures

It was especially the two words 'culture' and 'development', which in the 1970s came to be interwoven key terms in the LAL members' attempts to reconstruct – or in their own understanding: to create, protect and preserve – an identity as a rural dweller.

As for the concept of culture, there was a tendency to idealize a presumed traditional, rural culture based on collective values, in contrast to a decadent urban culture based on individualism and egotism. It was a case of a desire to 'preserve' or 'protect' village culture against the harmful effects of urban culture. In this connection, there was talk of the danger of the 'dissolution of village culture' of 'the community going up in smoke', of the necessity to 'protect the local community' and to 'save the traditional peasant culture'. Or as board member Niels Winther Petersen commented in October 1977: 'the unilateral emphasis on material goods [constitutes a danger for] independent, small, locally democratic communities [built upon] the cultural cornerstones, school, church, community hall, and a rich associational life and small artisan firms' (*Lb* 1977, no. 9: 14, our translation). Associations appeared whose only goal was to maintain the old village culture, for example, the Association for the Revitalization of Village Culture in Vesthimmerland (*Foreningen til levendegørelsen af landsbykulturen i Vesthimmerland*). Similarly, in some cases there was mobilization for the 'protection' or 'defence' of the villages' core institutions, such as occurred in February 1976 in the parish of Nørre Nærå-Bederslev. This defence took the form of a 'group for well-being' (*trivselsgruppe*). One of the group's founders, future LAL chairman Carsten Abild, explains:

> A year ago, when the residents in Nørre Nærå-Bederslev parish decided to stand together, it was indeed an entirely spontaneous and genuine expression of defence. A defence with the goal of saving the parish's priesthood, the school, associational life, the remaining three local shops, building locales for youth as well as the elderly – for residents as well as newcomers – the pride of the parish, the seven village ponds, the artisans, unity in the parish, traditions and values – in short, the future of Nørre Nærå-Bederslev. It is a defence of an environment – of a way of life and a culture, the Danish peasant culture. (*Lb* 1977, no. 1: 3, our translation)

Taking Abild's statement at face value, it should be expected that, in such crisis situations, a rapid and effective mobilization with broad support from all segments of the local population would take place. Thus, Abild concludes:

The situation in Nørre Nærå-Bederslev is not much different from the situation in other villages across the country. In some places they have grappled with the issue, as we have – in other places they tackle the issue differently. In some places they have given up, in other places nothing has yet been done. In some places much can still be saved. In no place is it yet too late. (ibid., our translation)

The notion that cultures can fall apart exists within social anthropology, where studies of non-European peoples may speak of threatened or dying cultures. From the 1970s, action was taken in many Danish rural districts to keep alive a dying culture, even resurrecting the dead cultures, precisely as anthropologists have endeavoured to keep alive dying non-European peoples or at least their culture's legacy.

6.4.5.   Natural Development

The result was that the 1960s' evolutionary terminology within the co-operative movement was retained, though in modified form. Rather than a global developmental race towards higher living standards, the word 'development' was now viewed as an effort to reach a higher degree of human happiness, which – as we have seen – could best be achieved via the communalism of the small society. Several of the new leading village inhabitants desired or even demanded 'well-being' and 'life quality' via human togetherness and an 'ecologically correct co-operation with nature', to use Glahn's terminology (for example, *Lb* 1978, no. 4: 13). He described 'natural development' as follows:

> In general, I could imagine that development would proceed so that people who especially want to be in step with others, for example, in agriculture or in connection with the exploitation of alternative energy, join together in villages, partly because the people who value community and solidarity higher than their own interests in their walled-off neighbourhoods [*ligusterkvarterer*] would tend to move to the villages. Here the legislation must not place itself as an obstacle to new forms of ownership in agriculture or new forms of land allocation, etc. On the contrary, it is one of LAL's tasks to ensure legislation, which supports such a development. (*Lb* 1978, no. 4: 8, our translation)

However, 'development' did not lose its meaning as progress in material living standards. Hence, the Abild article about Heltborg describes how a stagnating population and a rapidly declining number of school pupils had led to 'an acute need for development' (*Lb* 1977, no. 3: 1). In this connection, it was argued that the municipality should allow the selling off of new lots for single-family homes, such that the town could maintain its population and thus ensure its various services. Just as in the 1960s, the time factor was utilized in the argumentation. The development clock was ticking, and it was necessary to act before it was too late: 'Not everyone in Heltborg agrees that such a new housing area is the best solution to the village's problems. But on the other hand, it is primarily time that matters. Something has to happen in Heltborg, and it has to happen soon' (ibid., our translation).

For Abild, the main idea was that one should 'preserve and further develop the active village society', summarized in the concept of 'the village environment'. It later appeared that many of the village residents in Heltborg believed that the 72 house lots were too much all at one time. They did not want underdevelopment, that is, they did not want development to 'stagnate', but on the contrary neither did they want any 'overdevelopment' in the form of too much development (for example, *Lb* 1977, no. 3: 9ff.).

It appeared that several citizens' associations were struggling with the same problems as in Heltborg. At this point, the notion of 'natural development' was introduced into LAL's terminology – a somewhat diffuse concept, the function of which was to communicate the desire to simultaneously protect and further develop. Stand still, but keep moving. Look back to cultural roots, but nevertheless keep up with modern progress. Accordingly, in dealing with local authorities, LAL inspired, 'ruralized' villagers began to suggest 'natural development in the villages', 'natural development of democracy', 'even and calm development', 'a degree of development', 'a reasonable development' which could ensure that '[the village] did not slowly die out as an active local village society', and so on.

The problem here was clearly that the idea of a natural development was characterized by an ideologically determined content as part of a new discourse of rurality among the village population. Judging from the many conflicts between the newcomers and the native inhabitants during the last 30 years, such natural this and that had meaning only for the former group, whereas the latter was predominantly sceptical about the rhetoric of equality and naturalness.

6.5. FARMER PROTEST VERSUS NEWCOMER PROTEST

At an entirely general level, the rationalization of economic co-operation in the rural districts in the 1960s seemed to have led to greater dependence on people outside the rural district communities, in both economic and cultural terms.

Culturally, it was already the case that the waves of new residents and returnees, who began to settle in the more or less depopulated villages in the late 1960s, stimulated an urbanization process. This identity-oriented urbanization, or cultural urbanization, derived from the spread of an urban-style worldview regarding the good life in the countryside.

As we have seen, there was an effort to actualize this worldview – the dream of the active rural village society – via certain moral imperatives, which were viewed as 'natural' (nature, apparently, being valued more in recent years than it ever has been in history, at least discursively). These imperatives can be classed in terms of three specially unique and nevertheless internally connected concepts: an active citizen concept which touched upon the internal relations in the village (everyone ought to be active); an egalitarianism concept, which also affected the internal relations (everyone ought to be equal); and several concepts which could be summarized by what could be called a 'victimization syndrome', and which concerned the external relations (the locals are being repressed by non-local centralists).

Such a new rural dweller identity was – and *is* – formulated and promoted within and outside the villages by the new network of local activists, typically organized in citizens' associations, residents' associations, unofficial village councils, various networks of EU fundraisers and so on. During the last 25 years, nationwide organizations such as LAL, *Landsbyer i Danmark* (Villages in Denmark), *Landdistrikternes Fællesråd* (Joint Council of Rural Districts) and the *Folkeligt Institut for Udkantsforhold* (Popular Institute for Conditions in Marginal Areas) have contributed to coordinating and organizing these local efforts.

For example, in the village of Hellested on Zealand, new ex-urbanite residents have established a citizens' association and are trying to revolutionize the community by introducing new rural concepts, centred around words like 'green', 'active', 'shared' and the slogan that summarizes this worldview – 'a whole and active life in a whole and active local community' – as well as introducing new rural strategies, such as workshops, the establishment of green areas in the village centre, the preservation of cultural historic places and monuments, the arrangement of a multitude of social events 'for *all* inhabitants', and so on. However, in more than one instance, such urban terminology and practice have involved serious conflicts with the native population – in Hellested as well as in many other villages.

Moreover, as we shall discuss in Chapter 7, our current fieldwork on new rural groups in Denmark traces how this cultural urbanization process reveals itself in practice. In this study from the marginal rural area of Lolland, dramatic confrontations between ex-urbanites and natives have occurred. Here, quite another urban group consisting of poor uneducated, young families living on social security and attracted by cheap housing, that is, a kind of new rural proletariat, is increasingly being isolated and stigmatized by the native rural dwellers, who describe the urbanites' behaviour as 'chaotic' and 'abnormal', their speech as 'unintelligible' and their mentality as 'quarrelsome' and 'restless' and 'not like us at all'. At the same time, native politicians and public servants are using urban expressions, often inspired by

LAL and similar organizations, such as 'village environment' and 'active participation', although cleansed of Glahn–Marxist undertones.

As such, *all* contemporary Danish, rural identities can be seen as embedded in – or, at least, influenced by – urban terminology and practice. Furthermore, this process can be traced historically. Thus, several of these cultural urbanization tendencies can be traced back to agrarian protest movements where, as a supplement to the traditional core expressions, we find the use of terms such as 'struggle', 'equality', 'necessity to stand together' and 'solidarity'.

Such trade unionist expressions were pervasive in the publications issued by the well-organized agrarian protest movement of the 1930s known as *Landbrugernes Sammenslutning* (Farmers' Confederation, or LS). At its height in mid-1932, this rather aggressive interest organization had around 100,000 members, comprising about one-sixth of all Danish farmers (Brogaard 1965: 18). The trade union aspects were also prominent in LS's successor organization, the previously mentioned *Landbrugernes Fællesorganisation* (Joint Organization of Farmers, or LFO), whose publication, *Landbosamvirke* (Rural Co-operation) appearing from 1966, was a means of exerting political pressure and promoting narrow business economic interests.

What was the *content* of this cultural urbanization, of which LAL was an exponent? Examining, within a comparative perspective, issues of the LFO journal *Landbosamvirke* from the mid- to late 1960s, it is possible to find some kind of answer.

First, it is interesting to observe how the 'victimization syndrome' pervaded both *Landsbyen* in the years 1977–78 as well as *Landbosamvirke* during the years 1967–68. Hence, it is characteristic of both LFO and LAL a decade later that they felt themselves to be victims of an injustice imposed upon them by the outside society. Society had been guilty of 'neglect'. Furthermore, people in both groups felt that one reason they had been neglected was that they had been too trusting, too compliant with the rest of society. Hence, both forms of argumentation contain a more or less understated thesis that the country-dweller had been fooled by the city-dweller, and that it was time to remove the blinkers as quickly as possible and demand one's rights. 'We demand compensation', was thus the persistent slogan within the LFO. Hence, a February 1967 editorial entitled 'The situation is becoming acute!' raises the threat of a farmers' production strike:

> With regard to agriculture, we are again witnessing how other occupational groups with their ultimatum-type demands seek to arrange the economic social structure of the future without taking into consideration the conditions, which have dominated in the country's largest net foreign exchange generating occupation, agriculture. This occupation enters the picture much later, when people are busy

speaking of the necessity to exhibit public spiritedness . . . Time after time, [agriculture] has shown itself willing to show public spiritedness, and it has been very costly for the occupation, both in money, loss of agricultural workers, and in the form of increased labour input. (*Ls* 1967: 23, our translation)

Among both the LFO farmers and the LAL urban-cum-village activists, the demand for compensation (that is, money) was accompanied by considerable impatience. Both groups felt that they had been tolerant for too long, and that it was *getting too late* (the clock of 'the development' was ticking, and 'the development' was *not* going in the right direction!). In this connection, both groups viewed themselves as pioneers in a popular movement and, hence, as representatives of a new and better era. At an October 1968 LFO meeting in Denmark's second largest city, Aarhus, vice-chairman Alfred Larsen, himself a farmer, declared:

Now the signals must be changed. If the old men [the leaders of the agricultural organizations] will do it, then good. But if they won't, then a new man must stand on the farmer's croft, someone who dares to look forward and put in the work for the organization of agriculture, which will be needed by those who remain . . . Today's meeting . . . should portend a new era where farmers are no more to be considered, as before, a pariah caste. Danish agriculture can certainly be worthy of its history. (*Ls* 1968: 215, our translation)

Moreover, it is characteristic that both the LAL and LFO activists felt that the struggle was uneven, claiming that experts were to be found in the enemy camp.[3] As a counterweight to these false campaigns, one must therefore conduct effective counter campaigns. In both organizations, then, there was an effort to legitimate their words and their messages in the public debate.

So we understand why participants in the October 1968 LFO meeting became so bitter over the lack of media coverage. In the words of a report of the meeting in *Landbosamvirke*, one could 'justifiably fail to understand why they would not broadcast a meeting where up to a thousand farmers were assembled, when they are always on the spot if just half a dozen long-haired and long-bearded left-wingers are running together on a street corner in Copenhagen' (*Ls* 1968: 207, our translation).

Though there were clear similarities between the peasant protest movements of the 1960s and the newcomers' protests of the 1970s, there are nevertheless also decisive differences. The phrase 'the country's largest net foreign exchange generating occupation', cited above, seems most clearly to reflect the fundamental difference in the self-understanding of the two groups.

Whereas the newcomer-dominated interest organizations since LAL have demanded economic compensation on the basis of a moralistic–ethical argument (maintenance of countryside values), LFO concentrated almost exclusively on the economic–physiocratic argument. The other social groups should not 'fight over milking the Danish farmers', simply because they could not afford it (*Ls* 1967: 116). It was socio-economically demonstrable that the entire society 'needed' agriculture, such that farmers were and became society's most important providers or – as it was often expressed – 'pillars of society' (*Ls* 1967: 193, 167).

It was thus the simple urge for survival that prompted farmers in LS and subsequently in LFO to be inspired by the workers' movements of the cities, or as a member of LS's organizational committee, farmer A. Hartel (1934: 22), commented in 1934: 'to follow the same occupational path, which had advanced the workers' estate'. However, Hartel added remarks about a 'change in mentality . . . Only reluctantly will the liberally raised and thinking peasant acquire those obligations, which follow from membership in a trade union: solidarity, discipline and economic sacrifice'.

Thus the farmers, steeped in their own self-understanding, continued on the path of *duty* (not at all adopting the 'craving mentality' belonging to the urban population!). They were still in possession of a traditional rural identity, they were 'uncontaminated' by urban culture. They continued, as it was often expressed, to 'exhibit public spiritedness', though this willingness to sacrifice was grossly exploited by the rest of society, led by the industrial occupations and the growing group of functionaries in what was seen during the mid- to late 1960s as 'the dance around the golden calf' (*Ls* 1967: 163). Nor could one find any understanding on the part of the politicians. Thus, the LFO activists and several other farmers believed that they could be made 'scapegoats' for an overheated economy, which was caused by the other social groups' dance around the golden calf and *not* by the massive state subsidies given to Danish farmers (*Ls* 1967: 47).

That the farmers did not want to be lumped together with socially revolutionary, left-wing urban protesters, is also indicated in the minutes of the meeting held in Aarhus in October 1968. Significantly enough, this struggle over words at the meeting was followed by a protest march to a television studio in Aarhus, where an appeal was delivered to the media protesting about the lack of coverage by journalists and the farmers' subsequent bitterness about being 'silenced' (*Ls* 1968: 203).

In *Landbosamvirke*, the report of the meeting repeatedly mentions that 'everything took place in an atmosphere of calm and dignity', that 'the traffic regulations were respected' and that the farmers walked 'two by two' in perfect order, and so on (ibid., our translation). At this point, however, the LFO people were surrounded by (negatively-oriented) journalists, which in *Landbosamvirke* was found to be 'significant indeed':

[Now] when there was a bit of sensation in the air, the press showed up. The cameras flashed and the pens gave off sparks. Obviously sensation is needed in present-day society. We have to learn more from this if we want to be heard. We are simply much too nice people. (Ibid., our translation)

6.6.   WHAT SPEAKING MEANS: THE DISCOURSIVE ELEMENT

Thus, as we have just seen, the protesting farmers of the 1960s sincerely believed that on the basis of an *economic* argument about agriculture as 'the most important net foreign exchange earning occupation', they had a right to compensation. Such an argument is still popular today.[4]

The rationalization of local workplaces (and thereby also the social meeting places), however, meant that the non-agriculturalists among the rural population developed a potential legitimating problem with the Danish state, which since the early 1960s had increasingly transferred subsidies to the rural communities in the form of price supports for agricultural production, regional development subsidies and similar programmes directed towards what could be rightly called Denmark's 'domestically underdeveloped population', that is, those living in the countryside (Svendsen 2003a).

Since the 1960s, the rural population seems not to have been able to manage on their own, especially in pure economic terms. This general lack of economic sustainability has meant that the argument about the rural population as indispensable breadwinners and – as derived from this – important 'cultural bearers' has gradually lost its importance.

What other arguments can the rural dwellers marshal to continue to obtain a part of the welfare resources from the Danish state and from the EU? A newcomer-dominated and interest-group association such as LAL had already found a solution to the problem in the 1970s: the rural dwellers should systematically and continually conduct a symbolic struggle in the public debate. By utilizing slogans as weapons, they could legitimate a new rural dweller identity, which they could ultimately capitalize upon. The result is a new message: society (including the EU) has a moral duty to provide for the rural populations. This is the direct opposite of what had formerly been the predominant view among the protesting farmer-dominated population in the rural areas who were, themselves, providing for the rest of society.

In contrast to the era before 1970, the locally based, economic self-organization in the countryside has been definitively abandoned. Now words like 'natural', 'environment', 'equality', 'local democracy', 'cultural values', 'active village society' and 'well-being' play a central role in the new, powerful networks in the rural areas. This parallels the importance of 'structural changes', 'vertical integration' and 'rationalization' for the farmers of the 1960s. It thus seems primarily to be the very rhetoric, the concepts, which must act to release funds from the various public support schemes doled out by the surrounding society and thereby bring the rural population closer to their objective: *the right to development.*

Did this morally based, symbolic struggle have any effect on the political decision-making processes after 1970? Judging from the steadily increasing millions of DDK in Danish state funds released for regional development from 1970 to 1980, the campaign appears to have been successful. An even more concrete outcome of pressure from LAL and kindred organizations is the establishment of the so-called Rural District Foundation (*Landdistriktspuljen*) in 1994 – a permanent foundation that, according to the homepage of the Ministry of the Interior, was aimed at 'improv[ing] the possibilities of development in the rural areas', and which was allocated DKK 22 million in 2001.

Even more important, however, it appears that the LAL's formulations in fact slipped into the public debate and thereby had a permanent impact on the political agenda; 'the right to development' and the associated rhetoric came to be normal and natural concepts in the state production of knowledge, visible, for example, in the publications of the Danish Institute for Social Research (*Socialforskningsinstituttet*), in proposals, white papers, political agendas, and so on. This seemed to be the case, for example, with the 'active citizen' imperative, the idea of an egalitarian community and the thesis of 'natural development' (implying the 'victimization syndrome'). Another example is the Developmental Centre for Popular Enlightenment and Adult Education (*Udviklingscentret for Folkeoplysning og Voksenundervisning*), founded in 1986 with the purpose of evaluating the programme for adult education and popular enlightenment. The evaluation of the latter was published in the report *At overskride grænser* (Crossing boundaries), which according to an observer could just as well have had the title 'Back to the local community' (Korsgaard 1997: 431). Here it was concluded that the trend is 'heading back in the direction toward the community of neighbourhood and family' (ibid.). At a more general level, the new ideas were reflected in the Law on Leisure Time implemented in 1970, and which in reality was a law on subsidies for recreational activities.

However, it is important to add here that not all rural dwellers have taken the new terminology to their hearts although, obviously, they cannot possibly avoid having their own opinion on the subject. One typical example is the earlier mentioned village of Hellested in Stevns, a rural area south of Copenhagen on Zealand. Here, the board of the citizens' association – mainly consisting of newcomers from Copenhagen – apply a characteristic LAL-inspired rhetoric, whereas the indigenous people are clearly sceptical when listening to all these rather academic (although powerful, it is acknowledged!) words. Examples are the poor local participation in a workshop arranged by the citizens' association – a DKK 100,000 project funded by the *Landdistriktspulje* and hosting LAL's former vice-chairman and chairman Ole Glahn as guest speaker. Or the hostile attitude among the indigenous people against the boards' plans of allocating land to part-time smallholders in order to attract new settlers from the urban areas. At this point, the natives clearly feel that their village is being 'taken over' by invaders from the Copenhagen area. Clearly, symbolic struggles and symbolic violence have led to psychological distance between groups of newcomers and locals.

Certainly, as will also be seen in Chapter 7, such local antipathy against new formulations of rural identity and reality as we witness in Hellested, often involves conflicts between urban and agrarian-thinking groups – the former verbalizing rurality within a non-agriculturalist, the latter within a modernist–agriculturalist conceptual universe, although with clear overlaps.

So we see that, since the mid- to late 1970s, the LAL activists and their associates have increasingly challenged the farmers' way of conceiving and expressing rurality and rural life. As such, they have to a great extent succeeded in moulding the public debate in Denmark and thereby legitimating their own worldview in the public space with the possibility of harvesting the various forms of profit, which followed. Certainly, at the beginning of the new millennium, rural non-agriculturalist organizations like LAL tend to resemble more and more well-organized interest groups, the main purpose of which is to obtain state subsidies for their members – a tendency that is reflected in the LAL homepage May 2002 (LAL 2002). What did not completely succeed for the protesting farmers in the 1930s and 1960s seems to have been completely successful for the newcomers and returnees since the 1970s.

6.7.   SUMMARY

In the case of the post-war Danish co-operative movement (Chapter 5), we tried to show how powerful concepts contribute to change human thoughts and practice. In this context, we asked ourselves: what consequences follow from the absence of the term 'social capital' (or a similar word denoting a social production factor) in the public debate? Or, paraphrasing Bourdieu: what *does* speaking really mean? And what linkages do we find between discursive elements and social capital building?

Such issues were developed and discussed more thoroughly in this chapter, which sheds light on the construction of a non-agriculturalist conceptual universe during the 1970s and the subsequent conflicts between local people and newcomers that this entailed.

After the Introduction, we stressed the importance of the discoursive element for people's worldviews and practices and, thus, for social capital building. We argued for the existence of two distinct discourses of rurality in Denmark since the Second World War. These discourses have had significant influence on the identities, co-operative networks and physical reality of the rural population and, consequently, on human practice. The first one was called the agriculturalist discourse of rurality. Although still important today, its almost hegemonic power peaked during the 1960s. Based on keywords such as structural changes, structural development, vertical integration, rationalization and centralization, it mainly served to enhance production interests of farmers. However, since 1970 this agrarian terminology has been increasingly challenged by a second one: the non-agriculturalist discourse of rurality. This terminology is based on keywords such as village society, culture, active citizenship and environment, and mainly belongs to newcomers in the villages – often well-educated people, who want to promote recreational, environmental and local political interests, frequently at the expense of the farmers.

We then told the story of the so-called Danish village society movement of the 1970s. This rural red–green wave often implied severe cultural clashes between local people and urban newcomers and, hence, distance, distrust and bonding social capital – clashes that can be detected even today. First, we showed how, during the 1970s, a non-agrarian village society movement took shape, inspired by the red–green terminology prevailing at the Danish universities. More specifically, it was demonstrated how this new discourse of rurality was developed and promoted by the nationwide organization, the National Confederation of Village Communities (*Landssammenslutningen af Landsbysamfund* or LAL) that had been established in 1976. Thus, from the late 1970s, members of this organization were instrumental in creating and using a specific LAL vocabulary in their journal *Landsbyen* ('The village'). Second, it was explained how important elements of this LAL terminology were later to be disseminated among the population, and how this had real effects on rural identities and realities at the local level, as well as on rural political debates and agendas at the national level.

Finally, the LAL protest movement was compared to agrarian protest movements before 1970, and we briefly summed up the importance of the discoursive element in post-war Denmark, as being primarily linked to transformations of bridging into bonding types of social capital.

NOTES

1. We have encountered 30 of such reports and books published in the 1970s, not including a large number of publications on other rural issues, but with a similar rhetoric.
2. In presenting the very first issue of *Landsbyen*, one senses this degree of difference between the two. For example, Glahn explicitly characterizes the association as a tool for political pressure: 'Through the National Confederation we can spread our ideas and experiences and thereby alter the course of development, among other things by influencing the politicians' (Ole Glahn, cited in *Lb* 1977, no. 1: 3, our translation).
3. 'Agriculture cannot continue to be served by professors, wise men [expert advisers] and other theoreticians unilaterally asserting that the Danish social household can do without the occupation of agriculture, since the opposite is undoubtedly the case' (*Ls* 1968: 143, our translation).
4. This can be seen, for example, in a supplement in the national daily newspaper *Jyllandsposten* (5 May 2001) entitled 'Agriculture over all borders'. The supplement, written by the Danish Agriculture Council (*Landbrugsrådet*), was clearly an attempt to give Danish agriculture a better image among the population.

7. Bonding and Bridging Social Capital: A Contemporary Fieldwork Study

7.1. INTRODUCTION

In this chapter, we shall try to find out how social capital really is created and destroyed in situ, by actual living, thinking, feeling persons. By undertaking a contemporary fieldwork study, we shall learn from those who are striving to accumulate various types of social capital 'out there'. In particular, we wonder whether the notions of bridging and bonding social capital are relevant for contemporary everyday life.

Therefore, in this chapter, we shall link our theoretical and historical findings to a case of contemporary social capital building. In Denmark and in most other Western European countries, outlying municipalities have had to cope with an increasing number of newcomers on public support. Here, the clash between newcomers and the native rural population provides us with an illustrative case in the study of the formation of exclusive social networks and bonding social capital, although some bridging social capital building can also be detected.

In this context, our main purpose in this chapter is to shed light on a crucial question that until now has been neglected in the literature: what are the concrete human and economic costs stemming from excessive bonding social capital, and how could they be avoided? As our case study will show, such a question entails reflections on the erosion of bridging social capital and voluntary provision of collective goods resulting from a transition from generalized to particularized trust (Uslaner 2002), ultimately implying widespread distrust among different 'superglued' groups. This leads to the more specific and qualitatively oriented question: what are the costs of distrust, and how can growing distrust in a society be reduced?

In April 2003, one of the authors attended a council meeting in the Ravnsborg Municipality, a marginal rural area in the northwest of the island of Lolland, which is situated 150 kilometres southwest of the Danish capital of Copenhagen. Discussing the numbers of recent newcomers to the municipality, the author asked one of the municipality council members (who knew that we were doing a fieldwork study on the newcomers): 'However, are you not happy that you have newcomers *at all*?'. She replied promptly: 'Yes! But still it's a shame that we get the *wrong* newcomers!'.

This statement reflects the general scepticism among locals towards the many newcomers in Ravnsborg. The problem is that many of the newcomers come from Copenhagen and are relying on public transfer payments, thus becoming an economic burden as well. In this strict economic sense, the politician is clearly right because highly educated and better-off newcomers supporting rather than weakening the tax base are, of course, a better solution for the locals.

However, the purpose of this fieldwork study is to apply the theory of social capital and identify the possibilities for integrating the newcomers so that they can also contribute socially and economically. Here, we simply suggest that all citizens in Ravnsborg Municipality have a lot to gain from co-operation, that is, bridging social capital, and much to lose from isolating the newcomers, that is, bonding social capital. Such a case study at the micro level has general implications for a cultural clash between two different groups (that is, urban newcomers versus rural locals) by demonstrating the problems of a social capital mix where bonding social capital strongly prevails, at the expense of some bridging social capital.

First, we introduce the method of the fieldwork study within the bridging/bonding social capital framework. Then we briefly describe Ravnsborg Municipality and consider the newcomers in terms of an economic burden or a survival possibility due to depopulation. The subsequent sections analyse the social capital in the municipality by interviewing members of both the newcomer group and the local group, thus determining whether bonding and bridging social capital matters in daily life.

7.2.   SOCIAL CAPITAL AND ANTHROPOLOGICAL FIELDWORK

7.2.1.   Superglue and Lubricant

Our ethnographical survey reveals that the integration of urban newcomers has important implications for building social capital. As argued in Chapter 2, social capital is a production factor in the sense that when people voluntarily join together in groups and create cultural communities, then regular face-to-face interaction will create trust and bridging social capital in a healthy circle. Thus, the more people get to know each other in different social situations – for example when drinking coffee, chatting over a hedge, being among friends, at the workplace, in associational life, in the supermarket or the church and so on – the more 'bridges' are built between people who were formerly strangers (or even enemies).

Through this personal closeness, more trust is created in a society which, again, lubricates civic life. In this way, co-operative relations gradually become an important societal resource. The positive social capital generated by personal contacts, that is, by giving people a chance to get to know other people and thereby creating *trust* – is both a private good for the single individual (the more contacts, the better are the chances of getting a job, finding a helping hand, making social contacts and so on) and a societal good (information is spread rapidly, less intervention and monitoring from public authorities, general security, high life satisfaction and so on) (see Putnam 2000: 21).

Extensive trust in an area simply enhances the quality of life as we saw in the rural districts from the mid-nineteenth century, where the local population organized into co-operatives and the trust generated here spread to many economic, political and cultural movements (Chapters 3 and 4). A good example of bridging social capital was civic movements such as the agricultural co-operative movement. This rich civic life during the last decade of the 19th century is very similar to the 'Tocquevillean' virtues flourishing in the United States in the very same period, as recorded by Putnam (2000). Furthermore, the rise and decline of the Danish co-operative movement during the twentieth century resemble in many ways one of Putnam's main case studies in *Bowling Alone*, the American Civil Rights Movement, which culminated in the late 1960s – as noted in Chapter 2. In the original Danish, co-operative contract, *Andelskontrakten*, members committed themselves to an equal relationship – that is, balanced reciprocity – from the biggest to the smallest farmer. Furthermore, we have identified numerous examples of creating bridging social capital in rural Denmark as, for example, the building of sports halls in almost every parish (Chapter 4).

In contrast, as argued in Chapter 2, group isolation and general distrust leads to bonding social capital and exclusive networks that accentuate excluding identities and (too) homogeneous groups. This involves too much reprocity or social glue within a group – *superglue* – in contrast to more open, bridging types of social capital which function as *lubricants* in a society (ibid.: 22). So we see that networking within a group may create a social cohesion that is *too* strong and can, as such, be called superglue because it will make society less yielding. The creation of superglue – and the resulting 'drying up' of benevolent lubricants in civic life – not only has great human costs but will, eventually, also be measurable in pure economic terms.

In Chapter 5, we saw how religious and ethnic conflicts have often led to strong bonding social capital. One historical Danish example of a religious conflict is that between the Home Mission and Grundtvigianism at the end of the nineteenth century, which resulted in the forced establishment of superfluous Home Mission co-operative dairies, causing local conflicts and economic backlash (Haue 1977). Also in this context, recall the – largely generational – conflicts between traditionalistic and modernistic thinking farmers during the 1950s and 1960s, as well as the conflicts between locals and urban newcomers during the 1970s (Chapter 5). It is with these historical case studies in mind that this chapter, applying ethnographic data fresh from the field, links contemporary formation of bridging and bonding social capital in a fragmentizing marginal, rural community to the more structural aspects of social capital building, which can be deduced from our historical case studies.

7.2.2.   Fieldwork Method

Our anthropological fieldwork consists of 70 interviews undertaken in April and May 2003, for which we applied inductive, qualitative and explorative methodology (see Kvale 1996; Bernard 1998; Munck and Sobo 1998). The data from these 70 interviews are therefore loosely structured. Forty of them are taped, in-depth interviews lasting from one to three hours. Overall, newcomers and locals are equally represented and arbitrarily chosen (see Svendsen 2003b, for more details on findings and the set-up of survey).

The interviews are the result of an intense fieldwork, where one of the authors lived in the area, in a small cottage at the sea, which he borrowed from Ravnsborg municipality.

This mix of conversation and embedded questions in the forty in-depth interviews is known as 'informal' interviewing, following the definition of anthropologist David M. Fetterman:

> Informal interviews should be user friendly. In other words, they should be transparent to the participant after a short period of time. An informal interview is different from a conversation, but it typically merges with one, forming a mixture of conversation and embedded questions. The questions typically emerge from the conversation. In some cases, they are serendipitous and result from comments by the participant. In most cases, the ethnographer has a series of questions to ask the participant and will wait for the most appropriate time to ask them during the conversation (if possible) (Fetterman 1989: 49)

A crucial element in this method is to – sometimes immediately, sometimes after a long period of ('waiting' or 'waste') time – obtain a relaxed and unformal atmosphere between interviewer and interwiewee. This is done by *not* rushing but, rather, listening carefully and with concentrated patience, fully forgetting your own ego (but *all the time* thinking however, *strategically*, how to cover the subject areas in the best way by asking the right 'why', or 'what do you men by that?' at the right time, and with the right timing). In short, thinking strategically while keeping silent most of the time and, thus, *not* threatening the interviewee in any way. In our fieldwork, it is exactly this element, which more than anything else has secured the quality of the data. Fetterman comments:

> A multitude of significant nonthreatening questions can elicit the information the fieldworker seeks and create many golden moments in which to ask questions naturally, as part of the general flow of conversation. Planning and executing properly placed questions, while maintaining a flexible format, is the essence of good ethnography, ensuring the quality of the data and maintaining the participant's right to privacy. (ibid.: 50)

Such an informal technique has also been called 'unstructured' interviewing by anthropologist H. Russel Bernard and others.

> Unstructured interviews are based on a clear plan that you [the fieldworker] keep constantly in mind, but are also characterized by a minimum of control over the informant's responses. The idea is to get people to open up and let them express themselves in their own terms, and at their own pace. (Bernhard 1998: 209)

Thus, in contrast to the completely unstructured interview, the intention here is to modify the control of the interviewer to a limited sphere of conversation, within which the interviewed parties to a large extent are free to express themselves. More precisely, the interview technique we used – by asking certain questions when the opportunity arose – can be seen as a combination of what Bernard defines as the unstructured and the semi-structured interview. According to Bernard, the semi-structured interview must be regarded as a more formal interview form, which – though containing some elements of the flexibility from the unstructured interview – is clearly guided by an interview plan prepared by the fieldworker beforehand (ibid.).

In this survey, the embedded questions are directed towards seven target subjects, which were inductively detected during the first two weeks of the fieldwork. Both newcomers and locals were asked questions about these seven subjects (with the exception of the third which was addressed to only newcomers) to enable comparative studies:

1. *Background*: Why do the newcomers move to Ravnsborg Municipality? What were they doing before? What expectations did the newcomers have about the countryside and have these expectations been fulfilled?
2. *Networks*: What social networks did the newcomers have before they moved? What networks do they have now? How do they use their networks? What strategies do they have for building networks?
3. *The first month*: What were your experiences of the first month in Ravnsborg (newcomers only)?

4. *Newcomers versus locals*: Do you have contacts with your neighbours and do you help each other (newcomers only)? How do you see the newcomers/the locals? Are there any differences in mentality? If yes, then what are they?

5. *The role of the municipality*: What is the relationship between Ravnsborg Municipality and the newcomers? What are your experiences of the municipality (newcomers only)? What resources are available for newcomers? What could have been done better?

6. *Associational life*: Do the newcomers participate in the associational life? Do they participate in any other activities where they meet the locals?

7. *Future*: How can the newcomers contribute economically and socially? Do you want to stay in the municipality and what are your future plans (newcomers only)?

The intention – in line with Bernard's ideas on the unstructured interview – was to allow the interviewed person to control the choice of subjects as far as possible, ensuring that the elements meaning most to that person were highlighted. This safeguarded the inductive approach of the whole fieldwork study and our ambition of getting as close to reality and everyday life as possible. (For problems and advantages linked to this so-called interactive interviewing, see Davies 1999: 99.)

Also, our fieldwork consisted of participant observation (see, for example, Spradley 1980). Among other things, the one author living full-time in the area attended different social and cultural events, town hall decision making, fairs and so on, where there was participation of people from the whole of Lolland.

The overall methodological aim of interviewing different actors within the same subject areas was to take full advantage of our holistic approach and try to get the big picture of how newcomers are integrated into the municipality. Are they active in bridging social capital building or are they isolated without contact with the rest of the population? However, before we move on to the social capital analysis, we shall first introduce the municipality of Ravnsborg.

7.3.   THE CASE OF RAVNSBORG MUNICIPALITY

7.3.1.   Presentation

Ravnsborg Municipality was created in 1970 under the Local Government Act Reform, with the merging of 11 rural parishes. The municipal centre, Horslunde, is little more than a village and the whole municipality is an outlying rural area dominated by agriculture. In terms of area, Ravnsborg is the biggest municipality in Lolland and Falster. It is bounded to the North by the sea and surrounded by (the islands of) Zealand, Møn, Falster and Lolland. To the South, it borders on the municipalities of Nakskov and Maribo. Ravnsborg also includes the two bigger islands, Fejø and Femø. Since 1970, the population has declined by roughly one-third, from 8,000 to 5,600 (see Frantsen 2003: 3 for more details). Except for the districts around Kragenæs and Femø, the landscape is generally flat and dominated by agriculture, especially by the extensive sugar beet fields. In recent years, traditional fruit farming has prospered, especially with the use of ecological cultivation techniques on Fejø. Consequently, the cultural landscape on Fejø, for example, is characterized by more diversity and presents more of a 'romantic idyll' than the predominant 'sugar beet deserts' (as one newcomer from Fejø commented). Also, the fast-growing wind turbine industry has created many jobs in the region (Frantsen 2003: 3).

A rich cultural life exists in Ravnsborg mainly within the more than 60 registered voluntary associations. About two-thirds of these associations involve sports. In addition to this, civic, residents' and pensioners' associations dominate (*Lokalbogen* 2003 for Lolland: 25). Cultural life includes regular events such as concerts, local theatre, the cultural event 'Light over Lolland', a jazz festival on Femø, the market in Reventlow and the Horslunde Games (a big handball and football meeting for Danish and foreign schoolchildren).

7.3.2.   The Problem

Demographics show that for generations the population of Lolland has become accustomed to the arrival of many newcomers. These have included the Wends (a Slavonic tribe from Poland) from the early Medieval period and, later, people from Mecklenburg and Holstein, as well as German craftsmen. Around 1870, when emigration from the rural districts started, Lolland-Falster was severely hit. In the period from 1870 to 1900, for example, most Danes who emigrated to the United States left from this region (Boyhus 1973: 120–27). The resulting reduced labour force encouraged a massive immigration of Swedish rural workers to harvest the sugar beet. Around 1900, the Swedes were gradually replaced by Polish emigrants (Nellemann 1967; Tagmose 1973). During the 1960s and 1970s, many newcomers came from other parts of Denmark. Within the last two decades, groups of Bosnians and gypsies have arrived together with many Zealanders, especially from Copenhagen, and often dependent on social security. We know, for example, that half of all newcomers to Ravnsborg Municipality from Copenhagen in 2002 were fully dependent on social transfer payments (Frantsen 2003: 19).

Thus, Ravnsborg Municipality is arguably accustomed to significant emigration and migration and presumably has historical traditions for integrating new citizens. However, the systematic trend of newcomers relying on social security services has been a drain on the economy, not only through income transfers, but also administration and social obligations, for example placing children in care. Furthermore, the municipality is burdened by the general economic stagnation within the private sector, a low birth rate and a demographic structure with many retired people staying in the area, whereas the young people tend to leave the region. In total, the result has been severe budget deficits and a low public service level in spite of the fact that Ravnsborg has one of the highest taxation rates in Denmark.

One way of trying to stop the immigration of costly social clients has been to demolish the old and cheap housing that was seen as a source of attraction to these unwanted newcomers. However, in an attempt to attract more affluent people with good jobs, Ravnsborg has tried to beautify the area, for example, by restoring old villages, or by the preservation of rural amenities. These economic problems are typical in outlying municipalities in Denmark and in most other Western European countries. As we shall see below, the newcomers on income transfers have a bad reputation among the locals, resulting in general distrust and bonding social capital.

Many of the interviewees in the local group are annoyed that many newcomers relying on public support have chosen to live in 'the most beautiful municipality in Denmark'. A viable economic solution must be implemented in the long run – running deficits forever is not a feasible solution. Thus, the question is how can the resources of the newcomers be mobilized to the benefit of local wealth and development?

7.4.   BONDING SOCIAL CAPITAL IN RAVNSBORG MUNICIPALITY

How is a transition from bridging social capital and generalized trust to bonding social capital and particularized trust being achieved in Ravnsborg, and what are the costs?

Two dominant tendencies in Ravnsborg are, on the one hand, the creation of distrust and bonding social capital and, on the other, and to a lesser extent, the creation of extensive trust and bridging social capital. Both types build on personal contact and trust. However, as we have stressed before, whereas bridging social capital is based on personal closeness and contact with people across all group barriers (outwards directed), bonding social capital tends to be monopolized by a closed circle (inwards directed). The latter results in both a physical and mental distance to other societal groups.

7.4.1.   Distance and the Destruction of Social Capital

Our survey demonstrates overall, and surprisingly clearly, that the erosion of social capital is created by the pattern of distance both physically and mentally. Thus, above all, it seems to be the *experienced distance* that weakens civil engagement. Entrepreneurs gradually withdraw because they have no clear connection or common cause to work for. In this context, we should also remember Putnam's comments on the 'privatisation of leisure time' in the United States. Here it is primarily excessive TV watching and time spent in front of the computer that tend to extend the physical and psychological distance between people (see Putnam 1996: 47–8, 2000: 216).

A consequence of distance is less contact between citizens and less caring about each other: fewer neighbours recognize each other; fewer greet each other in the street; fewer meet in the physical meeting places, for example, at the football ground, the choral society, parent–teacher meetings, town council meetings or the general meetings in the local house-owners' association and so on. As a result, many common goods that had made life easier and more pleasant disappear. For example, minding each other's children or dogs, getting access to information by chatting with neighbours, keeping an eye on a neighbours' house during holidays, borrow a hedge cutter and so on.

Our fieldwork shows that, when newcomers were asked whether they knew their neighbours, they typically replied that the neighbours lived too far away. Thus, the physical distance and the lack of physical meeting places mean that newcomers and locals do not have the opportunity to get to know each other, thereby losing potential advantages from co-operation. For example, everybody might gain, if newcomers were welcomed into a local and very unformal 'firewood supply circle', that is, an exchange of firewood and other necessities in the winter period within a superglued group of locals. The fieldwork clearly reveals that at least *one* of the newcomers would be able to reprocitate by repairing the computers of farmers (and, for certain, this referred to Copenhagener has suffered from lack of firework during the winter!).

However, this is not so. For example, a young and very isolated girl from Copenhagen on social security, who lived with her boyfriend in a rented house in very poor conditions was asked: 'Where do the local people meet?'. 'Well, I don't really know', she answered reluctantly while staring out of the window at the desert-like fields. 'But I am sure they know each other, they *ought* to. So they must have a place to meet'. 'Do you know them?'. 'No . . .' (silence). 'But at least we greet each other . . .'.

The interviews also reveal the pattern of a 'cultural gap' where the expression 'differences in mentality' between the two groups was often used by representatives from both sides. Most dramatically, this distance to other people in physical and mental terms is illustrated by the relationship between urban newcomers from Copenhagen and the local rural population.

The locals generally have a negative attitude towards the urban newcomers from Copenhagen, 'The Copenhageners'. Locals emphasize that the newcomers do not contribute but only receive money from the municipality. Several locals even described them as 'spongers'. Note that the results from the interviews not only reflected these economic arguments.

The conflict between the local islanders of Lolland and the Copenhageners is also derived from historical contrasts between farmers and townspeople due to differences in mentality and behaviour. These differences are objectified in a thousand ways, only visible to the eyes of the locals. Thus, antipathies among the locals are being reinforced by, for example, observable factors such as how the Copenhagernes dress, what their housing is like, whether they have a garden and so on – however silent, for the native population a most significant language denoting a poor, shabby and idle *urban* life-form, which they disgust and disrespect. Most aggressively, a local commented on her young Copenhagener nabours sitting publicly, at the side of the road, drinking beer: that they are 'sick in their heads' and, being drunk, you 'can't even figure what they're saying'.

What regards he Copenhageners on social transfer incomes we interviewed, they are fully aware about being an economic burden for the municipality. Generally, they find this situation unsatisfactory themselves. Several newcomers used the word 'trap' or 'grey zone' about their own situation, implying that it is hard to get a job or to take a new initiative in doing something. People feeling lonely and isolated and/or badly treated by the municipality have a tendency to work against 'the system' rather than to contribute actively (see the theory on reciprocity in Chapter 2).

7.4.2.   Stereotypes and Theory Effects

When the Copenhageners were asked why they chose to move to Ravnsborg, almost everyone answered that the cheap housing was the deciding factor. Furthermore, more than two-thirds of respondents in the urban newcomer group said that they already had some sort of connection with the island of Lolland, through friends, relatives or the fact that they had once lived there. Generally, newcomers were strongly aware of having a social network close by, be it friends or family, and it was anticipated that these networks would be a useful source of mutual assistance and social contact.

For most of the newcomers, Ravnsborg can offer what they are looking for: beautiful countryside, tranquillity, good opportunities for a whole range of activities, good conditions for the children and so on. Typical statements were 'There are so many possibilities here', 'We wanted a less stressful life close to nature', and 'We wanted to grow things'. The general pattern from the interviews was that the desire of most newcomers to accumulate social capital was consistent with the dream of 'the good life in the countryside'. They chose to move to Ravnsborg because they see possibilities and have dreams for the future that they can fulfil here.

In contrast, most local attitudes towards social security recipients from Copenhagen seem largely based on stereotypes. The standard answers to the question asking locals to identify the newcomers included: 'I have nothing positive to say about them', 'They do not want to work', 'They are alcoholics', 'They are on drugs', 'They do not take care of their children', 'They talk too much and too quickly', 'They are naive', 'They hide in the fields', 'They do not contribute', 'They only show up on the first of the month to collect their social security', 'They have a "welfare" mentality'. When these sceptical locals were asked whether they actually *knew* the newcomers, they generally answered no – but, well, they had *heard* about them.

Similar stereotypical attitudes exist among the newcomers, who typically commented: 'The locals are self-sufficient', 'The locals always know somebody who knows somebody' and 'The locals are inbred'. One newcomer on social security, who had lived for eight years in Ravnsborg, was asked how she felt about the local community. She gave this rather puzzling answer:

> Well, I think . . . well. That is, the neighbours greet me and . . . Well, you see, I am accustomed to doing that myself. So . . . But, that is, if I meet them when I am out with my dog, then we also chat a little. Well, that is . . . chatting might not be the right word, we talk to each other's . . . *dogs*! (laughter). That's the way it is . . . Nothing can be done about it.

The result is that stereotypes or modern myths, mainly derived from distance and lack of knowledge, will work *against* bridging social capital. Basically, the absence of physical meeting places – platforms – can lead to misunderstandings between the two groups, so that the isolated networks of newcomers versus locals have formed without the crucial intergroup contact. Too much bonding social capital compared to the amount of bridging social capital is economically irrational for the municipality, since the cost of non-co-operation is – as we soon shall see – enormous.

7.4.3.   The Costs of Distrust

If physical meeting places or *platforms* are not facilitated so that the two groups get to know each other, not only will the groups fail to benefit from each other's resources but – even more seriously – generalized distrust will imply that the citizens will start working *against* each other. Here, Ravnsborg is also an illustrative example of how conflicts and bonding social capital can throw a spanner in the works, with serious economic consequences – just as the conflicts between Home Mission members and Grundtvigians did in the 1890s.

It is not easy to calculate how much distrust costs society. However, our interviews overall demonstrate that significant human costs arise among newcomers as a result of alienation, suspicion and total isolation. Clearly, the instances of visits to doctors and psychologists, early retirement, social worker involvement, children with behavioural problems and so on could presumably have been reduced if a newcomer had had access to a larger network, including local people with strong resources. Our interview with a doctor in the central hospital confirmed these suppositions.

An illustrative example is the rapidly growing number of disputes within the last few years between Copenhageners and locals. These disputes between neighbours typically concern trifling cases such as the positioning of a carport or the height of an end wall, and whereas normally they could have been settled by the parties themselves, they now result in extensive and costly litigation.

The pattern reflected in our interviews is that the Copenhageners and the locals are quick to start a war whenever there is something to fight about (as trivial as it may be). Rather than trying to co-operate, two neighbours will avoid each other and seek support from others of their own kind. Such social cohesion within the group results in the municipality all of a sudden receiving more complaints from other neighbours. Therefore, the amount of expensive public and professional third-party involvement escalates, with an increase in the workload for the police, lawyers, doctors, the regional psychiatric centre, the court, the investigation team, municipal family therapists, as well as a range of municipal, regional and national public administration institutions (that is, primarily the social work).

A specific example is a carport dispute that to date (May 2003) has lasted for two years and has escalated out of all proportion, with one party laying information against the other party and 'the whole lot' (as described by the municipal employee). Officially, 46 case reports have been filed so far and hundreds of public working hours have been poured into this rather absurd dispute. Such 'mud-slinging' is arguably initiated by what we have called physical and mental distance.

7.5.   BRIDGING SOCIAL CAPITAL IN RAVNSBORG MUNICIPALITY

Our interviews also revealed the opposite tendency of bonding social capital, namely bridging social capital. The lubricator of bridging social capital and inclusive networks makes it possible to co-operate across groups. Coleman has stated that it is not possible for a society to utilize a human capital (however big it may be) if the people who have it do not communicate, that is, in our case, if they never or only seldom meet. A *social* capital is the prerequisite for transferring human capital such as knowledge, ideas, learning processes and so on. This theory is valid not only in the relationship between children and their parents but also between the two 'ethnic' groups of Copenhageners and locals.

As one of the locals laconically commented in our interview, referring to the newcomers: 'You run the risk of missing a lot of expertise if you don't talk together'. Also, the common thread running through the interviews is that both groups would like to get to know members of the other group better and benefit from it. Typical statements such as the following confirm this: 'We could use those people [the newcomers]', 'Some of the newcomers are really active', or 'I think that the locals are most helpful'.

Already existing, potential platforms for social interaction between the two groups are the more than 60 voluntary organizations in the municipality. These organizations are – and have been through the last 150 years – the physical meeting places for different rural groups for solving practical matters or arranging cultural events. This is still the case in Ravnsborg, whether it involves football, lottery or amateur dramatics. The organizations also become an 'excuse' for doing a common activity and thereby getting to know each other. They provide a good opportunity for newcomers to integrate and become one of the privileged who 'knows someone who knows someone', that is, closure, resulting in common norms and social control – a tool for swift action and a safer environment.

The associational life seems the perfect platform for promoting closures and thereby integration, not just those for adults but also those for children, thereby obliging the parents to meet at sports matches and so on. Characteristic of all these places is that newcomers and locals meet regularly face to face and get to know one another. Everyone can contribute and the result is a societal benefiting, bridging social capital production. Thus, political decision makers should be aware of the important policy implication of this analysis, namely to encourage the opening of physical meeting places as the future platforms for successful integration and economic growth. However, right now – and, as always, we might add – they seem to be overlooking the social production factor.

7.6.   SUMMARY

In this chapter, we wanted to put into perspective our historical findings from Chapters 4, 5 and 6 by presenting the results of our most recent fieldwork study in Ravnsborg Municipality, a marginal rural area on the island of Lolland.

Our main purpose was, from 'within' and using the qualitative fieldwork method, to measure the human and economic costs stemming from excessive bonding social capital and widespread distrust between superglued groups, as well as to consider how distrust could be reduced.

In this, in many ways, impoverished and fragmented region of Denmark, serious cultural clashes between urban newcomers on social security and traditional, agrarian-oriented locals provide us with an interesting and illustrative case of the formation of exclusive social networks and bonding social capital. At the same time, and to a much lesser extent, we also witnessed some bridging social capital building. However, such bridging social capital in Ravnsborg, primarily in the many voluntary associations in the municipality, is insufficient to offset the social and economic burdens stemming from psychological and physical distance between groups of locals and newcomers, expressed in widespread distrust, prejudices (verbalized and non-verbalized), symbolic violence, group isolation, nepotism, superglue and lack of co-operation (if not outright opposition).

Methodologically, we used an inductive, qualitative and explorative approach. Thus, the case study was based on 70 loosely structured, personal interviews undertaken in April and May 2003, of which 40 were taped interviews lasting from one to three hours. Both locals and newcomers – the latter mostly people on social security from Copenhagen – were equally represented and arbitrarily chosen.

The overall methodological aim of our fieldwork study was to apply the theory of social capital in situ, to people in the throes of building various types of social capital, in order to identify possibilities for integrating the newcomers so that they, too, can contribute socially and economically. We hypothesized that all the inhabitants of Ravnsborg Municipality have much to gain from co-operation, that is, bridging social capital, and much to lose from isolating the newcomers, that is, bonding social capital.

Such a case study at the micro level has general implications for a cultural clash between two different groups (that is, urban newcomers versus agrarian-oriented locals) by demonstrating the complexity of a social capital mix where bonding social capital strongly prevails, ultimately leading to serious social and economic costs.

Thus, overall, the interviews suggested that significant human costs arise among newcomers as a result of alienation and isolation, mainly because of physical as well as psychological *distance* from native 'superglued' groups. Such patterns of bonding social capital were clearly reinforced by prejudices and symbolic violence towards the Copenhageners. The economic losses of such bonding social capital could be measured in various ways, for example, a drastic increase in visits to the doctor, early retirement, the number of children with social problems, neighbourhood disputes and so on. Distrust certainly costs. Bonding social capital costs. Consequently, in order to promote integration of newcomers, widespread co-operation and generalized trust, we recommended the building of what we have called *platforms*, that is, physical meeting places that ensure a mix of different groups and, thus, of the creation of bridging forms of social capital. In Ravnsborg, as well as in the rest of Denmark, voluntary associations have traditionally been some of the most important platforms capable of bridging social groups. In a social capital context, it is necessary to recognize the importance of these associations, as well as build and promote other platforms.

8. Conclusion

The main motivation for writing this book was to demonstrate that there has been a gap or 'missing link' in economic debates. The human sciences simply overlooked a production factor! In line with more traditional production factors such as physical, financial and human capital, this forgotten production factor can be called 'social capital'.

A crucial distinction was that of bridging and bonding social capital. We defined bridging social capital as a positive externality enhancing economic growth whereas excessive bonding social capital was defined as a negative externality detrimental to economic growth.

Thus, we defined the creation of social capital as being equal to the creation of *bridging* social capital, understood as inclusive types of co-operative networks transcending group cleavages and 'lubricating' co-operative relations within civic life so as to enhance economic growth. In contrast, we saw the destruction of social capital as the transformation of beneficial bridging social capital into harmful *bonding* social capital, implying strategies of exclusion, distrust between groups and – 'stiffening' society as though it were superglued – ultimately leading to economic decline. In other words, the economic problem arose in our model if the optimal balance between the stocks of bridging and bonding social capital in a society was upset by 'too much' bonding social capital.

The missing link of social capital, that is, bridging social capital, had to be added as an important production factor when considering entrepreneurship, group action, economic growth and the net outcome of any economic solution such as economies of scale and centralization of production. We considered bridging social capital as a new production factor, which must be added to the conventional concepts of human and physical capital. Thus, in contrast to bonding social capital which implies group isolation, lack of co-operation and fragmented societies, bridging social capital is productive because it increases the level of both abstract and specific trust in a society and allows more transactions to take place without third-party enforcement. The implication of such a discovery was a re-evaluation of traditional economics and we thus proposed a new socio-economics, 'Bourdieuconomics', in respectful memory of the great French sociologist. Allowing for cross-disciplinary analyses of both material and non-material forms of capital, we proposed that such a Bourdieuconomics should concentrate on the study of social capital.

Consequently, the main research question we raised was how social capital is created and destroyed. Overall, we answered this question in the following way. First, Chapter 2 defined the theoretical background of social capital and entrepreneurship. Chapter 3 then turned to empirical evidence by comparing the general emergence of co-operative movements and our new survey results on the present level of beneficial bridging social capital in two different political systems (Denmark and Poland). Chapters 4–7 moved on by focusing on entrepreneurship and bridging/bonding social capital in Danish rural communities. Here, the case of Denmark generally reflects the present and the future of democracies in the Western world as more and more rural areas have undergone the same kind of transformation in recent years. The implications of this cross-disciplinary investigation ranging from political economy, sociology, history and anthropology are arguably of general interest to human scientists.

We now conclude the book by suggesting a general model for explaining the creation and destruction of social capital. Figure 8.1 extracts the four main lessons derived from the preceding seven chapters, namely the political, civic, organizational and discoursive elements, and relates them to the bridging/bonding social capital building process.

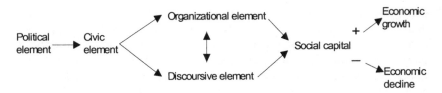

Source: The authors.

Figure 8.1   General model for the creation and destruction of social capital

By 'political element' we mean the political set-up, that is, democracy or communism, as well as all formal institutions linked to it and its economic systems, for example capitalism or planned economy. By 'civic element' we mean the accumulated traditions of civic virtues, skills and participation belonging to a population. By 'organizational element' we mean infrastructure, physical planning (including economic and cultural buildings) and voluntarily self-enforced, formal institutions within a civic society ('written rules of the game'). Finally, by 'discoursive element', we mean dominating terminologies in the public sphere, often involving symbolic violence (both tacitly and in words) between different groups, thus reinforcing psychological distance and bonding social capital.

Before developing these elements in our review of the main contributions from each specific chapter, we first give a brief and simplified outline of our methodological approach in relation to the model. As indicated in Figure 8.1, we compressed the main findings concerning our mix of theoretical and empirically observed elements that determine the creation and destruction of social capital into a general model. First, theory in Chapter 2 and theoretical evidence in Chapter 3 made it plausible to regard the political system and all formal institutions linked to it (political element), as a background variable for both civic participation (civic element) and social capital, as shown in Figure 8.1. Second, after this deductive approach, we shifted to an inductive approach, observing patterns within the actual general social capital framework. Here, Chapter 4 basically pointed to the importance of the civic and organizational elements whereas Chapters 5, 6 and 7 primarily established the importance of the organizational and discoursive elements (see Figure 8.1).

Note that the model depicts both bridging social capital contributing to economic growth and excessive bonding social capital contributing to economic decline. If, for example, the political system is highly centralized (as was the case of Russia, for example, before 1989) then this institutional set-up will also affect civic society (as reflected by low scores of civic participation). The civic element again influences the organizational and discoursive elements eventually resulting in some proportion of primarily bonding social capital and economic decline (–). In contrast, the opposite result would occur if political power is decentralized (as is the case of United States, for example). Then there would be room for civic society and free entrepreneurship to develop in relation to the organizational and discoursive elements, eventually resulting in some proportion of primarily bridging social capital and economic growth (+).

We shall now elaborate on the contributions from each chapter. The main purpose in Chapter 2 was to give a theoretical background for social capital and entrepreneurship. We argued that bridging social capital could be analysed as a positive externality, implying economic net gains for society overall. Bridging social capital was accumulated as the result of the potential of social sanctioning plus open and inclusive populations with regular face-to-face interaction, that is, reciprocal relations in accordance with the principle of personal closeness, fostering predictable behaviour, democratic debate, and mutual obligations and trust. Theory therefore led to the general recommendation that any loss in bridging social capital must be deducted from the economic gain that followed from free-market forces.

Deciding whether bridging social capital is a positive externality or not, we first detected the link between economics and culture, involving Bourdieu's theory of material and non-material forms of capital and the importance of entrepreneurship. Next, we presented the concept of social capital, linked to reciprocity and trust, as an important future contribution within the new socio-economics, 'Bourdieuconomics'.

Concerning entrepreneurship, we argued that regular face-to-face interaction within a group made it possible to impose extra social sanction costs on non-cooperative members in a group, thus ensuring co-operation and trust-building between members, eventually leading to successful group action. The presence of social sanction costs arguably solved the collective action problem because the individual net gain from free riding and not contributing to voluntary collective good provision now turned negative when the private costs were subtracted from a social sanction. This contribution filled a gap in economic literature. Moreover, in order to develop a framework for studying such socio-economic practice in situ we presented Bourdieu's extended definition of capital and his theory of the 'economy of practice', implying a methodology operating with various material and non-material capitals at the same level.

Examining the classical question of why some countries are rich and others poor, suggested that traditional production factors could not explain the observed differences in the wealth of nations. Rather, differences in the quality of formal institutions were arguably crucial to economic wealth. However, this type of political economy theory accentuating the role of formal institutions could not stand on its own – the non-material and informal dimension of institutions had to be added. In fact, one could argue that social capital and trust compensate for a lack of information, thereby offering a solution to the fundamental problem raised by new institutional economics, namely the presence of asymmetrical information. The presence of bridging social capital presumably lubricates civic society and the outcome is a voluntary provision of collective goods, such as common norms, predictability in human exchanges and trust. In this way, bridging social capital reduces transaction costs in society, thereby enhancing economic growth and consequently the creation of differences in the wealth of nations.

Here, we combined the new institutional economics and social capital approaches by arguing that the level of power decentralization in a political system (political element) was a crucial background variable for the creation and destruction of social capital because dictatorships, such as those identified in Central and Eastern Europe before 1989, tended to eliminate the building of trust, entrepreneurship and voluntary group action. In contrast, democratic countries with decentralized power left room for self-selection of entrepreneurs and trust building. Furthermore, we suggested how self-selection of local leaders could take place in a non-hierarchical setting, such as self-selection among a number of potential entrepreneurs in, for example, the locally based and voluntary co-operative movements. Such a process was arguably based on reputation.

Overall, we found it useful to supplement the approach in new institutional economics and its focus on formal institutions with Bourdieu's idea of material and non-material forms of capital. 'Bourdieuconomics' implies the usage of a capital theory that, methodologically, operates with material and non-material forms of capital at the same level. Here, we stressed the variable of civicness (civic element), that is, those civic traditions, skills and virtues belonging to a population which clearly are deeply rooted in non-material capitals, not least social capital, and which act as a crucial incentive or barrier to bridging social capital building. This implied thoroughgoing, inductively and qualitatively based in situ analyses of both historical and contemporary case studies, with a special focus on the role of civic movements in social capital building processes. Here, one non-material form of capital embedded in civic traditions and practices, namely social capital, appeared to be of particular importance when explaining differences in economic growth and institutional set-ups. Thus, in contrast to formal institutions ('written rules of the game'), invisible social capital entailing real visible effects could be localized as institutionalized but informal human exchange within civic life ('unwritten rules of the game'). Future research should therefore be directed towards this new field of Bourdieuconomics and, within such a framework, highlight the missing link of social capital and voluntary entrepreneurship.

Chapter 3 raised the general question whether a political system, that is, the formal institutional set-up in a country, matters to the level of social capital and civic life in practice (political and civic elements). We tested this hypothesis by comparing the historical and parallel emergence of co-operative movements in Denmark and Poland (before communism) and by undertaking new social capital surveys in Denmark and Poland (after communism).

First, we identified possible empirical roots by linking social capital building to rural development and comparing the cases of agricultural co-operative movements in Denmark and Poland. Arguably, valuable stocks of bridging social capital were built in both countries through a lengthy process during the nineteenth century via the well-developed co-operative movement in Denmark, as well as in Poland, prior to the Second World War. Most of the farmers' operations were based on trust and voluntary co-operation.

After the Second World War, Denmark continued to follow a democratic path of economic development; the democratic co-operative movement was not proscribed and continued to play a crucial role in the success of agriculture. In contrast, Poland was obliged to follow a totalitarian rule. First fascists, then communists, tried to resist the co-operative idea, and then to infiltrate and subordinate it. Since co-operative movements play a crucial role in building a capitalistic and democratic society, it is no surprise that their abolition was one of the first measures taken by the communist government.

Therefore, these voluntary organizations in Poland were brought under the control of the party, and people got used to obeying orders rather than making their own decisions, presumably destroying the stock of beneficial bridging social capital and leading to fewer voluntary organizations compared to the case of Denmark. The massive state intervention in the Polish economy during communism established heavy bureaucratic systems that monopolized the right to approve all actions in society. Arbitrary use of central power intimidated the citizens and taught them to trust no one. Also, it created room for corruption among bureaucrats, party officials and state monopolies, undermining the citizens' trust in formal institutions.

Second, the actual measurement of the social capital level in contemporary Denmark and Poland supported our hypothesis that the political system matters. Our empirical findings overall suggested that the level of bridging social capital is significantly higher in Denmark than in Poland. The average Dane is a member of 12 times more voluntary organizations than the average Pole. Being a member of a voluntary organization gives Danes, in addition to achieving the purpose of organization, a platform for social mingling and the exchange of other information. Concerning trust among citizens, Danes trust other Danes three and a half times more than the Poles trust other Poles, and Danes would in general trust 'a great deal' the four most important formal institutions (legal system, police, administration and government) ten times more than the Poles do. Finally, like the case for membership of voluntary organizations, we would expect more civic participation and entrepreneurship in a capitalist country than in a communist country, where entrepreneurs were persecuted as potential threats to the system due to their capability of organizing resistance. Accordingly, we found that Danes – having, in contrast to Poles, both long and uninterrupted traditions of civic engagement – participate in twice as many civic actions as do the Poles.

Thus, the empirical findings seemed to confirm the theoretical idea that different political systems (political element) will lead to different levels of traditions of civic participation (civic element), which, ultimately, will have a direct impact on the levels of bridging/bonding social capital among a population, as summarized in Figure 8.1. In this case, democracy and capitalism maintained and built bridging social capital whereas communist dictatorship destroyed it, that is, transformed stocks of bridging social capital into bonding types of social capital, ultimately leading to generalized distrust, fragmented societies and economic decline. The lack of bridging social capital in Central and Eastern Europe could therefore be one explanation for the rather disappointing economic results and hardships of transition so far.

Chapter 4 analysed the building of beneficial bridging social capital in the rural part of Denmark, a capitalist northern European country, since the beginning of the nineteenth century. Here, we saw that initial accumulation of strong traditions of civic virtues, civic skills and active civic participation (civic element), rooted in a newly established Danish civic society dating back to the late eighteenth century, led to the formation of an organizational structure (organizational element) which clearly improved bridging social capital building and, thus, facilitated subsequent building of other capitals (physical, economic, human). As the empirical data suggested, this organizational structure was found in both a *visible* part consisting of infrastructure, shared buildings (platforms) and formal institutions (written rules of the game), as well as an *invisible* part consisting of informal institutions (unwritten rules of the game) involving conscious, socio-economic social capital strategies among peasants.

The building of 'civicness' and an organizational structure promoting local entrepreneurship and inclusive co-operative networks were traced within the Danish co-operative movement before the Second World War. Next, we localized the continuity of civic engagement and inclusive civic organization in a more recent stock of bridging social capital in rural Denmark, namely the one stemming from the so-called sports halls movement during the 1960s and 1970s. Overall, the main question was: is bridging social capital really a production factor and why do entrepreneurs provide it voluntarily in practice? We answered this question in two steps.

First, we presented an example of the rise of positive or beneficial social capital (bridging social capital) in the emergence of strongly inclusive peasant networks. These were mainly organized within the co-operative movement during the second half of the nineteenth century, and should be seen as being embedded in a civic society initially founded at the beginning of the century, although with strong roots in the late eighteenth century.

Regarding the organizational element, we found that the initial establishment of networks – what we called the 'cytogenesis' of bridging social capital – is contingent upon the existence of the three key elements: democracy, trust and the equal possibility of making a profit. Here, we saw a dynamic interplay between the physical and non-physical part of the organization. Thus, it was demonstrated that the building of productive bridging social capital was enhanced by improvements in infrastructure, by the purely physical organization of the co-operative village, *Andelslandsbyen*, involving a great number of cultural and economic buildings ('platforms') shared by members across group boundaries, *as well as* by widely agreed upon, formal institutions (written rules of the game) in the form of the standardized founding statutes of co-operative associations facilitating ('kick-starting') viable and durable peasant co-operation. As an outcome of this process, entrepreneurs provided collective goods, contributing to economic growth and education in formerly poor, rural areas.

Furthermore, the historical material suggested that it was mainly these written rules of the game, which made possible a self-organization of rural districts that entailed a rapid accumulation of bridging social capital and, consequently, of other forms of capital, and which ultimately achieved great socially beneficial significance.

Gradually, as farmers got used to following the written rules of the game, the formalized framework for co-operation became 'naturalized', that is, diffused into informal exchange as well. In this way, co-operation according to the rules of the game, implying collective good provision secured by agreed-upon sanctions, became a natural way of acting, that is, normal behaviour which the peasants no longer questioned. The rules were internalized, that is, turned into informal and unwritten rules allowing the actors to formulate socio-economic strategies. In other words, they were turned into a specific habitus, which again would further speed up the accumulation of bridging social capital and promote the recruitment of future generations of local entrepreneurs. In this way, a healthy circle of bridging social capital building was secured. Also, the spread of networks – or, in our terminology, the 'mytosis' of bridging social capital – was, and *is*, contingent upon entrepreneurship at local, regional and national levels, facilitated by numerous decentralized platforms and good infrastructure.

These two stages in the cycle formed what we have termed 'bridging social capital building'. The common goods achieved in this way consisted of a significant increase in productivity from the beginning of the 1880s. This occurred in a broader context of increased communication between people – most importantly facilitated by improved infrastructure from about 1870, for example, the building of railways and roads – at local, regional and national levels, in spite of international economic crises and the governmental scepticism towards the co-operative dairies.

Second, we turned to more recent stocks of bridging social capital in rural Denmark, most prominently a case study belonging to the twentieth century but which still today, in the new millennium, has a great impact on rural life: the sports halls movement of the 1960s and 1970s. Like the co-operative movement from the mid-1860s to the mid-1960s, the sports halls movement involved an organizational structure promoting strongly inclusive, bridging networks, which clearly were embedded in previously established civic traditions, implying voluntary self-organization as an offshoot of civic virtues (civic and organizational elements). Furthermore, and seemingly in a much more radical way than ever before, these *ildsjæle* or 'public-spirited entrepreneurs' consciously aimed to plan, build and run shared (cultural) buildings or 'platforms' (organizational element) in order to create meeting places for *all* groups, across social, generational, professional or religious boundaries. Thus, the overall aim of building a sports hall in every rural parish was, it was said, to ensure that 'people met and learned from each other' – which, in our terminology, means: to secure the future existence of a comprehensive valuable bridging social capital in the local communities.

While characterized by being embedded in invisible forms of capital involving idealistic and unselfish motives, civic participation and the 'fantastic building of sports halls' from the middle of the 1960s to 1980 was only possible due to the common initiative of energetic entrepreneurs. These included local people born in the villages and, not least, newcomers. Together, these rural dwellers undertook an enormous amount of voluntary work during these two decades.

However, the sports associations behind the new sports halls rather quickly became dependent on state subsidies, which in more radical cases seemed to destroy entrepreneurship by diminishing people's pleasure in – spontaneously and voluntarily – doing good things for their fellow citizens or, in sum, their enjoyment in pursuing an enthusiasm of their own. In other words, these people would no longer feel that they were participating in indispensable, local co-operation for 'our' hall and, hence, their feeling of responsibility and their interest would quickly diminish. Therefore, we suggested that too many public subsidies tend to ruin stocks of bridging social capital.

Chapter 5 traced market centralization processes and transformations of beneficial bridging social capital, built by energetic entrepreneurs before the Second World War, into excessive harmful bonding social capital after the war. Hence, our main purpose was to ask whether social capital really has been forgotten in market processes, and whether a subsequent and substantial transformation from bridging to bonding social capital really has been going on since the Second World War.

After briefly recounting an important example of early bonding social capital about 1900, due to religious conflicts, and resulting in a duplication of formerly shared buildings in many rural Danish parishes (discoursive and organizational elements), we highlighted the destruction of bridging social capital within the post-war Danish co-operative movement, leading, during the 1960s, to massive shutdowns of shared economic and cultural buildings of vital socio-economic significance for the local communities (organizational element). We also observed how mergers of agricultural enterprises and centralization of production took place on the initiative of primarily national agricultural leaders, applying a modern agricultural economic terminology (discoursive element).

First, empirical evidence was presented, suggesting that the old Danish saying 'A word is a word' used to be valid in the Danish countryside. However, the level of trust presumably decreased when agricultural production was centralized after the Second World War, most dramatically within the Danish co-operative dairy sector, where important local and regional platforms in the form of local parish dairies – previously the fabrics of bridging social capital – were shut down in great numbers during a dramatic period of transition in the 1960s (organizational element).

Thus, we drew attention to the fact that any loss in bridging social capital must be deducted from the economic gain following economies of scale (for example, centralization of dairy production). We suggested that alternative possibilities should be considered further, taking the production factor of inclusive and lubricating bridging social capital into account, because it is uncertain whether the net gain is positive or whether another way of organizing production – and maintaining the high level of bridging social capital, established by a co-operative dairy movement deeply embedded in a nineteenth century decentralized, rural civic society – would significantly have increased economic growth further.

The market centralization debates, imbued by abstract terminology borrowed from classical economics – and applied by national agricultural leaders to obtain power at the expense of local leaders – highlighted the consequences of the absence of the term 'social capital' (or a similar word denoting a social production factor) in the public debate. Thus, in the formulation of Bourdieu, we see *ce que parler veux dire*. Speaking matters! This was clearly illustrated by the disappearance of a whole social group in rural Denmark, the smallholders, who, although being 'social capitalists' *par excellence* and thus lubricators of their local community, were struck by 'aphasia' from the mid 1960s (discoursive element).

Second, in Chapter 6 we used the case study of the Danish village society movement of the 1970s to further explore the linkage between discoursive elements and social capital building. Once again, we saw that this entailed severe cultural clashes between local people and newcomers and, hence, of distance, distrust, symbolic violence and bonding social capital (discoursive element). Thus, processes of symbolic violence leading to a reinforcement of bonding social capital were highlighted by the construction of a non-agriculturalist conceptual universe (or 'discourse of rurality') during the 1970s, and the subsequent conflicts between local people and newcomers this entailed.

Thus, similar to the spread of powerful agricultural, *classical economic* terminology on the initiative of professional and centralized leadership during the 1950s and 1960s, an urban and non-agriculturalist terminology of the 1970s – now borrowed from the *social* sciences and mainly belonging to the newcomers from the cities – has been disseminated among the Danish population to this very day. And, like the agriculturalist discourse of rurality, this has clearly had a considerable effect on rural identities and realities at the local level, as well as on rural political debates and agendas at the national level.

However, through the whole period, using either conventional economic or social science terminology, opponents against one-sided and excessive market centralization among the rural population have basically been left defenceless because they did not possess the keywords 'social capital', which would have enabled them to present a convincing economic counterargument. Consequently, the importance of the power of words in these market centralization debates based on the agriculturalist and non-agriculturalist discourses of rurality (discoursive element) was explained.

In sum, market centralization processes in a capitalist society may eventually fragmentize and thus destroy bridging social capital if the positive externality of local production and social capital is not taken into account. Excessive bonding social capital in Denmark after the Second World War seemed, in contrast to sports hall building, for example, to facilitate the formation of exclusive networks, distrust and lack of co-operation across group boundaries. Centralization of production may pay, of course, when economies of scale are present. However, our argument was that too much market centralization would occur from the perspective of society if the positive externality of bridging social capital was not considered when undertaking an overall cost–benefit analysis. Thus, the aspect of bridging social capital should be taken into account by academics, politicians, firm managers and other decision makers just like other positive externalities such as the promotion of education or better environmental quality.

In Chapter 7, we wanted to find out whether social capital really is created and destroyed in everyday life, testing in this way whether contemporary fieldwork in rural Denmark confirms or rejects the idea of bridging and bonding social capital. More specifically, we asked ourselves the question: what are the costs of distrust and excessive bonding social capital, and how can these costs be reduced? Thus, in our latest fieldwork study we have analysed strategies of co-operation and confrontation between rural groups in a marginal rural area in Denmark: Ravnsborg Municipality in the northwest of the island of Lolland, which is situated 150 kilometres southwest of the capital of Copenhagen.

As we were soon to discover, a severe conflict between urban newcomers and locals in rural areas prevailed, much in line with the case study in Chapter 6. Newcomers and locals alike frequently emphasized this conflict. Therefore, the fieldwork study indeed demonstrated that the concepts of bridging and bonding social capital were relevant for cultural clashes between two different groups, in this case urban newcomers versus agrarian-oriented locals. Overall, such an analysis is of general interest as regional municipalities in Denmark and most other Western European countries have had to contend with the migration of more and more newcomers supported by the public purse.

The complexity of a social capital mix was identified, in which excessive bonding social capital strongly prevailed, ultimately leading to serious social and economic costs among a population. Significant human costs arise among newcomers from alienation and isolation, mainly as a result of physical as well as psychological distance to native 'superglued' groups (organizational element). Such patterns of bonding social capital were clearly reinforced by prejudices and symbolic violence towards the 'wrong newcomers' (discoursive element).

The economic losses of such bonding social capital were displayed in a number of different ways, for example, in the form of a drastic increase in surgery visits, early retirement, children with social problems, neighbourhood disputes and so on. Distrust and excessive bonding social capital certainly increase costs, implying economic decline.

At the same time, but to a much lesser extent, we witnessed a production of bridging social capital, which primarily was built in the many voluntary associations in the municipality, thus acting as platforms securing a steady mix of different groups (organizational element). However, it remained clear that such production of 'lubricants' far from counterbalanced the social and economic burdens stemming from physical and psychological distance between locals and newcomers, and which ultimately have led to distrust, symbolic violence, group isolation and lack of co-operation. Overall, our fieldwork clearly identified important patterns of social capital building. Furthermore, by observing and discussing the benefits from producing bridging social capital and the costs of excessive bonding social capital it has demonstrated that social capital matters in everyday life.

Our main concern in this book has been to formulate and bring to the reader this new insight: that social capital *matters* and that it can be seen as the missing link for understanding economic and civic well-being. We hope that such insight will be able to guide future research and decision-making towards the crucial role of entrepreneurship and voluntary organizations. Last, but not least, it promises a bright new millennium for humanity, gained through communication, trust and co-operation across narrow group and national boundaries.

Bibliography

Ab (*Andelsbladet. Fællesorgan for de Danske Andelsselskaber*) (*The Co-operative Magazine. Journal of the Central Co-operative Committee of Denmark*), 1904, 1959–67 and 1969–70.

Almås, R. (1999), *Rural Development – a Norwegian Perspective*, Report no. 9/99, Centre for Rural Research, Trondheim.

Anderson, Jr., B.M. (1940), 'Governmental economic planning', *American Review of Economics*, **30** (1), 247–62.

Anheier, H.K., J. Gerhards and F.P. Romo (1995), 'Forms of capital and social structure in cultural fields: examining Bourdieu's social topography', *American Journal of Sociology*, **100** (4), 859–903.

Appadurai, A. (1986), 'Introduction: commodities and the politics of value', in A. Appadurai (ed.), *The Social Life of Things*, Cambridge: Cambridge University Press, pp. 3–63.

Balle-Petersen, M. (1976), 'Foreningstiden' [The era of associations], *Arv og Eje*, Year Book, 43–68, Copenhagen: Dansk Kulturhistorisk Museumsforening.

Balle-Petersen, M. (1977), 'Guds folk i Danmark' [God's people in Denmark], *Folk og Kultur*, Year Book, 78–124. Copenhagen: Foreningen Danmarks Folkeminder.

Becker, G. (1968), 'Crime and punishment. An economic approach', *Journal of Political Economy*, **76** (2), 169–217.

Becker, G. (1996), *Accounting for Tastes*, Cambridge, MA: Harvard University Press and New York: Cambridge University Press.

Ben-Porath, Y. (1980), 'The *F*-connection: families, friends, and firms and the organization of exchange', *Population and Development Review*, **6** (1), 1–30.

Bernard, H.R. (1998), *Research Methods in Anthropology. Qualitative and Quantitative Approaches*, Thousand Oaks, CA: Sage.

Bjerre, P. (1974), *Landsbypolitik – Samfundspolitik* [Village Politics – State Politics], Dansk Byplanlaboratoriums skriftserie, no. 8, Copenhagen.

Bjørn, C. (1982), 'Dansk mejeribrug' [Danish dairywork], in C. Bjørn (ed.), *Dansk Mejeribrug 1882–2000* [Danish Dairywork 1882–2000], Odense, Denmark: De Danske Mejeriers Fællesorganisation, pp. 11–188.

Bjørn, C. (ed.) (1988), *Det Danske Landbrugs Historie* [History of the Danish Agriculture], vol. 3, Copenhagen: Det Danske Landboselskab.

Bjørn, C. (1997), 'Andelstiden. Produktionsanlæg og sociale bygninger' [The era of cooperative associations. Production buildings and social buildings], in *De Kulturhistoriske Interesser i Landskabet* [The Cultural-Historical Interests in the Landscape], Copenhagen: S & N-styrelsen, pp. 309–25.

Bjørnskov, C. (2003), 'The happy few. Cross-country evidence of social capital and life satisfaction', *Kyklos*, **56** (1), 3–16.

Bjørnskov, C. (2004), 'The economic use of social capital: the income relation', in M. Paldam and G.T. Svendsen (eds), *Trust, Social Capital and Economic Growth: An International Comparison*, Cheltenham, UK: Edward Elgar, Ch 7 (forthcoming).

Blinkenberg Nielsen, O. (1950), *De Danske Sognesparekasser 1865–1914* [The Danish Parish Savings Banks 1865–1914], Copenhagen: Sparevirkes Forlag.

Boix, C. and D.N. Posner (1998), 'Social capital: explaining its origins and effects on government performance', *British Journal of Political Science*, **28** (4), 686–93.

Bonanno, A. (1993), 'Some reflections of Eastern European agriculture' *Agriculture and Human Values*, **1**, 2–10.

Bourdieu, P. (1971) 'The thinkable and the unthinkable', *The Times Literary Supplement*, 15 October, pp. 1255–6.

Bourdieu, P. (1977), *Outline of a Theory of Practice*, Cambridge: Cambridge University Press.

Bourdieu, P. (1979a) 'Le capital social' [Social capital], *Actes de la recherche en sciences sociales*, **31**, 2–3.

Bourdieu, P. (1979b), 'Les trois états du capital culturel' [The three states of cultural capital], *Actes de la recherche en sciences sociales*, **30**, 3–6.

Bourdieu, P. (1980), 'The production of belief: contribution to an economy of symbolic goods', *Media, Culture and Society*, **2** (3), 261–93.

Bourdieu, P. (1982), *Ce que parler veut dire: L'économie des échanges linguistiques* [What Speaking Means: The Economy of Linguistic Exchanges], Paris: Arthème Fayard.

Bourdieu, P. (1983a) 'Ökonomisches Kapital, kulturelles Kapital, soziales Kapital' [Economic capital, cultural capital, social capital], in R. Kreckel (ed.), *Soziale Ungleichheiten* [Social Inequalities], *Soziale Welt*, vol. 2, Göttingen: Schwartz, pp. 183-198.

Bourdieu, P. (1983b), 'The field of cultural production, or: the economic world reversed', *Poetics*, **12** (4/5), 311–56.

Bourdieu, P. (1985), 'The social space and the genesis of groups', *Social Science Information*, **2**, 195–220.

Bourdieu, P. (1986), 'The forms of capital', in J.G. Richardson (ed.), *Handbook of Theory and Research for the Sociology of Education*, New York, Westport, CT and London: Greenwood Press, pp. 241–58.

Bourdieu, P. (1989), *Distinction: A Social Critique of the Judgement of Taste*, London: Routledge.

Bourdieu, P. (1990a), *In Other Words: Essays towards a Reflexive Sociology*, Cambridge: Polity.

Bourdieu, P. (1990b), *The Logic of Practice*, Cambridge: Polity.

Bourdieu, P. (1997), 'Le champ économique' [The economic field], *Actes de la recherche en sciences sociales*, **119**, 48–66.

Bourdieu, P. (1998), *Practical Reasons*, Cambridge: Polity.

Bourdieu, P. (2000), *Les Structures Sociales de L'économie* [The Social Structures of the Economy], Paris: Seuil.

Bourdieu, P. (2003), *Firing Back. Against the Tyranny of the Market*, New York: New Press.

Bourdieu, P. and L.J.D. Wacquant (1992), *An Invitation to Reflexive Sociology*, Chicago: University of Chicago Press.

Boyhus, E.-M. (ed.) (1973), *Sukkerroer. 100 År på Lolland-Falster* [Sugar Beets. 100 Years in Lolland-Falster], Maribo, Denmark: Lolland-Falsters Historiske Samfund.

Brogaard, P. (1965), *Landbrugernes Sammenslutning* [Farmers' Confederation], MA thesis, University of Aarhus.

Buksti, J. (1982), 'Dansk mejeribrug 1955–82' [Danish dairywork 1955–82], in C. Bjørn (ed.), *Dansk mejeribrug 1882–2000* [Danish Dairywork 1882–2000], Odense, Denmark: De Danske Mejeriers Fællesorganisation, pp. 309–480.

Calhoun, C. (1993), 'Habitus, field, and capital', in C. Calhoun, E. LiPuma and M. Postone (eds), *Bourdieu: Critical Perspectives*, Cambridge: Polity, pp. 61–88.

Carter, J. and A. Ghorbani (2003), 'Towards a Formalization of Trust', Working paper, Faculty of Computer Science, University of New Brunswick, Fredericton, Canada.

Chloupkova, J. (2002a), 'Polish agriculture: Organisational structure and impacts of transition', Unit of Economics Working Paper 2002/3, Royal Veterinary and Agricultural University, Copenhagen.

Chloupkova, J. (2002b), 'European Cooperative Movement: Background and Common Denominators', Unit of Economics Working Paper 2002/4, Royal Veterinary and Agricultural University, Copenhagen.

Chloupkova, J. and C. Bjørnskov (2002a), 'Counting in social capital when easing agricultural credit constraints', *Journal of Microfinance*, **4**, 17–36.

Chloupkova, J. and C. Bjørnskov (2002b), 'Could social capital help Czech agriculture?', *Agricultural Economics (Zemedelska Ekonomika)*, **48** (6), 245–9.

Chloupkova, J., G.L.H. Svendsen and G.T. Svendsen (2003), 'Building and destroying social capital: The case of cooperative movements in Denmark and Poland', *Agriculture and Human Values*, **20** (3), 241-252.

Christensen, J. (1983), *Rural Denmark 1750–1980*, Copenhagen: The Central Co-operative Committee of Denmark.

Christensen, J. (1985), *Landbostatistik. Håndbog i Dansk Landbohistorisk Statistik 1830–1900* [Rural Statistics. Handbook in Danish Rural Historical Statistics 1830-1900], Copenhagen: Landbohistorisk Selskab.

Christiansen, P.O. (1982), *En Livsform på Tvangsauktion?* [A Life-mode on Forced Sale?], Copenhagen: Gyldendal.

Coase, R.H. (1937), 'The nature of the firm', *Economica*, **6**, 386–405.

Coase, R.H. (1960), 'The problem of social cost', *Journal of Law and Economics*, **3** (1), 1–44.

Coleman, J.S. (1988a), 'Social capital in the creation of human capital', *American Journal of Sociology*, **94**, 95–121.

Coleman, J.S. (1988b), 'The creation and destruction of social capital: implications for the law', *Journal of Law, Ethics & Public Policy*, **3**, 375–404.

Coleman, J.S. (1990), *Foundations of Social Theory*, Cambridge, MA: Harvard University Press.

Coleman, J.S. (1994), 'A rational choice perspective on economic sociology', in N.J. Smelser and R. Swedberg (eds), *The Handbook of Economic Sociology*, New York: Princeton University Press, pp. 166–78.

Coleman, J.S. and T.B. Hoffer (1987), *Public and Private Schools: The Impact of Communities*, New York: Basic Books.

Current Contents Database (2003).

Danmarks Idræts-Forbund (The Danish National Sports Confederation) (2001), 'Oplysninger om lovgivning og offentlige tilskud' [Information about laws and public subsidies], www.dif.dk, access date: November 14, 2001.

Daugbjerg, C. and G.T. Svendsen (2001), *Green Taxation in Question*, Basingstoke: Macmillan (Palgrave).

Davies, C.A. (1999), *Reflexive Ethnography. A Guide to Researching Selves and Others*, London, New York: Routledge.

DGI-byen (2002), 'Fakta om DGI-byen, februar 2002' [Facts about the DGI city, February 2002], www.dgi-byen.dk, access date: March 22, 2002.

DL (Dansk Landbrug) (Danish Agriculture), a magazine issued by The Danish National Confederation of Farmers' Associations (De Samvirkende Danske Landboforeninger), 1962 and 1967.

Dollerup, P. (1966), *Brugsforeningerne 1866–1896. Sociale, Økonomiske og Politiske Undersøgelser i de Danske Brugsforeningers Historie fra 1866 til 1896* [The Co-operative Wholesale Societies 1866-1896. Social, Economic and Political Investigations in the History of the Danish Co-operative Wholesale Societies from 1866 to 1896], Albertslund, Denmark: Det Danske Forlag.

DU (Dansk Udsyn) (Danish Outlook), a yearbook issued by the folk high school association 'Askov lærlinge', Askov, Denmark, 1955.

DU (Dansk Ungdom) (Danish Youth), a journal issued by The Danish National Confederation of Youth Associations (De danske Ungdomsforeninger, DdU), 1952, 1959 and 1964.

DUI (Dansk Ungdom og Idræt) (Danish Youth and Athletics), a journal issued by The Danish National Confederation of Gymnastics and Youth Associations (De Danske Gymnastik- og Ungdomsforeninger, DDGU), 1967–68, 1971–73, 1988, 1990 and 1997.

Durkheim, E. (1908), 'Débat sur l'économie politique et les sciences sociales' [Debate on the political economy and the social sciences], electronic version by Jean-Marie Tremblay, pages.infinit.nct/sociojmt, access date: March 27, 2002.

Durkheim, E. ([1888] 1951), *Suicide: A Study in Sociology*, translated by George Simpson and John A. Spaulding, New York: Free Press.

Durkheim, E. ([1893] 1984), *The Division of Labour in Society*, New York: Free Press.

Edwards, B. and M.W. Foley (1997), 'Social capital and the political economy of our discontent', *American Behavioral Scientist*, **40** (5), 669–78.

European Commission (1998), *Agricultural Situation and Prospects in the Central and Eastern Countries: Summary Report*, Directorate General for Agriculture, Brussels.

Fabricius, B. (1991), *Vi Byggede Selv Vores Samfund* [We Built our Society Ourselves], Esbjerg, Denmark: Odder Museum.

FAO (Food and Agriculture Organization) (1994), *Reorienting the Cooperative Structure in Selected Eastern European Countries: Summary of Case-studies*, Central and Eastern Europe – Agriculture in Transition 1, Food and Agriculture Organization of the United Nations.

Feldbæk, O. (1988), 'Kongen bød – Enevælden og reformerne' [The king commanded – The absolute monarchy and the agricultural reforms], in C. Bjørn (ed.), *Landboreformerne – Forskning og Forløb* [The Agricultural Reforms – Research and Course], Odense, Denmark: Landbohistorisk Selskab, pp. 9–29.

Fetterman, D.M. (1989), *Ethnography Step by Step*, Newbury Park, CA, London, New Delhi: Sage.

Fink, T. (1999), *Båndene Bandt* [Unbroken Ties], 2 Volumes, Aabenraa, Denmark: IFG Press.

Flora, J.L. (1998), 'Social capital and communities of place', *Rural Sociology*, **63** (4), 481–506.

Frantsen, S. (2003), *Befolkningsudviklingen i Ravnsborg Kommune. Udvikling eller afvikling?* [The Demographic Development in Ravnsborg Municipality. Development or Depopulation?], Unpublished Paper Exercise, Danmarks Forvaltningshøjskole, Copenhagen.

Frey, B. and A. Stutzer (2002), *Happiness and Economics. How the Economy and Institutions Affect Human Well-being*, Princeton, NJ: Princeton University Press.

Fukuyama, F. (1995a), *Trust. The Social Virtues and the Creation of Prosperity*, London: Hamish Hamilton.

Fukuyama, F. (1995b), 'Social capital and the global economy', *Foreign Affairs*, **74** (5), 89–103.

Gartman, D. (1991), 'Culture as class symbolization or mass reification? A critique of Bourdieu's distinction', *American Journal of Sociology*, **97** (2), 421–47.

Glahn, O. (1985), 'Landdistriktets kulturelle tilbud' [Cultural service institutions in the rural area], in LOK (ed.), *Mellem Land og By – om Landdistrikter og Levevilkår* [Between Countryside and City – about Rural Districts and Life Conditions], Copenhagen: LOK, pp. 167–196.

Gluckman, M. (1958), *Analysis of a social situation in modern Zululand*, Rhodes-Livingstone paper no. 8 (reprinted from *Bantu Studies*).

Goffman, E. (1959), *The Presentation of Self in Everyday Life*, New York: Anchor-Doubleday.

Granovetter, M.S. (1973), 'The strength of weak ties', *American Journal of Sociology*, **78**, 1360–80.

Granovetter, M.S. (1974), *Getting a Job: A Study of Contacts and Careers*, Cambridge, MA: Harvard University Press.

Granovetter, M.S. (1985), 'Economic action, social structure and embeddedness', *American Journal of Sociology*, **9**, 481–510.

Granovetter, M.S. (1990), 'The old and the new economic sociology', in R. Friedland and A.F. Robertson (eds), *Beyond the Marketplace*, New York: Aldine de Gruyter, pp. 89–112.

Granovetter, M.S. (1995), 'The economic sociology of firms and entrepreneurs', in A. Portes (ed.), *The Economic Sociology of Immigration*, New York: Russell Sage, pp. 128–65.

Green, D.P. and I. Shapiro (1994), *Pathologies of Rational Choice. Theory. A Critique of Applications in Political Science*, New Haven, CT: Yale University Press.

Haagard, H.R. (1911), *Rural Denmark and its Lessons*, London: Longmans Green & Co.

Hacking, I. (1999), *The Social Construction of What?*, Cambridge, MA and London: Harvard University Press.

Halfacree, K. (2001), 'Constructing the object: taxonomic practices, "counterurbanization" and positioning marginal rural settlement', *International Journal of Population Geography*, 7, 395–411.

Halfacree, K., I. Kovach and R. Woodward (2002), *Leadership and Local Power in European Rural Development*, London: Ashgate.

Hansen, A.H. (1937), 'The situation of gold today in relation to world currencies', *American Review of Economics*, 27 (1), 130–40.

Hansen, C.B. and P.D. Rasmussen (1995), *Hvor Blev Mejeriet af?* [Where Has the Dairy Gone?], Auning, Denmark: Dansk Landbrugsmuseum.

Hansgaard, T. (1981), *Landboreformerne i Danmark i det 18. Århundrede. Problemer og Synspunkter* [The Agricultural Reforms in 18th Century Denmark. Problems and Opinions], Viborg, Denmark: Landbohistorisk Selskab.

Hartel, A. (1934), *L. S. En kort Fremstilling af Bevægelsen: 'Landbrugernes Sammenslutning', dens Organisation og Fremtidsplaner* [L.S. A Brief Presentation of the Movement: 'Farmers' Confederation', its Organisation and Future Perspectives, Copenhagen: Steen Hasselbalchs Forlag.

Haue, H. (1977), 'Mejerikrigen' [The Dairy War], *Fortid og nutid*, 2 7 (1977–78), 359–90.

Hb (Højskolebladet) (The Folk High School Magazine), issued by The Independent Institution 'Højskolebladet', 1958.

Hellevik, O. (1980), *Forskningsmetode i Sosiologi og Statsvitenskap* [Research Method in Sociology and Political Science], 4th Edition, Oslo: Universitetsforlaget, Norway.

Helliwell, J.F. and R.D. Putnam (2000), 'Economic growth and social capital in Italy', in P. Dasgupta and I. Serageldin (eds), *Social Capital: A Multifaceted Perspective*, Washington DC: World Bank, pp. 253–68.

Herbert-Cheshire, L. (2000), 'Contemporary strategies for rural community development in Australia: a governmentality perspective', *Journal of Rural Studies*, 16, 203–15.

Hertel, H. (1917), *Andelsbevægelsen i Danmark* [The Co-operative Movement in Denmark], Copenhagen: Gyldendalske Boghandel-Nordisk Forlag.

Hh (Husmandshjemmet) (Smallholders' Magazine), issued by The Danish National Confederation of Smallholders' Associations (De samvirkende danske husmandsforeninger), 1960, 1964–65.

Hjøllund, L., M. Paldam and G.T. Svendsen (2001), 'Social capital in Russia and Denmark: a comparative study', Department of Economics, Aarhus School of Business, Working Paper 01–13.

Hofferth, S.L. and J. Iceland (1998), 'Social capital in rural and urban communities', *Rural Sociology*, **63** (4), 574–98.

Hoggart, K. and A. Paniagua (2001), 'What rural restructuring?', *Journal of Rural Studies*, **17**, 41–62.

Hoggart, K. et al. (1995), *Rural Europe: Identity and Change*, London: Arnold.

Højrup, T. (1983), 'The concept of life-mode. A form-specifying mode of analysis applied to contemporary Western Europe', *Ethnologia Scandinavica*, **23**, 15–50.

Højrup, T. (1989), *Det Glemte Folk. Livsformer og Centraldirigering* [The Forgotten People. Life-modes and Central Governance], Hørsholm, Denmark: Statens Byggeforsknings Institut.

Honoré, P. (ed.) (1994), *Fredericia-Hallen i 25 År* [The Fredericia Sports Hall in 25 Years], Fredericia, Denmark: Fredericia-Hallen.

Hume, D. ([1739] 1984), *A Treatise of Human Nature*, New York: Penguin Books.

Hunek, T. (1994), *Reorienting the Cooperative Structure in Selected Eastern European Countries: Case-study on Poland*, Central and Eastern Europe – Agriculture in Transition 5, Food and Agriculture Organization of the United Nations.

ICA (International Co-operative Alliance) (1993), *Poland: Cooperatives in Eastern and Central Europe*, ICA Studies and Reports, Geneva.

ICA (International Co-operative Alliance) (1999), www.coop.org/ica, access date: December 12, 2000.

Inglehart, R., M. Basañez and A. Moreno (1998), *Human Values and Beliefs: A Cross-cultural Sourcebook. Political, Religious, Sexual, and Economic Norms in 43 Societies*, Findings from the 1990–93 World Values Survey, Ann Arbor, MI: University of Michigan Press.

Inglot, S. (1966), *Zarys Historii Polskiego Ruchu Spó_dzielczego* [An Outline of the History of Polish Cooperatives], Warsaw.

Jenkins, R. (1992), *Pierre Bourdieu*, London: Routledge.

Johannisson, B. and M. Mønsted (1997), 'Contextualizing entrepreneurial networking. The case of Scandinavia', *International Studies of Management and Organization*, **27** (3), 109–36.

Johannisson, B. and A. Nilsson (1989), 'Community entrepreneurs: networking for local development', *Entrepreneurship and Regional Development*, **1** (1), 3–19.

Kaser, M.C. and E.A. Radice (1985), *The Economic History of Eastern Europe 1919–1975*, Oxford: Clarendon.

Katz, P. and V. Scully (1994), *The New Urbanism: Toward an Architecture of Community*, New York: McGraw-Hill,

Korsgaard, O. (1997), *Kampen om Lyset. Dansk Voksenoplysning gennem 500 År* [The Struggle for Light. Danish Adult Education through 500 Years], Copenhagen: Gyldendal.

Kortelainen, J. (ed.) (1997), *Crossing the Russian Border. Regional Development and Cross-border Cooperation in Karelia*, Joensuu: Julkaisuja Publications.

Kuhnert, S. (2001), 'An evolutionary theory of collective action: Schumpeterian entrepreneurship for the common good', *Constitutional Political Economy*, **12**, 13–29.

Kurrild-Klitgaard, P. and G.T. Svendsen (2003), 'Rational bandits: plunder, public goods, and the Vikings', *Public Choice*, **117** (3/4), 255–272.

Kvale, S. (1996), *Interviews. An Introduction to Qualitative Research Interviewing*, Thousand Oaks, CA: Sage.

LAL (Landssammenslutningen af Landsbysamfund) (The National Confederation of Village Communities) (2002), www.lal.dk, access date: March 2, 2002.

Landau, Z. and J. Tomaszewski (1985), *The Polish Economy in the Twentieth Century*, London and Sydney: Croom Helm.

Lash, S. (1993), 'Cultural economy and social change', in C. Calhoun, E. LiPuma and M. Postone (eds), *Bourdieu: Critical Perspectives*, Cambridge: Polity, pp. 193–211.

Latour, B. (1999), *Pandora's Hope: Essays on the Reality of Science Studies*, Cambridge, MA: Harvard University Press.

Lauridsen, H.R. (1980), *Det Religiøse–Kulturelle Liv i Stationsbyerne* [The Religious–Cultural Life in the Market Towns], Copenhagen: Statens humanistiske Forskningsråd.

Lauridsen, H.R. (1986), *Folk i bevægelse. Folkelig vækkelse, politik og andelsfællesskab i Nordvestjylland* [People in Movement. Religious revival, Politics and Co-operatives in Northwestern Jutland], Struer, Denmark: Landbohistorisk Selskab.

Lazega, E. and M.-O. Lebeaux (1995), 'Capital social et contrainte latérale' [Social capital and lateral enforcement], *Revue française de sociologie*, **36** (4), October–December.

Lb (*Landsbyen. Tidsskrift for Landsbysamfundsbevægelsen*) (*The Village. Journal of the Village Community Movement*), a journal issued by The National Confederation of Village Communities (Landssammenslutningen af Landsbysamfund, LAL), 1977–78.

Lebaron, F. (2000), *La Croyance Économique* [The Economic Belief], Paris: Le Seuil.

Lebaron, F. (2003), 'Pierre Bourdieu: Economic models against economism', *Theory and Society*, **32** (5/6) (special double issue in memory of Pierre Bourdieu), 551–565.

Leisner, J. (1988), 'Den oplyste enevælde. Historien om en dansk succes' [The enlightened monarchy. The history of a danish success], in C. Bjørn (ed.), *Landboreformerne – forskning og forløb* [The Agricultural Reforms – Research and Course], Odense, Denmark: Landbohistorisk Selskab, pp. 30–43.

Lemieux, V. (2001), 'Social capital in situations of co-operation and conflict', *Isuma*, **2** (1), Spring, www.isuma.net/v02n01/lemieux/lemieux_e.shtml, access date: January 15, 2002.

Lerski, G.J. (1996), *Historical Dictionary of Poland 966–1945*, Westport, CT and London: Greenwood.

Lijphart, A. (1975), 'The comparable-cases strategy in comparative research', *Comparative Political Studies*, **8**, 158–77.

Lindberg, K. and J. Paldam (1954), 'Fagforeningerne og samfundet' [The trade unions and the society], in J.O. Krag (ed.), *Tidehverv og samfundsorden. En socialistisk orientering* [Epoch and Social Order. A Socialist Orientation]. Copenhagen: Forlaget Fremad, pp. 104–26.

Lokalbogen for Lolland (The Local Telephone Directory for Lolland) (2003), Rødovre, Denmark: TDC Forlag A/S.

Ls (Landbosamvirke) (Farmers' Union), a journal issued by The Joint Organization of Farmers (Landbrugernes Fællesorganisation, LFO), 1967–68.

Luhman, N. (1979), *Trust and Power: Two Works by Niklas Luhmann*, Chichester: John Wiley.

Mahar, C., R. Harker and C. Wilkes (1990), 'The basic theoretical position', in Harker, Mahar and Wilkes (eds), *An Introduction to the Work of Pierre Bourdieu*, London: Macmillan, pp. 1–25.

Maliszewski A. (1995), 'The fall of the co-operative movement in Poland: causes and consequences', International Co-operative Information Centre, *ICA Review*, **88** (1), http://www.wisc.edu/uwcc/icic/orgs/ica/pubs/review

Manøe-Hansen (ed.) (1972), *Hjedding Andelsmejeri 1882–1905* [Hjedding Co-operative Dairy 1882–1905], Ansager, Denmark: Ølgod museum.

Marx, K. ([1849] 1968a), Karl Marx and Friedrich Engels, *Werke* [works], vol. 6, Berlin/DDR: Dietz Verlag.

Marx, K. ([1863] 1968b), Karl Marx and Friedrich Engels, *Werke* [works], vol. 26.2, Berlin/DDR: Dietz Verlag.

Marx, K. ([1867] 1968c), Karl Marx and Friedrich Engels, *Werke* [works], vol. 23, Berlin/DDR: Dietz Verlag.

Marx, K. and F. Engels ([1848] 1947), *The German Ideology*, New York: International.

Marx, K. and F. Engels ([1848] 1948), *The Communist Manifesto*, New York: International.

Mauss, M. ([1925] 1969), *The Gift*, London: Routledge & Kegan Paul.

May, T. (1996), *Situating Social Theory*, Buckingham, UK and Philadelphia, PA: Open University Press.

Mayer, R., J. Dave and F. Schoorman (1995), 'An integrative model of organizational trust', *Academy of Management Review*, **20**, 709–34.

Meert, H. (2000), 'Rural community life and the importance of reciprocal survival strategies', *Sociologia Ruralis*, **40** (3), 319–38.

Milgrom, P.R., D.C. North and B.R. Weingast (1990), 'The role of institutions in the revival of trade: the law merchant, private judges and the champagne fairs', *Economics and Politics*, **2** (1), 1–23.

Mingione, E. (1991), *Fragmented Societies: A Sociology of Economic Life Beyond the Market Paradigm*, Oxford: Basil Blackwell.

Ministeriet for Kulturelle Anliggender (The Ministery for Cultural Issues) (1966), *Betænkning Vedrørende Kulturcentre* [Report Concerning Cultural Centres], Report no. 412, Copenhagen: Ministeriet for Kulturelle Anliggender.

Mlcoch L. (2000), 'Od institucionalizace neodpovednosti' [From the institutionalism of unaccountability to the institutionalism of accountability], presented at the conference 'Institucionalizace (ne)odpovednosti: globalni svet, evropska integrace and ceske zajmy' (Institutionalism of (un)accountability: global world, European integration and Czech interests), Prague, 30 November–2 December.

Mogensen, G.V. (1970), *De sociale konsekvenser af landbrugets strukturændringer* [The Social Consequences of the Structural Changes in the Agricultural Sector], Socialforskningsinstituttet, report no. 46, Copenhagen: Teknisk Forlag.

Mogensen, G.V., H. Mørkeberg and J. Sundbo (1979), *Småbyer i Landdistrikter* [Small Villages in Rural Areas], Socialforskningsinstituttet, report no. 86, Copenhagen: Teknisk Forlag.

Møllgaard, J. (1984), *Landbrugets Livsformer* [Agricultural Life-modes], Copenhagen: Statens Byggeforskningsinstitut.

Mormont, M. (1987), 'The emergence of rural struggles and their ideological effects', *International Journal of Urban and Regional Research*, **7**, 559–78.

Mormont, M. (1990), 'Who is rural? Or, how to be rural. Towards a sociology of the rural', in T. Marsden, P. Lowe and S. Whatmore (eds), *Rural Restructuring: Global Processes and their Responses*, London: David Fulton, pp. 21–45.

Mt (*Mejeritidende*) *(Dairy News)*, a magazine issued by The Danish National Dairymen's Association (Dansk Mejeristforening), 1964 and 1969.

Mueller, D.C. (1989), *Public Choice II*, Cambridge: Cambridge University Press.

Müller, H.-P. (1986), 'Kultur, Geschmack und Distinktion: Grundzüge der Kultursoziologie Pierre Bourdieus', in F. Neidhardt, M.R. Lepsius and J. Weiss (eds), *Kultur und Gesellschaft* [Culture and Society], Opladen: Westdeutscher Verlag, pp. 162–90.

Munck, V.C. de and E.J. Sobo (1998), *Using Methods in the Field. A Practical Introduction and Casebook*, London, New Delhi: Altamira Press.

Nellemann, G. (1967), *Den Polske Indvandring til Lolland-Falster* [The Polish Migration to Lolland-Falster], Maribo, Denmark: Lolland-Falsters historiske Samfund.

Nelson, H.D. (1983), *Poland – a Country Study*, Washington, DC: Foreign Area Studies, The American University.

Nordstrand, R., A.K. Andersen and K.B. Larsen (2001), *Regional Udvikling af Indkomst og Beskæftigelse* [Regional Development in Outcome and Occupation], Copenhagen: AKF Forlaget.

North, D.C. (1990), *Institutions, Institutional Change and Economic Performance*, Cambridge, UK: Cambridge University Press.

North, D.C. and B.R. Weingast (1989), 'Constitutions and commitment: the evolution of institutions governing public choice in seventeenth century England', *Journal of Economic History*, **49** (4), 803–32.

Nyhan, D. (2000), 'Book review of *Bowling Alone*' in *Boston Globe*, www.BowlingAlone.com/reviews.php3, access date: September 20, 2000.

Odgaard, K. and J. Simonsen (1998), *Slægtskabssystemet og de intellektuelle i Kazakstan* [The Kinship System and the Intellectuals in Kazachstan], Aarhus, Denmark: University of Aarhus.

OECD (Organization for Economic Co-operation and Development) (1995), *Poland: Review of Agricultural Policies*, Centre for Co-operation with the Economies in Transition, Paris: OECD.

Olsen, A. (1998), 'Stevnshallerne' [The Stevns Sports Halls], in V. Buck (ed.), *Store Heddinge Før og Nu* [Store Heddinge Now and Before], vol. 6, Store Heddinge, Denmark: Stevns Lokalhistoriske Arkiv, pp. 73–82.

Olson, M. (1965), *The Logic of Collective Action*, Cambridge: Cambridge University Press.

Olson, M. (1982), *The Rise and Decline of Nations*, New Haven, CT: Yale University Press.

Olson, M. (1993), 'Dictatorship, democracy, and development', *American Political Science Review*, **87**, 567–76.

Olson, M. (1996), 'Big bills left on the sidewalk: why some nations are rich, and others poor', *Journal of Economic Perspectives*, **10** (2), 3–24.

Olson, M. (2000), *Power and Prosperity: Outgrowing Communist and Capitalist Dictatorships*, New York: Basic Books.

Ordeshook, P.C. (1993), 'The development of contemporary political theory', in W.A. Barnett, M.J. Hinich and N.J. Schofield (eds), *Political Economy: Institutions, Competition and Representation*, Cambridge, MA: Cambridge University Press.

Ostrom, E. (1965), 'Public entrepreneurship: a case study in ground water basin management', PhD dissertation, Department of Political Science, University of California-Los Angeles.

Ostrom, E. (1990), *Governing the Commons. The Evolution of Institutions for Collective Action*, Cambridge: Cambridge University Press.

Ostrom, E. (1992), *Crafting Institutions for Self-governing Irrigation Systems*, San Francisco, CA: Institute for Contemporary Studies Press.

Ostrom, E. (1994), 'Constituting social capital and collective action', *Journal of Theoretical Politics*, **6** (4), 527–62.

Ostrom, E. (1998), 'A behavioral approach to the rational choice theory of collective action', *American Political Review*, **92** (1), 1–22.

Ostrom, E. and T.K. Ahn (eds) (2003), *Foundations of Social Capital. Critical Studies in Economic Institutions*, Cheltenham, UK and Northampton, MA, USA: Edward Elgar Publishing.

Ostrom, E., R. Gardner and J. Walker (1994), *Rules, Games, and Common-pool Resources*, Ann Arbor, MI: University of Michigan Press.

Ostrom, V. (1985), 'Worker self-management in American society', Working paper no. W85–2 prepared for workshop in political theory and policy analysis, Indiana University, Bloomington, IL.

Paldam, M. (2000), 'Social capital: one or many? Definition and measurement', *Journal of Economic Surveys*, Special Issue on Political Economy, **14** (5), 629–53.

Paldam, M. (2002), *Udviklingen i Rusland, Polen og de Baltiske Lande: Lys Forude efter den Store Ændring af det Økonomiske System* [The Development of Russia, Poland and the Baltics: Light Ahead after the Change of the Economic System], Aarhus, Denmark: Rockwoolfonden.

Paldam, M. and G.T. Svendsen (2000), 'An essay on social capital: looking for the fire behind the smoke', *European Journal of Political Economy*, **16**, 339–66.

Paldam, M. and G.T. Svendsen (2002), 'Missing social capital and the transition in Eastern Europe', *Journal of Institutional Innovation, Development and Transition*, **5**, 21–34.

Paldam, M. and G.T. Svendsen (eds) (2004), *Trust, Social Capital and Economic Growth: An International Comparison*, Cheltenham, UK and Northampton, MA, USA: Edward Elgar (forthcoming).

Passeron, J.-C. (2001), 'Entre économie et sociologie: rationalité, formalisme et histoire', in J.-Y. Grenier, C. Grignon and P.-M. Menger (eds), *Le modèle et le récit*, p. 99-138. Paris: Éditions de la Msh.

Polanyi, K. (1944), *The Great Transformation: The Political and Economic Origins of our Time*, Boston, MA: Beacon Hill.

Polanyi, K. (1968), *Primitive, Archaic and Modern Economics*, New York: Doubleday.

Polanyi, K., C. Arensberg and H. Pearson (1957), *Trade and Markets in the Early Empires*, New York: Free Press.

Portes, A. (1998), 'Social capital: origins and applications', *Annual Review of Sociology*, **24**, 1–24.

Portes, A. (2000), 'The two meanings of social capital', Sociological Forum, **15** (1), 1-12.

Portes, A. and P. Landolt (1996), 'The downside of social capital', *American Prospect*, **26**, May–June, 18–21.

Portes, A. and J. Sensenbrenner (1993), 'Embeddedness and immigration: notes on the social determinants of economic action', *American Journal of Sociology*, **98** (6), 1320–50.

Produktions- og Raastofkommissionen (The Production and Raw Material Commission) (1949), *Betænkning Angaaende Rationel Kraft- og Varmeforsyning* [Report Concerning Rational Power and Heat Supply], Copenhagen: Produktions- og Raastofkommissionen.

Putnam, R.D. (1993a), *Making Democracy Work. Civic Traditions in Modern Italy*, Princeton, NJ: Princeton University Press.

Putnam, R.D. (1993b), 'The prosperous community. Social capital and public life', *American Prospect*, **13**, Spring, 35–42.

Putnam, R.D. (1995), 'Bowling alone: America's declining social capital', *Journal of Democracy*, **6** (1), 65-78.

Putnam, R.D. (1996), 'The strange disappearance of civic America', *American Prospect*, **24**, Winter, 34–48.

Putnam, R.D. (2000), *Bowling Alone. The Collapse and Revival of American Community*, New York, London, Toronto, Singapore: Simon & Schuster.

Rasmussen, J.D. (1982), 'Dansk mejeribrug 1914–55' [Danish dairywork 1914–55], in C. Bjørn (ed.), *Dansk Mejeribrug 1882–2000* [Danish Dairywork 1882–2000], Odense, Denmark: De Danske Mejeriers Fællesorganisation, pp. 189–308.

Ravnholt, H. (1943), *Den danske Andelsbevægelse* [The Danish Co-operative Movement], Copenhagen: Det Danske Selskab.

Ray, C. (1998a), 'The relationship between cultural identities and social and economic development', in P. Lowe, C. Ray, N. Ward, D. Wood and R. Woodward (eds), *Participation in Rural Development: A Review of European Experience*, Centre for Rural Economy Research, report commissioned by the European Foundation for the Improvement of Living and Working Conditions. Newcastle: University of Newcastle upon Tyne.

Ray, C. (1998b), 'Culture, intellectual property and territorial rural development', *Sociologia Ruralis*, **38** (1), 3–20.

Rørdam, T. (1983), *Fra Andelssamfundets Barndom*. [From the Childhood of the Co-operative Society], Jelling, Denmark: Dansk Friskoleforening.

Rose, R. (2000), 'Getting things done in an anti-modern society: social capital networks in Russia', in P. Dasgupta and I. Serageldin (eds), *Social Capital, A Multifaceted Perspective*, Washington, DC: World Bank, pp. 147–71.

Rotberg, R.I. (ed.) (2001), *Patterns of Social Capital. Stability and Change in Historical Perspective*, Cambridge: Cambridge University Press.

SAEPR/FAPA (2000), *Stereotypes in the European Union concerning Polish Agriculture*, Foundation of Assistance Programmes for Agriculture, Agricultural Policy Analysis Unit, Warsaw, Poland.

Sandefur, R.L. and E.O. Laumann (1998), 'A paradigm for social capital', *Rationality and Society*, **10** (4), 481–501.

Schjødt, E.B. and G.T. Svendsen (2002), 'Transition to market economy in Eastern Europe: interest groups and political institutions in Russia', *Nordic Journal of Political Economy*, **28** (2), 181–94.

Sen, A. (1999), Development as Freedom. Oxford: Oxford University Press.

Shaw, A. and G.T. Svendsen (2003), 'Religion, social capital and economic growth – the case of India', unpublished working paper.

Simmel, G. ([1908] 1955), *Conflict and the Web of Group Affiliations*, New York: Free Press.

Simon, H.A. (1993), 'Altruism and economics', *American Economic Review*, **83** (2), 156–61.

Smart, A. (1993), 'Gifts, bribes, and guanxi: a reconsideration of Bourdieu's social capital', *Cultural Anthropology*, **8** (3), 388–408.

Smith, A. ([1776] 1991), *The Wealth of Nations*, New York: Everyman's Library, A.A. Knopf.

Snook, I. (1990), 'Language, truth and power', in R. Harker, C. Mahar and C. Wilkes (eds), *An Introduction to the Work of Pierre Bourdieu. The Practice of Theory*, London: Macmillan, pp. 160–79.

Sobel, J. (2002), 'Can we trust social capital?', *Journal of Economic Literature*, **40**, March, 139–54.

Solvang, G. (1984), *Husmandsliv. En Etnologisk Skildring af Livsvilkårene i Rønhave-kolonien på Als 1925–80* [Smallholder Life. An Ethnological Account of the Living Conditions in the Rønhave Smallholder Colony on Als 1925–80], Odense, Denmark: Landbohistorisk Selskab.

Solvang, G. (1997), 'Nye perspektiver for lokalsamfundet i landdistrikterne' [New perspectives for the local rural community], in N.H. Jessen, A. Myrtue, P.G. Møller and E. Porsmose (eds), *Landdistrikterne 1950–2050*, Odense, Denmark: Odense Universitetsforlag, pp. 65–84.

Solvang, G. (1999) *Husmandsliv under Afvikling. Udvikling og Forandring i et Sønderjysk Landbosamfund 1975–2000 med Hovedvægt på de Nye Tilflyttere* [Dying Smallholder Life. Development and Change in an Agricultural Community in Southern Jutland 1975–2000, with a Focus on the Newcomers], Viborg, Denmark: Landbohistorisk Selskab.

Sonne, H.C. (1867), *Om Arbejderforeninger. Til Oplysning og Veiledning* [About Workers' Associations. For Enlightenment and Instruction], Copenhagen: Louis Kleins Bogtrykkeri.

Spradley, J.P. (1980), *Participant Observation*, New York, Toronto, London, Sydney: Holt, Rinehart & Winston.

Svendsen, G.L.H. (2000), 'Fra selvorganisering til statsregulering. Omkring Smørmærkeforeningens samarbejde med staten 1900–1912' [From self-organisation to state regulation. About the co-operation between the Danish butter label association and the Danish state], *Bol og By*, (2), 73–95.

Svendsen, G.L.H. (2001), 'Historien anskuet som et kapitalmarked. Selvorganiseringen i de danske landdistrikter 1800–1900' [History analysed as a capital market. Self-organisation in the Danish rural districts 1800-1900], *Fortid og Nutid*, (1), 23–51.

Svendsen, G.L.H. (2002), 'Conceptual hegemonies in rural Denmark 1945–2002', *Space and Planning*, (4), 355–9.

Svendsen, G.L.H. (2003a), 'The right to development. Construction of a non-agriculturalist discourse of rurality in rural Denmark', *Journal of Rural Studies*, **20** (4), 79-94.

Svendsen, G.L.H. (2003b), '*Vi hilser da på hinanden... De nye tilflyttere i Ravnsborg Kommune: Problemer og muligheder*' [But at least we greet each other... The Newcomers in Ravnsborg Municipality: Problems and possibilities], Working paper 5/03, Danish Centre for Rural Research and Development, Southern University of Denmark, Esbjerg.

Svendsen, G.L.H. and G.T. Svendsen (2000), 'Measuring social capital: the Danish co-operative dairy movement', *Sociologia Ruralis*, **40** (1), 72–86.

Svendsen, G.L.H. and G.T. Svendsen (2001), 'Alleviating poverty: entrepreneurship and social capital in rural Denmark 1800–1900', *Belgeo*, **1** (3), 231–46.

Svendsen, G.L.H. and G.T. Svendsen (2003), 'The wealth of nations: Bourdieuconomics and social capital', *Theory and Society*, **32** (5/6) (special double issue in memory of Pierre Bourdieu), 607–631.

Svendsen, G.T. (1998), *Public Choice and Environmental Regulation: Tradable Permit Systems in the United States and CO_2 Taxation in Europe*, New Horizons in Environmental Economics, series, Cheltenham, UK and Lyme, USA: Edward Elgar.

Svendsen, G.T. (1999), 'US interest groups prefer emission trading. A new perspective', *Public Choice*, **101**, (1/2), 109–28.

Svendsen, G.T. (2003), *The Political Economy of the European Union: Institutions, Policy and Economic Growth*, Cheltenham, UK and Northampton, MA, USA: Edward Elgar.

Swartz, D. (1997), *Culture and Power: The Sociology of Pierre Bourdieu*, Chicago, London: University of Chicago Press.

Swedberg, R. (1994), 'Markets as social structures', in Neil Smelser and Richard Swedberg (eds), *The Handbook of Economic Sociology*, Princeton, NJ: Princeton University Press, pp. 255–82.

Tagmose, K.E. (1973), 'Jysk Arbejdskraft' [Workers from Jutland], in E.-M. Boyhus (ed.), *Sukkerroer. 100 År på Lolland-Falster* [Sugar Beets. 100 Years in Lolland-Falster], Maribo, Denmark: Lolland-Falsters Historiske Samfund, pp. 138–40.

Tange, K.K. (1965), *Fra Skummeske til Centrifuge. Erindringsbilleder* [From Skimmer to Cream Separator. Pictures from the Memory], Copenhagen: Rosenkilde & Bagger.

Thomassen, H.K. (1999), *Holgers Saga* [Holger's Saga], Store Heddinge, Denmark: Stevns Lokalhistoriske Arkiv.

Thugutt, S. (1937), *Spó_dzielczo__: Zarys ideologii* (Co-operatives, an Outline of Ideology), Warsaw.

Tietenberg, T.H. (2002), *Environmental and Natural Resource Economics*, 6th Edition, Reading, MA: Addison Wesley Longman Higher Education.

UfL (*Ugeskrift for Landmænd*) (*Weekly Magazine for Farmers*), issued by The Danish Agronomist Association (Dansk Agronomforening), 1963.

Uslaner, E. (2002), *The Moral Foundations of Trust*, New York: Cambridge University Press.

Vedholm, H. (1995), *Kernen i Mejeribruget. MD Foods fra 1970–1995* [The Core of the Danish Dairy Sector. MD Foods from 1970–1995], Silkeborg, Denmark: MD Foods.

Vestergaard, T. (1991), 'Are artisanal fisheries backward? Artisanal fisheries in modern society, the example of Denmark', in J.-R. Durand, J. Lemoalle and J. Weber (eds), *La Recherche Face à la Pêche Artisanale*, II, Paris: Orstom, pp. 781–8.

Vk (*Vestkysten*) (*The West Coast* (*newspaper*)), May 8, 1973; December 2 and 24, 1974.

Wacquant, L.J.D. (1998), 'Negative social capital: state breakdown and social destitution in America's urban core', *Netherlands Journal of Housing and the Built Environment*, **13** (1), 25–40.

Weber, M. ([1922] 1947), *The Theory of Social and Economic Organization*, New York: Free Press.

Williamson, O.E. (1975), *Markets and Hierarchies: Analysis and Antitrust Implications*, New York: Free Press.

Woods, M. (1997), 'Discourses of power and rurality. Local politics in Somerset in the 20th century', *Political Geography*, **16** (6), 453–78.

Woods, M. (1998), 'Researching rural conflicts: hunting, local politics and actor-networks', *Journal of Rural Studies*, **14** (3), 321–40.

Woodward, R. (1999), 'Gunning for rural England: the politics of the promotion of military land use in the Northumberland National Park', *Journal of Rural Studies*, **15**, 17–33.

Woodward, R. (2001), 'Khaki conservation: an examination of military environmentalist discourses in the British Army', *Journal of Rural Studies*, **17**, 201–17.

Woolcock, M. (1998), 'Social capital and economic development: toward a theoretical synthesis and policy framework', *Theory and Society*, **27**, 151–208.

World Bank (1990), *An Agricultural Strategy for Poland*, Washington, DC: World Bank.

World Bank (1999), www.worldbank.org/poverty/scapital/library/index.htm, World Bank Task Force, International Bank for Reconstruction and Development, World Bank, Washington, DC, access date: January 10, 2000.

World Bank (2002), http://www.worldbank.org/data/onlinedatabases/online-databases.html, World Development Indicators, Washington, DC, access date: January 12, 2003.

Wrong, D. (1961), 'The oversocialized conception of man in modern sociology', *American Sociological Review*, **26** (2), 183–93.

Yin, R.K. (1989), *Case Study Research: Design and Methods*, Newbury Park, CA: Sage.

Subject Index

Author Index